Upper intermediate B2

James Greenan

@work

Teacher's Book

Richmond

 **Richmond**

58 St Aldates
Oxford
OX1 1ST
United Kingdom

© 2014, Santillana Educación, S.L. / Richmond

Publisher: Ruth Goodman
Editor(s): Nicola Gardner, David Cole-Powney
Digital Publisher: Luke Baxter
Senior Digital Editor: Belen Fernandez
Design Manager: Lorna Heaslip
Cover Illustration & Design: This Ain't Rock'n'Roll
Design & Layout: Dave Kuzmicki

ISBN: 978-84-668-1415-7

First edition: 2014
Printed in Spain
DL: M-8275-2013

No unauthorised photocopying

All rights reserved. No part of this book may be reproduced, stored in a retrieval system or transmitted in any form by any means, electronic, mechanical, photocopying, recording or otherwise, without the prior permission in writing of the Publisher.

Photocopies may be made, for classroom use, of pages 72 and 75 without the prior written permission of the Publisher. However, please note that the copyright law, which does not normally permit multiple copying of published material, applies to the rest of the book.

Publisher acknowledgements:

The Publisher would like to thank the following reviewers for their invaluable feedback on @work. We extend our thanks to the many other teachers and students around the world whose input has helped us to develop the materials.

Reviewers:
Angela Lilley, The Open University, Oxford, United Kingdom;
Manuel Hidalgo Iglesias, QUILL Language Learning, Mexico City, Mexico;
Marion Grussendorf, ACADIA GmbH, Cologne, Germany;
Paulo Henrique Vaz Lopes, Cultura Inglesa, Belo Horizonte, Brazil;
Radmila Petrova Kaisheva & Anna Rumenova Boyadzhieva-Moskova, University of National and World Economy, Sofia, Bulgaria;
Andrew Archer, Independent Publishers International, Tokyo, Japan

Every effort has been made to trace the holders of copyright before publication. The Publisher will be pleased to rectify any errors or omissions at the earliest opportunity.

Contents

Student's Book contents map	page	4
Introduction to the course	page	6
Unit 1 People	page	22
Unit 2 The best way to work	page	30
Unit 3 The future	page	37
Unit 4 Getting a job	page	45
Unit 5 New products and services	page	54
Writing emails	page	62
Unit 6 Meetings	page	67
Unit 7 Culture	page	76
Unit 8 Marketing and selling	page	82
Unit 9 Problems and solutions	page	89
Unit 10 The rules of work	page	97
Tracklist	page	105

Student's Book contents map

	Language			Skills			
	Grammar / Functions	Vocabulary	Fluency	Listening	Reading	Speaking	Writing
1 People p4							
Partners	Past tense review	Describing relationships			Two famous partnerships	Talking about relationships	
First impressions	Present perfect	Describing people		Candidates for a sales job	Five surprising ways to make a good first impression	Forming impressions of job candidates / Interviewing your partner	
Making contact	Starting and maintaining conversations		Sentence stress	Five short conversations	An introductory email	Starting and maintaining conversations	Introducing yourself by email
Scenario: The right judges — Finding candidates for a literary judging panel							
2 The best way to work p12							
Working too hard?	Articles	Describing a typical day		A typical day in the life of two product designers	Work/life balance questionnaire	Discussing work/ life balance	
How efficient are you?	Words that are used before nouns	Talking about productivity		Two product designers discuss how they keep productive at work	The Slow Movement	Discussing your strengths and weaknesses in productivity	
How have I done?	Giving effective feedback on work			An HR consultant discusses ways of giving feedback	Performance reviews: good or bad?	Discussing performance reviews and effective feedback / Giving feedback	
Scenario: Downsizing — Which staff should be promoted, kept and let go?							
3 The future p20							
Planning ahead	*be going to* and present continuous for future arrangements	Planning and managing change		Two business people discuss their attitudes towards planning for the future	Futurescaping	Discussing plans and arrangements / Futurescaping	
The uncertain future	Making predictions			The changing future of four industries	Future challenges	Making predictions about certain events	
The future of communication	Digital communication	Using social media		Four extracts from video or phone conferences	How digital media has changed the way business professionals communicate	Presenting advice on how to phone-/video- conference succesfully	
Scenario: Facing the future — How can an arts centre turn its fortunes around?							
4 Getting a job p28							
Career jumpers	Question forms	Describing jobs		Two career jumpers describe their old and new jobs	Two career jumpers	Interviews about career changes made	A profile of a career jumper
What employers look for in you		Describing positive professional qualities / Word families	Fillers	An HR manager talks about recruitment tests	A personality test	Analysing and giving feedback on personality test results	
Getting the job	Improving your interview technique / Dealing with difficult questions			Six answers from a job candidate	The psychology of interviews	Asking and answering interview questions	
Scenario: Arctic venture — Who should manage a new outdoor clothing store in the Arctic?							
5 New products and services p36							
Appropriate technology	Passive	Describing a product		The 'free wheelchair'		Presenting an appropriate technology product	
Giving customers what they want	Verb forms related to the passive	Describing changes to buildings and rooms		How a service was improved	Customer reviews on a consumer website	Planning a new business venture	
Presenting	Key presentation phrases / Planning a presentation		Linking words	A conversation about a bad presentation		Tips for presenting / Planning a presentation	
Scenario: Eco-activity centre — Choosing a site for a new holiday centre							

Writing emails p44

More practice = more practice available on the digital and print Workbook

	Language			Skills			
	Grammar / Functions	Vocabulary	Fluency	Listening	Reading	Speaking	Writing
6 Meetings p56							
My worst meeting		Describing and organising meetings		Unconventional ideas for improving meetings	My worst meeting	Best practice for meetings	
He said, she said	Reported speech Reporting verbs	Reporting verbs		Two meetings to investigate a complaint against a employee		Reporting what someone said	Minutes of a meeting
Getting heard	Making your point assertively			Four meeting extracts	How to get heard in a meeting	The interrupting game	
Scenario: Meeting mayhem Can the Zicu Foundation improve its meetings?							
7 Culture p64							
Culture shock in California		Cultural values Communication styles			Culture shock in California	Discussing working styles in business culture	
Cultural sensitivity	Second and third conditional			The Hermes project		Discussing cross-cultural misunderstandings	
When things go wrong	Apologising	Making mistakes and apologising	Tone of voice	Five apologies	What to do when you 'screw up' spectacularly	Apologising	
Scenario: Losing Luis Lima Can an American hockey team persuade their Brazilian star to return?							
8 Marketing and selling p72							
Legalised lying?	Comparatives and superlatives	Marketing and advertising			Three ingenious marketing campaigns	Discussing marketing and advertising	
Why the brand matters	Extreme adjectives	Brands and branding		Five famous brands	Why the brand matters	Discussing different marketing techniques	
The art of persuasion	Persuasive presentations Rhetorical techniques	Powerful words	Emphatic stress	Five sales presentation techniques		Preparing an introduction for a persuasive presentation	
Scenario: Rebranding Ibiza Joy Can a holiday company find a new market?							
9 Problems and solutions p80							
Creating	Verb patterns			An interview with an inventor	Inspiration or desperation	Talking about entrepreneurs	
Adapting		Phrases using prepositions		An economy expert talks about adapting to different markets	Wrong-footing your customers	Deciding how to adapt and market a product in different countries	
Group problem-solving	Suggesting and agreeing solutions			A group reaches a decision about an end-of-term party	Groupthink	Making a group decision about a fund-raising idea	
Scenario: Breaking into America Can a UK supermarket break into the US market?							
10 The rules of work p88							
Office relations	Modal verbs	Honesty and responsibility	Weak and strong forms	A radio show about a dilemma	An email about a workplace dilemma	Discussing workplace dilemmas	
Whistleblowing	Past form of modals	Unethical work practices		A whistleblower tells his story		Re-telling and discussing the story of a whistleblower	
The right rules	Expressing rules and expectations	Describing sanctions		Two people talk about rules in different workplaces	Trust me I'm an employee	Discussing workplace rules	
Scenario: Environmental dilemma What should be done about a polluting chemical company?							

Pairwork p96   Grammar p108   Irregular verbs p116   Audioscripts p118

Introduction to the course

About the course

@work is a course designed for working adults and students who need, or will need, English in their professional lives. The course focuses on practical English used in the workplace and would suit institutions teaching general English, although it is easily adaptable to cover the needs of students with more specific learning goals.

The objective of *@work* is to give **all** students the language skills they need to function in the workplace in a lively and aspirational way. This is how it's done:

- **Cohesive blended learning:** The digital resources are integrated with the print material, allowing students and teachers to move between different formats inside and outside the classroom. This means that the learning situations are fully exploited in a rich and engaging way.

- **Student and teacher flexibility**: *@work* has been specially designed so that teachers can customise the course to the available teaching hours and learning goals of the class. In addition, individual students can 'pick and mix' extra components to get the exact blend of skills that they need to work effectively in English.

- **People-focused:** This course brings a humanistic approach to professional English. It avoids the dryness of the corporate world and motivates learners by presenting language in contexts that all students can relate to.

- **Get-the-job done language:** The skills-development syllabus helps learners to construct the practical professional language and skills needed around the world in the 21st-century workplace.

- **Learning bites:** Optional components are available via apps and the *@work* Learning Platform, giving today's professionals and students access to engaging, useful content wherever, whenever and however they want.

Course components

Student's Book

The Student's Book is divided into ten units and provides over 60 hours of teaching material. This can be expanded with additional resources and digital add-ons, allowing teachers to customise the course to the number of contact hours and the students' requirements.

- Each unit contains three double-page lessons and a business scenario.

- New language is introduced in realistic contexts and students are given plenty of opportunity to practise this in communicative situations and pairwork activities.

- Each unit links to the Writing emails section, giving students practice and tips for communicating effectively via email.

- A grammar reference section looks at important grammar points in more detail.

Introduction to the course

Workbook and eWorkbook

The Workbook can be used in conjunction with the Student's Book in class, or it can be used by students independently as a self-study tool.

The eWorkbook is a fully interactive version of the Workbook and can be linked to the Richmond VLE (Virtual Learning Environment), letting students share their progress with teachers.

- All the key language and vocabulary from the Student's Book lessons are covered, so students gain confidence.
- A range of activities helps students develop all the key skills, including pronunciation and extra listening practice.
- Progress tests let students assess their own learning.
- An interactive grammar bank takes students through key grammar rules and gives extra practice.

@work Learning Platform
www.richmondatwork.net

Students and teachers using @work can access the @work Learning Platform. This contains additional digital content for both students and teachers and access to a Virtual Learning Environment (VLE).

- For students, there are email templates, unit tests and the Workbook answer key.
- Teachers have access to wordlists, role play task sheets and IF mapping.
- The VLE allows students to work online and for teachers to monitor their students' progress.

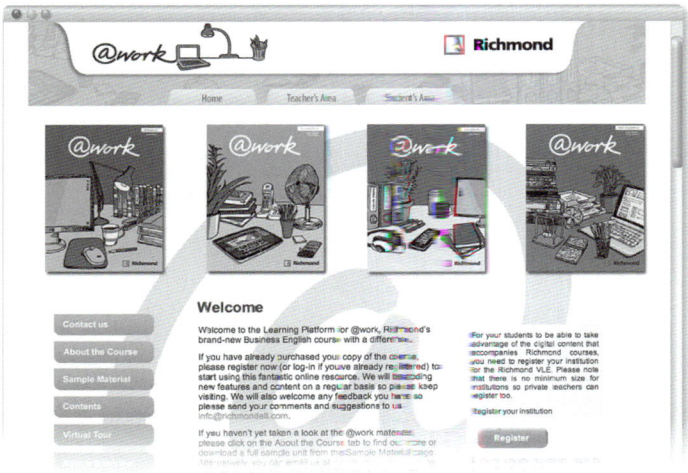

Additional digital materials

A range of value-added content is also available, giving students the opportunity to personalise their learning, try out innovative learning methods and develop particular business skills.

- Richmond Mazes are fun, interactive readers set in working environments, where students can determine how the story develops.
- Business Skills video modules give students practice in specific business skills, such as giving presentations, attending meetings and negotiating in English.

Student's Book Lesson 1

Every lesson of the topic-driven units starts with an opportunity for students to talk generally about the subject, before exploring it in more detail.

The first lesson introduces the unit topic with engaging reading and listening texts, involving the students in the topic and giving them the chance to see the target language and vocabulary in context.

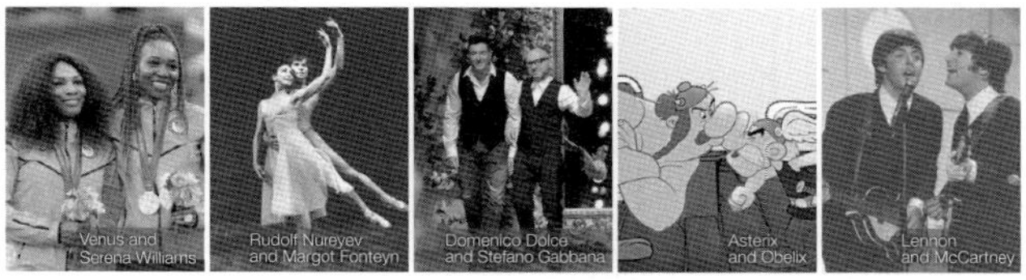

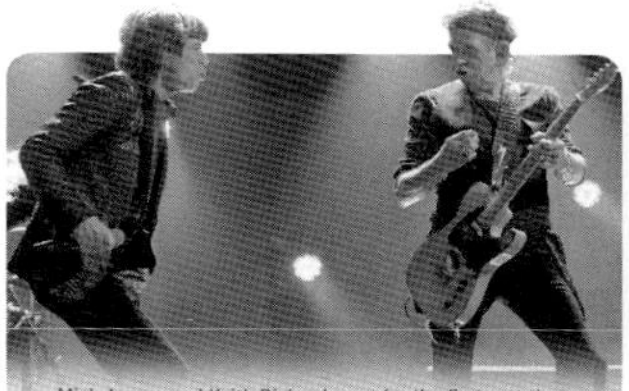

Concise grammar presentations appear within the units, reinforcing key concepts and providing students with a quick reference to the target language.

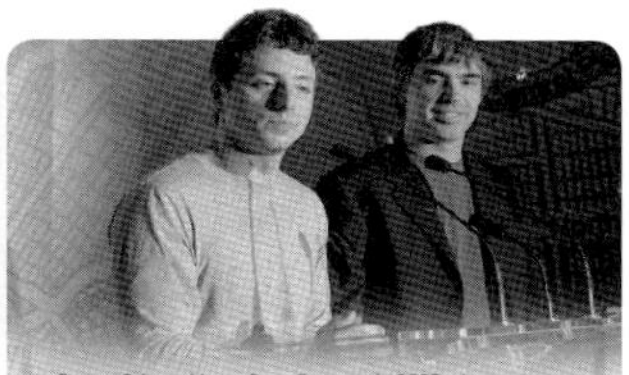

Engaging practice and personalised speaking activities let students gain confidence with the new language in a meaningful context.

 This icon shows where students can find further practice on one of the many digital add-ons.

The @work Student's Book comes with an access code for the digital materials.

'Fluency' provides an opportunity to identify and practise pronunciation by focusing on individual phonemes and stress patterns.

All the lessons finish with a production exercise, where students can use the target language in a spoken conversation or a written piece of work.

Introduction to the course

For more in-depth explanations and further examples of the grammar covered in each unit, a grammar reference section can be found at the back of the book. This can be used in class as part of the grammar presentations, or referred to whenever students have a doubt.

There are many listening activities throughout the course, allowing students to develop this essential skill. The listening texts often take the form of lively conversations and include a variety of international accents to ensure students are exposed to a range of different speakers and nationalities.

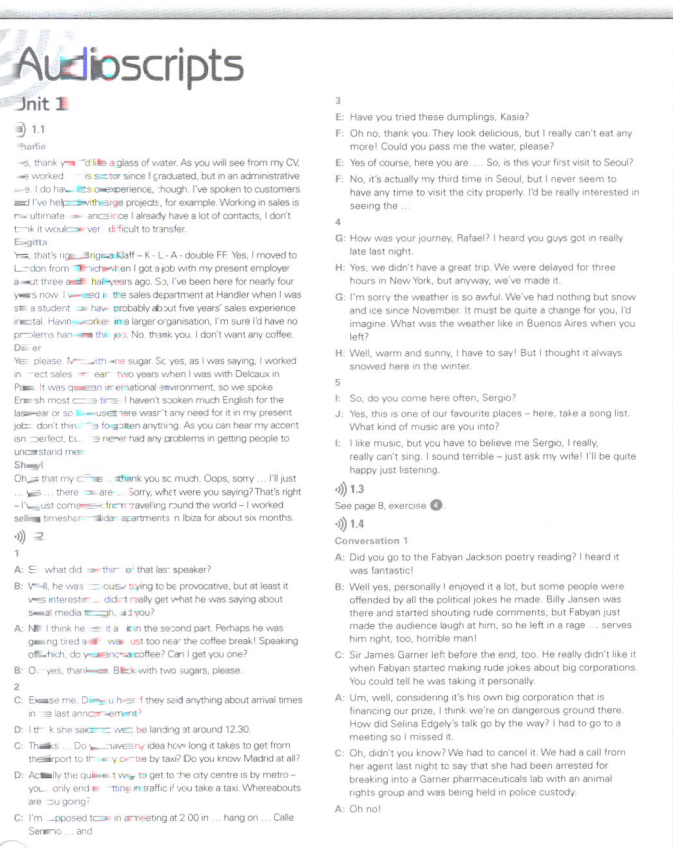

The Student's Book audioscripts are provided at the back of the coursebook for students to refer to.

Student's Book Lesson 2

The second lesson extends the unit topic and again begins with a general speaking activity to generate interest.

Students analyse an interesting reading or listening text which reinforces the language from the previous lesson and acts as a springboard to look at additional lexical sets and build on grammar points.

New lexis and grammar points are presented within boxes, providing a useful reference for students.

There is a variety of activities which let students practise new language in context and develop all the key skills.

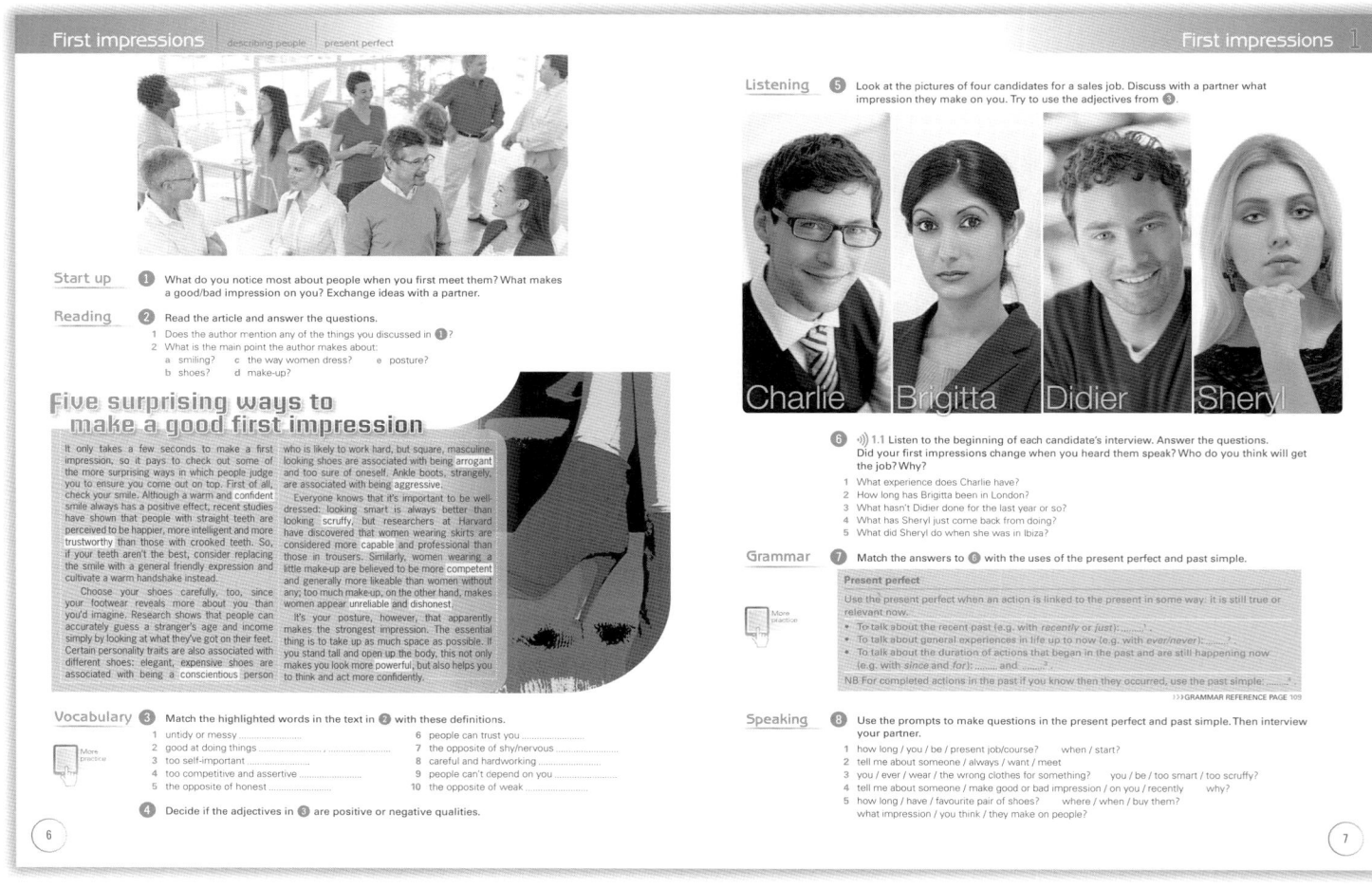

The two-page lesson finishes with a speaking task which rounds up the lesson with a personalised focus or a role play, allowing students to make use of the language they have learnt.

Introduction to the course

Throughout the lessons students practise their communication skills with tasks that can be carried out in pairs or in groups.

Dedicated activities provide an attractive stimulus to get students communicating among themselves.

The speaking tasks, which take the form of role plays or simple discussion questions, allow students to practise target language, as well as build their confidence when communicating with others.

Pairwork

Unit 1 page 4

Venus (born 1980) and **Serena Williams** (born 1981) are sisters and arguably two of the greatest tennis players of all time. In their careers so far, not counting their individual victories in singles matches, they have won the Australian Open women's doubles four times, the French and the US Open twice, Wimbledon five times and have taken the gold medal in the Olympic Games three times.

Rudolf Nureyev (1938–1993) and **Margot Fonteyn** (1919–1991) were ballet dancers. When they met, Margot Fonteyn was about to retire, but she invited 24-year-old Rudolf, a political dissident from the Soviet Union, to dance in the ballet *Giselle* with her in London as an experiment. It was the beginning of a 17-year-long professional relationship which produced some of the most beautiful and emotional classical ballet performances ever.

Domenico Dolce (born 1958) and **Stefano Gabbana** (born 1962) are Italian fashion designers. They presented their first collection of women's clothing at the 1985 Milan fashion week and opened their own store in Milan in 1986. They have been commissioned as costume designers for singers such as Madonna, Beyoncé and Kylie Minogue. Dolce & Gabbana have also been very successful in menswear and perfume, and their partnership has become a huge, multinational fashion brand.

Asterix and **Obelix** are cartoon characters living in a small village in the ancient Gaul (which corresponds to the region of Brittany in modern France) during the time of the Roman occupation around 50 BC. Asterix is a warrior and loves going on adventures and fighting the Romans with his best friend, the enormous Obelix. The pair have many adventures and save the village many times from the Romans and other enemies.

John Lennon (1940–1980) and **Paul McCartney** (born 1942) are the song-writing team from the Beatles, one of the most famous pop bands ever. There exist more than 180 songs written by Lennon-McCartney, most of which were recorded by the Beatles, including classics as *Yesterday*, *Ticket to Ride*, *Yellow Submarine* and *All you need is Love*.

Unit 1 page 5
Student A

Complete the text with the verbs in brackets. Use the past simple, past continuous or past perfect.

Bill Clinton and Hillary Rodham Clinton have been described as the 'world's ultimate power couple' and they have both enjoyed brilliant political careers. They _____¹ (meet) when they _____² (study) law at Yale University in 1971 and _____³ (bond) over their shared passion for politics. Despite having very different personalities – Bill was friendly and sociable whilst Hillary was quieter – there _____⁴ (be) a strong attraction between them right from the beginning. Hillary said of Bill that he was the first man she _____⁵ (meet) who wasn't afraid of her – and they _____⁶ (marry) four years later in 1975. They _____⁷ (settle) in Little Rock in Arkansas and during their first two decades of married life, _____⁸ (manage) to each build successful careers in their own right. While Bill _____⁹ (rise) through the ranks of the Democratic Party to become state governor and finally president, Hillary _____¹⁰ (build) her own successful legal career. Bill helped to promote his wife's political career after his own _____¹¹ (end) and she eventually became Secretary of State in the first Democratic government after the Clinton regime.

Unit 1 page 10
Student A

You have met the three authors below. Read about them and answer your partner's questions in ❷.

Jo-Jo Heller – popular comedian and singer who appears regularly on TV. Has published two comic novels about young women in modern life for Arbour House in the last two years. They have sold very well, but are not well written. If in the panel, she could give the prize more appeal at the less literary end of the market. She is funny and entertaining, but very young and inexperienced – does she have the literary knowledge to be a judge?

Billy Jansen – very well-known/respected political writer. He has written six political biographies for Arbour House over the last 15 years. The last one was published last year and was a best-seller. He is also editor of a famous satirical magazine and appears regularly in a popular TV quiz show. As a judge, he could create a lot of extra publicity for the prize. He has a very strong personality and comes across as arrogant. He regularly offends people with his sarcastic remarks and jokes.

Selina Edgely – one of Arbour House's most popular, best-selling authors for last 20 years. She writes historical romantic fiction – one book a year, and has huge sales. Her profile is ideal – she has mass appeal, but work is considered to have literary value. However, she is very passionate about animal rights and is against animal testing. Garner Pharmaceuticals does not have a good record in this respect as they still test cosmetics on animals.

Unit 1 page 11
Student A

Take these two different author roles when Student B tries to speak to you.

1 You're Jo-Jo Heller. You're trying to order coffee in the very crowded bar. You're delighted to be asked about being a judge, but don't want to seem too eager so will try to give the impression that you're very busy next spring, but you might have some time. Make sure though that the editor's last impression is that you're available.

2 You're Della Lane. You've been listening to an acceptance speech by the author who won a prize for the novel that you think you should have won, so you're feeling grumpy. You would hate to be on the judges' panel because you're too shy. You're sure that Lizanne Grey has been asked. You say that you'd be very pleased to as long as it doesn't mean you have to work with her because you fell out with some time ago and are no longer on speaking terms.

Unit 2 page 19

	of Tomek's major strengths
	too much attention to detail, while not seeing the big
	attention to routine administrative tasks
	main targets to be to work on record-keeping
	consistently produce work of the highest standard
	close attention to the smallest detail means that quality is
	efficient use of
	the needs of the customer
	clients have complained of having to wait
	must arrive punctually for appointments
	time consistently produces
	be relied on to find creative solutions
	come up with many of our most successful innovations
	Joseph could improve efficiency by prioritising his
	more careful scheduling

The situations in the pairwork activities are all based around typical working situations, so students will feel confident taking what they learn in class and transferring it to their professional lives.

Student's Book Lesson 3

The third lesson in the unit focuses on functional language and gives students the opportunity to improve their communication skills by learning and practising chunks of useful language.

The functional language items are included for their usefulness in a wide variety of professional contexts. They are presented visually for students to understand quickly and refer back to if necessary.

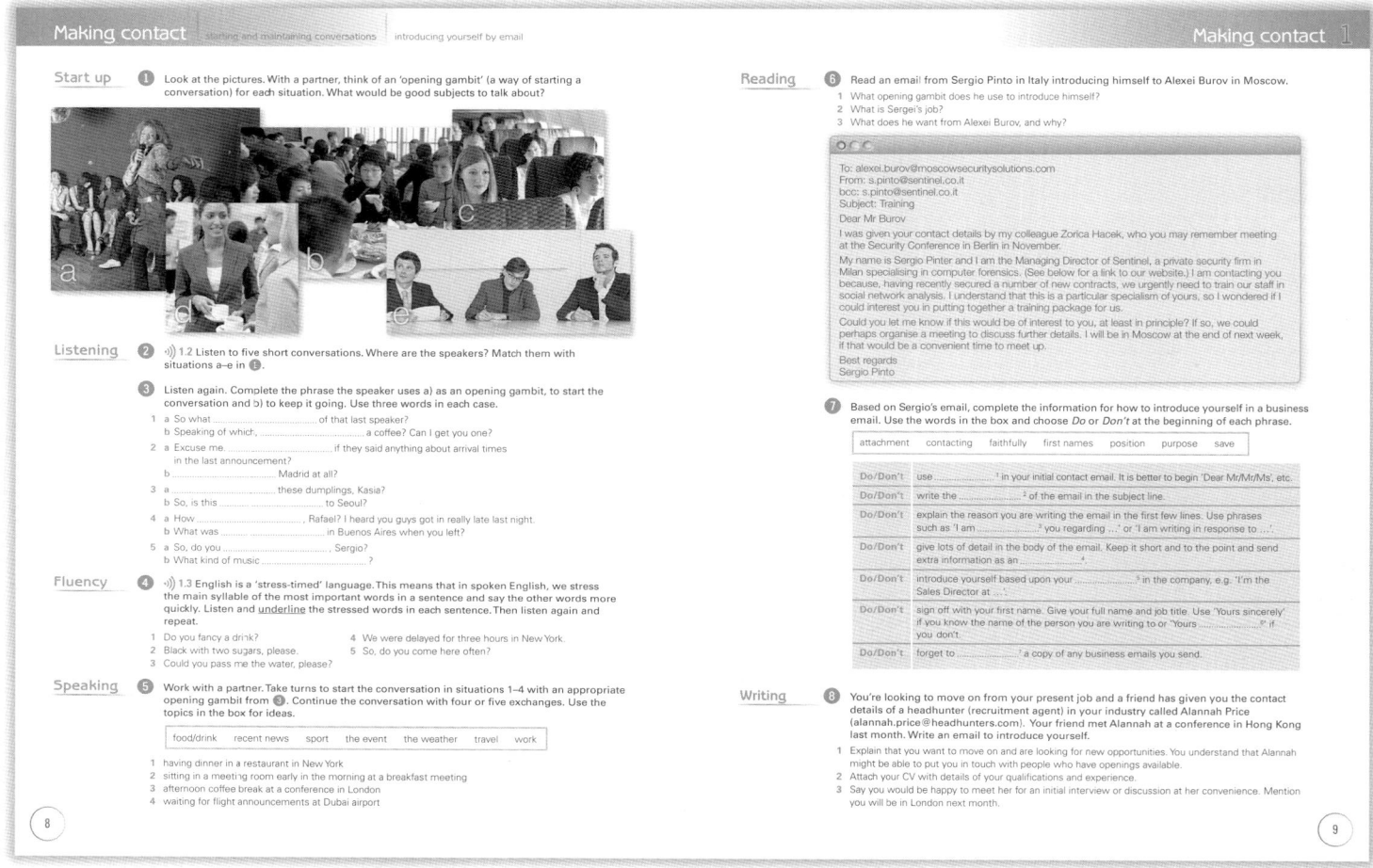

As always, the lesson begins with a speaking activity to introduce the topic.

Students can then see the functional language in context in a range of reading and listening exercises.

The lesson finishes with a speaking or role play activity to personalise and practise the language, so students can go away feeling comfortable and ready to communicate in English in a variety of situations.

Introduction to the course

Student's Book Scenarios

In the fourth and final lesson of the unit, students practise both the language and the skills that they have developed throughout the preceding lessons in a motivating real-life context in the form of a scenario.

Students interpret information from a wide range of sources including reports, emails, newspaper articles, phone messages, webpages, market research, as well as excerpts from conversations, meetings and job interviews.

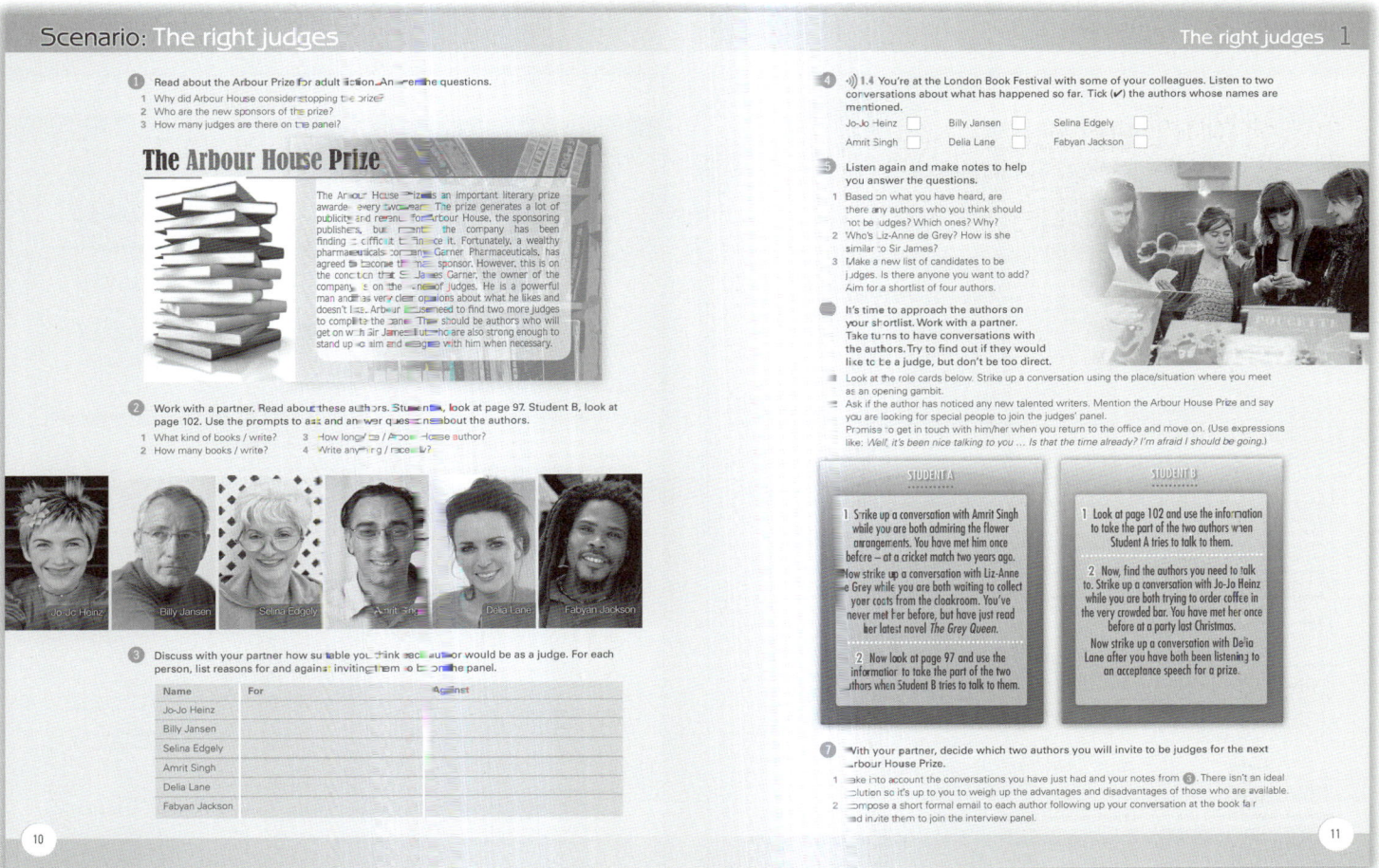

The scenario has a narrative thread, which sustains interest and links all the tasks together. Students acquire information about the situation in stages through listening and reading tasks until they have the overall picture of the situation. Students have opportunities to review what they have understood at each stage, before progressing to the final activity, where they have to resolve a problem.

Students are encouraged to work in pairs and in small groups and are given different role plays to practise the language of the lesson. These rolecards can be found in the unit pages and at the back of the book.

Student's Book Writing emails

In the middle of the Student's Book is the extensive Writing emails section, which provides templates and writing practice opportunities.

Each Writing emails lesson is topic driven and relates to one of the units in the Student's Book.

A collection of useful phrases is supplied for students to refer to when compiling their own emails. The phrases are broken down into categories for easy reference.

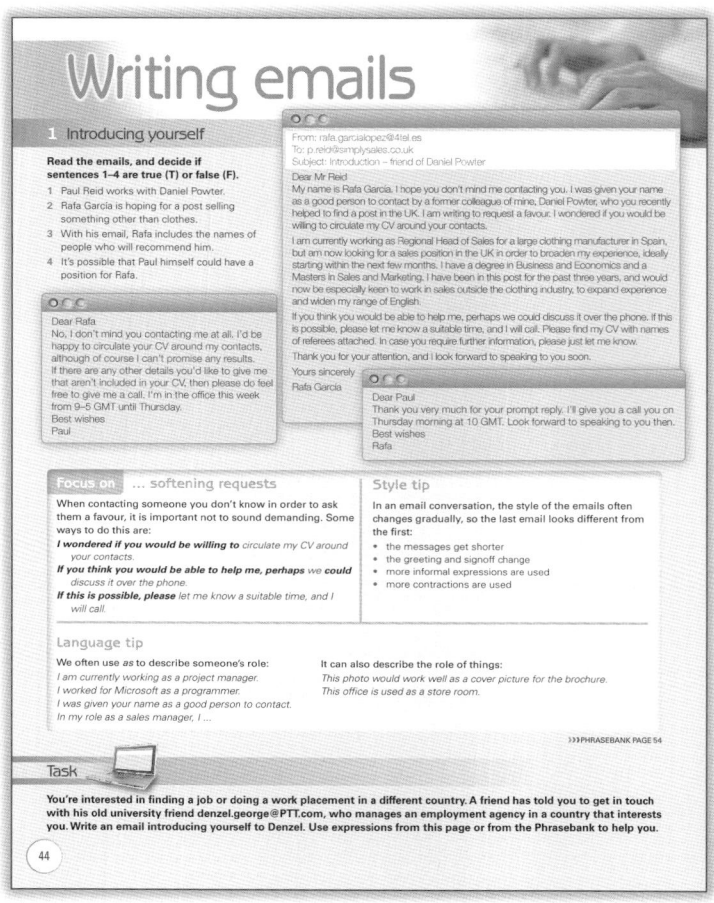

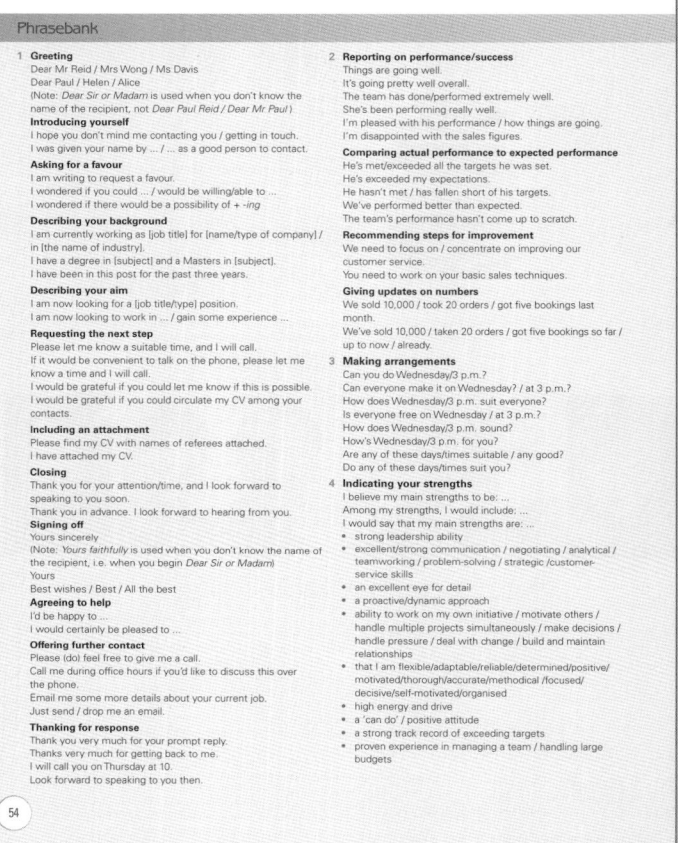

Students can refer to email writing tips which cover areas such as: style, tone, formal and informal language, grammar, punctuation and spelling.

They then put these tips into practice by carrying out an email writing task.

Introduction to the course

Workbook

The @work Workbook can be used in the classroom to extend the course or be used independently by students for self-study.

The Workbook is divided into ten units, which correspond to the Student's Book, and contains a range of activities to review the language from the Student's Book and further develop key skills.

The Workbook contains exercises to review the grammar and key vocabulary from each lesson, as well as extra listening practice and activities to improve pronunciation and use functional language.

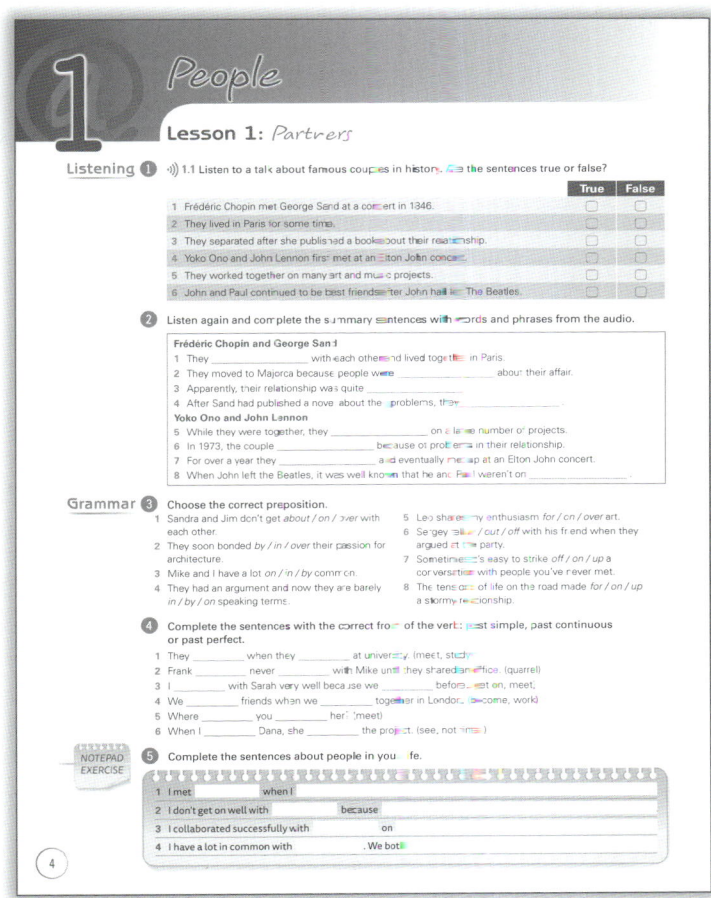

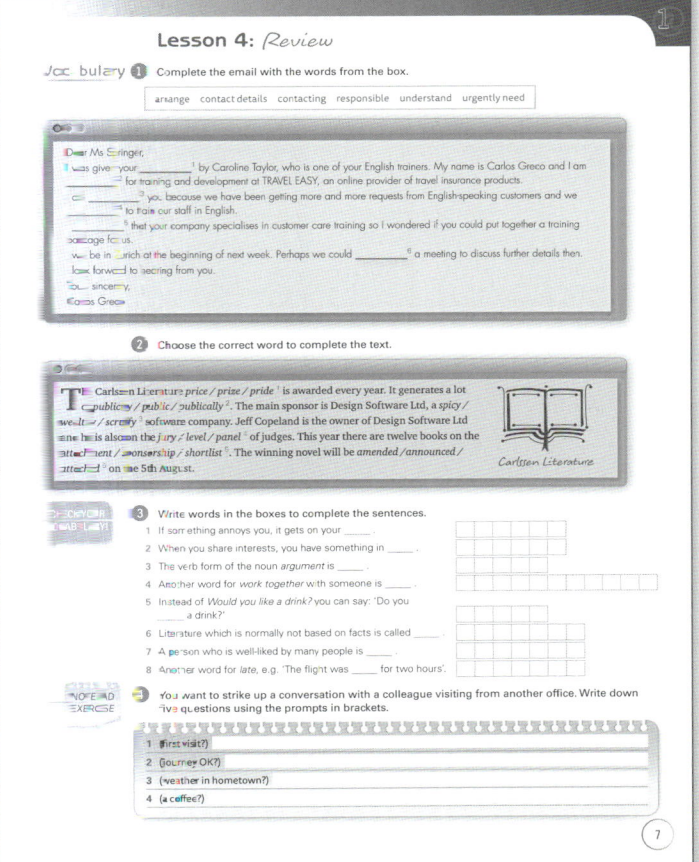

Notepad exercises make the language relevant to students and give them the opportunity to personalise their learning. When put together, these activities will form a personal profile for the students to refer to whenever they want.

Key vocabulary from the unit is reviewed in fun activities, such as crosswords and wordsearches.

At the end of every unit there is a test for students to assess their learning. Students answer 20 multiple-choice questions on different parts of the language from each unit.

To check students understand the grammar points from the Student's Book, there is also an interactive grammar section. Students are invited to complete the grammar rules and then practise them by doing the extra activities.

Test yourself

Choose the correct answer. For every correct answer you score one point.

1. I _____ lunch in the canteen when my boss phoned with an urgent question.
   a had
   b did have
   c was having

2. They had a big argument last week and since then they _____ to each other.
   a haven't spoken
   b didn't speak
   c don't speak

3. I noticed that they _____ to the speech.
   a don't really listen
   b haven't really listened
   c weren't really listening

4. I realised that I _____ Andrew at the sales conference last year.
   a met
   b had met
   c was meeting

5. Tell me about someone _____ to meet.
   a always you've wanted
   b you've always wanted
   c you've wanted always

6. A: Your laptop looks pretty old. How long _____ it?
   B: I bought it about five years ago.
   a have you had
   b did you have
   c do you have

7. If you don't speak to another person, you aren't on speaking _____ with them.
   a levels
   b conditions
   c terms

8. Another word for *working together with someone* is _____.
   a combining
   b collaborating
   c connecting

9. She had never _____ out with anyone in her life until recently.
   a fallen
   b fell
   c fall

10. A: What's Gina like?
    B: She's a really nice person, very warm and _____.
    a liking
    b likely
    c likeable

11. He's hardworking, accurate and careful not to make any mistakes. He's very _____.
    a confident
    b conscientious
    c crooked

12. *Smart* and *well-dressed* is the opposite of _____.
    a capable
    b scruffy
    c confident

13. A: Is Sebastian honest?
    B: Oh yes. He's very _____.
    a trustworthy
    b trusting
    c distrustful

14. Using software to analyse large databases is called data _____.
    a finding
    b mining
    c collecting

15. When writing an email, always send extra information as _____.
    a a copy
    b a file
    c an attachment

16. In formal emails, don't sign _____ with just your first name.
    a on
    b under
    c off

17. Use _____ when you start a formal email with 'Dear Mr Jones'.
    a Yours sincerely
    b Best wishes
    c Yours faithfully

18. Always _____ a copy of any business emails you send.
    a secure
    b save
    c safe

19. A: Excuse me. Did you hear what the last _____ said?
    B: Yes, I did. They said the flight to L.A. has been delayed.
    a statement
    b announcement
    c argument

20. I need to get to Cannon Street. I'm _____ to be in a meeting at 9.30.
    a supposed
    b planned
    c imagined

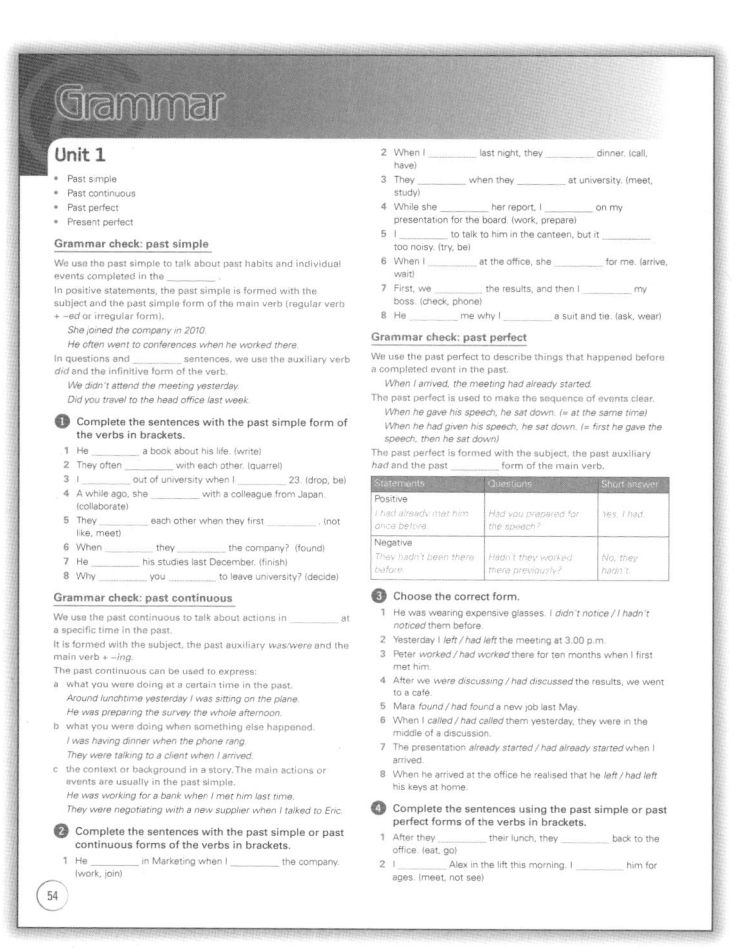

Score: _____ / 20 points

Grammar

Unit 1

- Past simple
- Past continuous
- Past perfect
- Present perfect

Grammar check: past simple

We use the past simple to talk about past habits and individual events completed in the _____.
In positive statements, the past simple is formed with the subject and the past simple form of the main verb (regular verb + –ed or irregular form).
  She joined the company in 2010.
  He often went to conferences when he worked there.
In questions and _____ sentences, we use the auxiliary verb *did* and the infinitive form of the verb.
  We didn't attend the meeting yesterday.
  Did you travel to the head office last week.

1 Complete the sentences with the past simple form of the verbs in brackets.

1. He _____ a book about his life. (write)
2. They often _____ with each other. (quarrel)
3. I _____ out of university when I _____ 23. (drop, be)
4. A while ago, she _____ with a colleague from Japan. (collaborate)
5. They _____ each other when they first _____ (not like, meet)
6. When _____ they _____ the company? (found)
7. He _____ his studies last December. (finish)
8. Why _____ you _____ to leave university? (decide)

Grammar check: past continuous

We use the past continuous to talk about actions in _____ at a specific time in the past.
It is formed with the subject, the past auxiliary *was/were* and the main verb + –ing.
The past continuous can be used to express:
a what you were doing at a certain time in the past.
  Around lunchtime yesterday I was sitting on the plane.
  He was preparing the survey the whole afternoon.
b what you were doing when something else happened.
  I was having dinner when the phone rang.
  They were talking to a client when I arrived.
c the context or background in a story. The main actions or events are usually in the past simple.
  He was working for a bank when I met him last time.
  They were negotiating with a new supplier when I talked to Eric.

2 Complete the sentences with the past simple or past continuous forms of the verbs in brackets.

1. He _____ in Marketing when I _____ the company. (work, join)

2. When I _____ last night, they _____ dinner. (call, have)
3. They _____ when they _____ at university. (meet, study)
4. While she _____ her report, I _____ on my presentation for the board. (work, prepare)
5. I _____ to talk to him in the canteen, but it _____ too noisy. (try, be)
6. When I _____ at the office, she _____ for me. (arrive, wait)
7. First, we _____ the results, and then I _____ my boss. (check, phone)
8. He _____ me why I _____ a suit and tie. (ask, wear)

Grammar check: past perfect

We use the past perfect to describe things that happened before a completed event in the past.
  When I arrived, the meeting had already started.
The past perfect is used to make the sequence of events clear.
  When he gave his speech, he sat down. (= at the same time)
  When he had given his speech, he sat down. (= first he gave the speech, then he sat down)
The past perfect is formed with the subject, the past auxiliary *had* and the past _____ form of the main verb.

Statements	Questions	Short answer
Positive		
I had already met him once before.	*Had you prepared for the speech?*	*Yes, I had.*
Negative		
They hadn't been there before.	*Hadn't they worked there previously?*	*No, they hadn't.*

3 Choose the correct form.

1. He was wearing expensive glasses. *I didn't notice / I hadn't noticed* them before.
2. Yesterday I *left / had left* the meeting at 3.00 p.m.
3. Peter *worked / had worked* there for ten months when I first met him.
4. After we *were discussing / had discussed* the results, we went to a cafe.
5. Mara *found / had found* a new job last May.
6. When I *called / had called* them yesterday, they were in the middle of a discussion.
7. The presentation *already started / had already started* when I arrived.
8. When he arrived at the office he realised that he *left / had left* his keys at home.

4 Complete the sentences using the past simple or past perfect forms of the verbs in brackets.

1. After they _____ their lunch, they _____ back to the office. (eat, go)
2. I _____ Alex in the lift this morning. I _____ him for ages. (meet, not see)

All the audioscripts from the Workbook activities are supplied at the back of the book.

Answers to all the activities are available on the *@work* Learning Platform.

This Workbook is also available in digital format. Details can be found on the *@work* Learning Platform at: www.richmondatwork.net.

Introduction to the course

 ## The @work Learning Platform

The *@work* Learning Platform is where students and teachers can go to use *@work* online. Students and teachers will find extra resources as well as access to the Virtual Learning Environment (VLE). To start, go to: **www.richmondatwork.net**.

Any institution that has adopted a Richmond course can register for the *@work* Learning Platform by simply clicking on the 'Register' button of the course homepage and following the registration process. An 'institution' can consist of just a private teacher. As part of the registration process, at least one Training Manager must be allocated.

Training Managers administer the institution's Richmond VLE. They can create classes and add teachers and students. Once a student is added, they can log in using the Access Code found at the back of their Student's Book. They will then have access to the Student's Area and the additional digital material on the VLE.

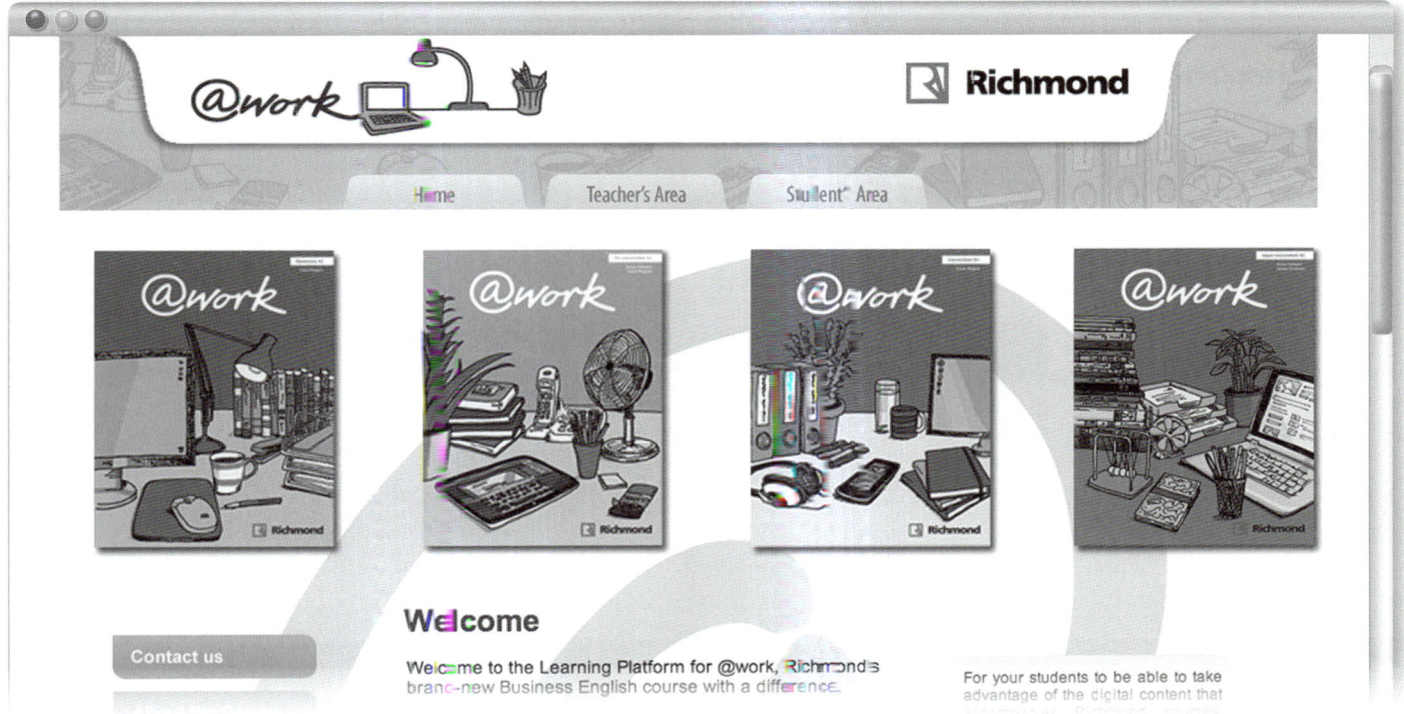

The Teacher's Area includes:

- Wordlists
- Student's Book audioscripts in Word format
- Role play task sheets
- Role play teacher's notes
- Workbook answers
- CEF mapping documents
- Access to the VLE

The Student's Area includes:

- Email templates
- The Business English Widget
- Links to useful learning sites
- Workbook unit tests
- Access to the VLE

The Virtual Learning Environment

The VLE allows an institution to manage all their classes online. Teachers are able to create their own blended course by communicating with students, setting assignments, monitoring progress and much more.

Richmond provides each student with extra digital content in the VLE to complement their course. Students have access to unit tests taken from the Workbook and interactive email activities that extend the email section in the Student's Book.

New products, such as the eWorkbook or the Video Modules, can also be accessed via the VLE using the Access Codes found with these products.

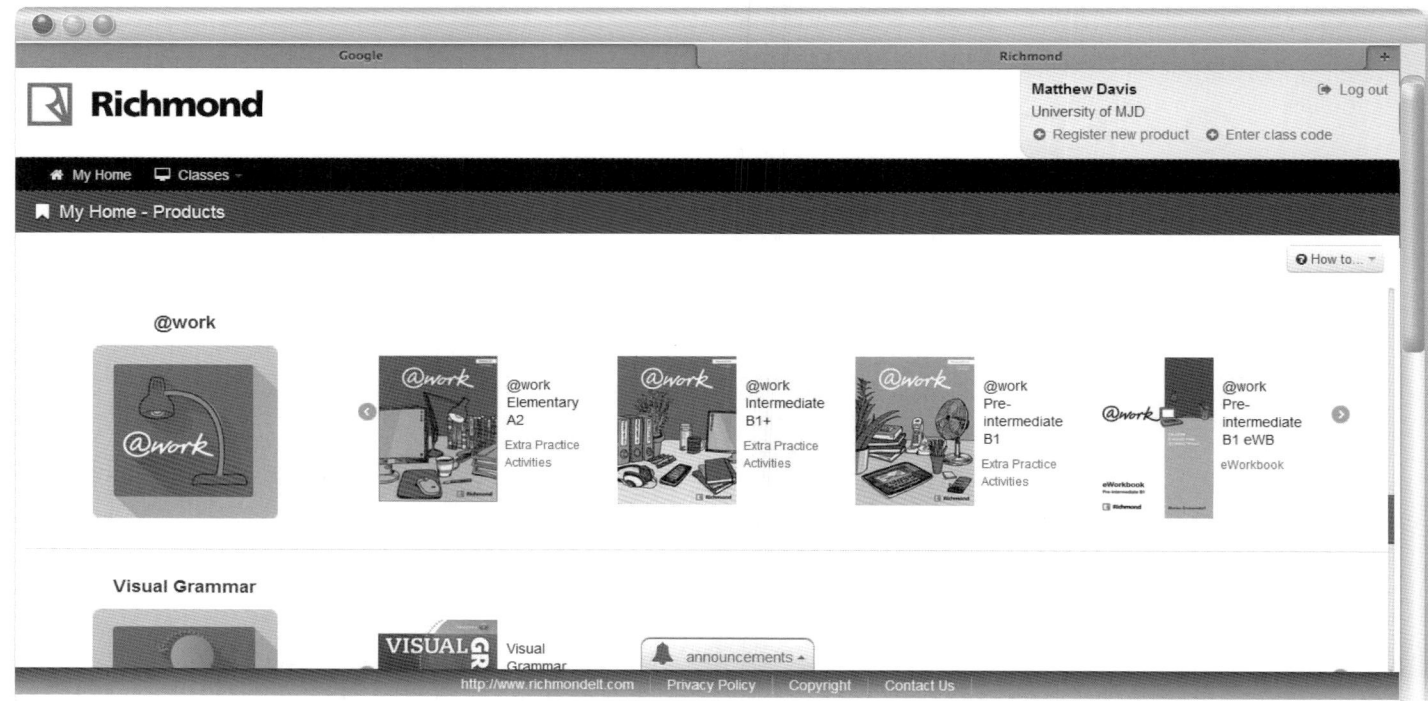

The VLE is organised into six different areas:

- **Materials** lets teachers manage the digital resources, such as unit tests and workbook activities, by giving access to students when appropriate.

- **Library**, where teachers can share useful documents with their classes and colleagues.

- **Forum** lets teachers and students create topics and comment on them. An excellent way to get students using English and participating in the learning process.

- **Participants**, where teachers can manage the students in their classes.

- **Assignments** lets teachers set work for their students.

- **Markbook** lets teachers monitor their students' progress so that as students complete activities, their results are updated automatically.

Introduction to the course

Additional digital materials

Richmond Mazes

The Richmond Mazes are entertaining and interactive short stories set in the world of work. Students must decide which route to take, creating their own adventure and dealing with English throughout.

These innovative and fun stories give students the chance to see and react to the language they have learnt throughout the course in a captivating real-life story.

The Richmond Mazes are available as apps for Apple and Android devices.

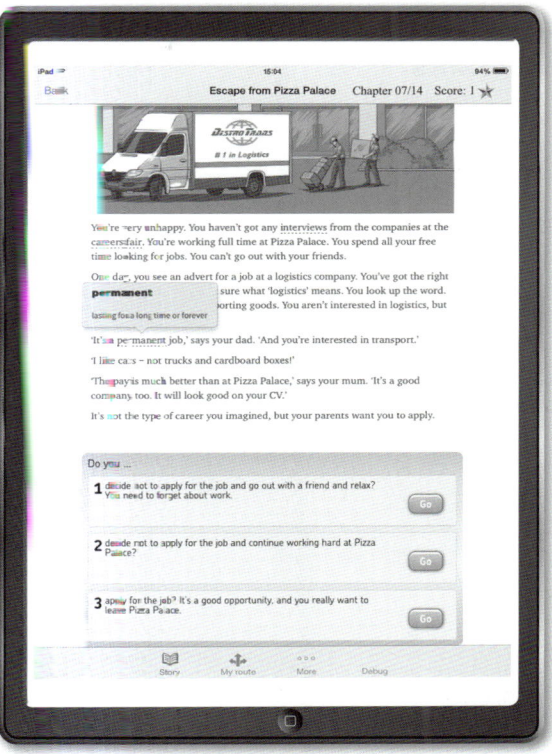

The eWorkbook

For students who wish to practise their English on the move, a digital version of the Workbook is available as a CD-ROM or via the @work Learning Platform. The eWorkbook is fully interactive and includes all audio tracks and answers.

The eWorkbook is linked with the Teacher's Markbook on the VLE so that teachers can monitor students, progress and identify any problem areas.

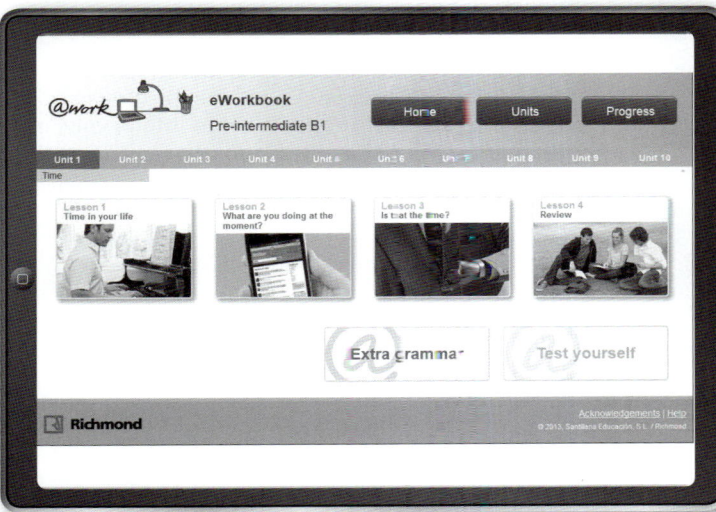

19

Business Skills

These modules are perfect for students who need practice in specialised business skills or for anyone who wants to use English professionally.

Extensive video clips and interactive activities focus on a range of skills, including:

- Presentations
- Negotiations
- Socialising
- Communications
- Meetings

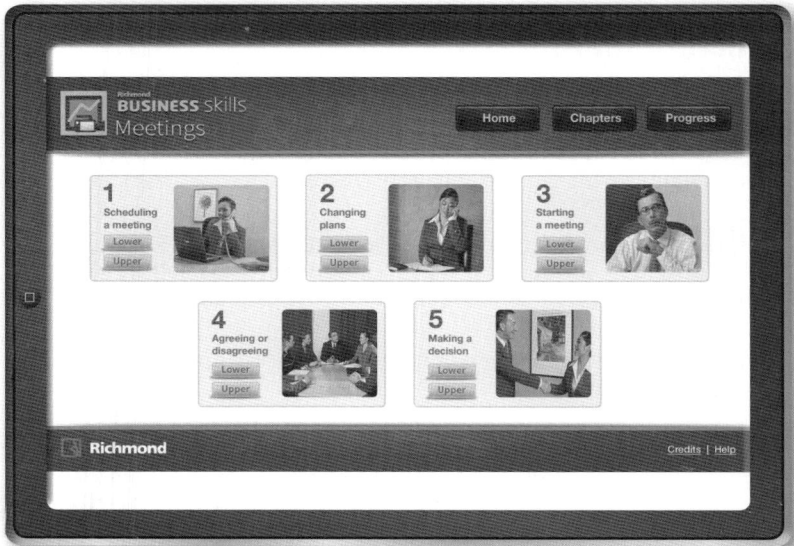

Students watch professional situations where these important skills are used and then analyse and practise the target language. This boosts the students' confidence, giving them the tools they need to deal with these situations where getting English right can be vitally important.

Students can work through the material in conjuction with the *@work* course, or they can focus on individual modules more intensively, in preparation for a specific purpose.

Richmond Business Theories

The Richmond Business Theories are a collection of apps which explore a range of important business theories and concepts. Available across four levels, the apps are all based on mini-lectures written by business specialists and university lecturers. They feature practice activities where students can test the theories and concepts in question plus a range of additional activities that will help students expand their business vocabulary.

Topics include team work, change management and motivation, and will suit both business students and working professionals.

The Richmond Business Theories apps are available for Android and Apple devices.

An institutional version is also available for each level, offering trackable access to all five theories for up to twenty students. Please contact your local Richmond representative for more details.

People

UNIT OBJECTIVES:

Students will practise ...
past tenses
present perfect
describing relationships and people

and they will learn how to ...
start and maintain a conversation
introduce themselves by email

Lesson 1: Partners, page 4

LESSON OBJECTIVES:

Students will learn and practise ...
describing relationships
past tenses

Warm up

Write down the names of some famous partnerships, living or dead, on separate pieces of paper (e.g. John Lennon on one piece, and Yoko Ono on another). You'll need enough for one per student plus one for you. Demonstrate the activity by taking a piece of paper and talking about the person on it, without saying their name. If a student guesses correctly, give him/her the piece of paper. Give out the pieces of paper and ask the students to walk round and pair up, introducing their person and exchanging papers after guessing correctly (or giving up). In this way they do a different person each time. When everyone has had several turns, ask the students to stop and find their partner, for example the person with *John Lennon* would join *Yoko Ono*. Then ask each pair to say why the couple are famous.

Start up

1 Focus on the pictures and ask the students to work in pairs to discuss the questions. Allow a few minutes for discussion, then ask the class to quickly read about the partnerships on page 96. After a few minutes ask the students to turn back to page 4. Ask them what they learnt about the Williams sisters – nominate an enthusiastic student to briefly summarise their achievements, then ask for ideas on why they have been so successful. Continue in the same way with the other partnerships. Involve as many students as possible.

Reading

2 Focus on the pictures. Ask the students what band Mick Jagger and Keith Richards were founder-members of (The Rolling Stones), and what company Sergey Brin and Larry Page founded (Google). Pre-teach *quarrel* (to disagree in an angry way; argue). Ask the students to read the questions first, then quickly read the texts to find the answers. Check the answers.

ANSWERS

1 Brin and Page 2 Jagger and Richards 3 Jagger and Richards 4 Jagger and Richards 5 Brin and Page

Vocabulary

3 Draw attention to the highlighted expressions in the text in **2**. Look at the example with the class, then ask the students to complete the exercise. As you check the answers, elicit simple definitions of the highlighted expressions (e.g. *share a passion* means 'be very interested in the same thing', and *bond* means 'become friends').

ANSWERS

1 shared his passion 2 tensions 3 had a lot in common 4 get on with, bonded 5 speaking terms 6 got on each other's nerves 7 collaborating 8 fall out 9 shared a vision

Students can find more activities at www.richmondatwork.net

Grammar

4 Focus on the **Grammar** box. Ask the students to complete the rules with the names of the tenses. Draw their attention to the grammar reference on page 108, which they can use for help or to expand the information in the grammar box. Check the answers then give the students a few minutes to find three examples of each of the different tenses in the text. Let the students compare answers in pairs before checking in class.

ANSWERS

1 past simple
e.g. Mick Jagger and Keith Richards met for the first time, They struck up a conversation, Keith noticed the rare (for the time) Muddy Waters records
2 past continuous
e.g. Mick was carrying [records] under his arm, they were both studying for a PhD, they were working on the same research project
3 past perfect
e.g. He had never met anyone, he hadn't visited Mick's dressing room, both had fallen in love with computers

5 Divide the class in two halves, A and B. Ask the students on side A to work in pairs to complete the text on page 96, and the students on side B to do the same with the text on page 101. Monitor as they do this and deal with any doubts or problems.

22

People 1

ANSWERS

Student A: 1 met 2 were studying 3 bonded 4 was
5 had met 6 married 7 settled 8 managed 9 was rising
10 was building 11 had ended (or ended)
Student B: 1 met 2 were both studying 3 had never known
4 shared 5 were spending 6 began 7 was building
8 was becoming 9 supported 10 had agreed 11 lasted

Students can find more activities at www.richmondatwork.net

Speaking

6 Ask the students to work together in the same AA, BB pairs to prepare the questions and agree on how they will answer the questions. Tell Student As that, as the people they are going to ask about are no longer alive, they need to use the past tense for the questions; tell Student Bs that they need to use the present tense in places, as the people are still alive.

ANSWERS

1 What are/were they?
2 What do/did they do?
3 Why are/were they famous?
4 Where did they meet?
5 What were their first impressions of each other when they first met?
6 What do/did they have in common?
7 Why do/did they get on well?
8 What tensions are/were there in the relationship?

7 Ask the students to work in AB pairs to ask and answer the questions they prepared in **6**. When they have finished, ask them to swap books to read the other student's text and check the tenses used. Only give answers if there is disagreement. Finally, ask one or two students to give a brief summary of their partner's text. Give the students a chance to discuss the couples in the text further (e.g. ask if students know what the Clintons are doing now, or whether they have read anything by Sartre or de Beauvoir).

8 Demonstrate the activity yourself first: ask a student to choose a number 1–5, and use the prompts for the number they choose to talk about a real person in your life. Expand on the prompts and encourage questions. Then ask the students to do the same in pairs, taking turns to nominate a number for the other to talk about.

Extra activity

Ask the students to write about a special friendship, either in class or for homework, describing how they met, how the friendship developed and their best memories from their time with the person.

Lesson 2: First impressions, page 6

LESSON OBJECTIVES:
Students will learn and practise …
describing people
present perfect

Warm up

Write on the whiteboard:
You can't judge a _____ by its cover.
First impressions are _____ lasting.
Tell the class that these are sayings (traditional phrases that express something many people believe is true about life). Ask the students to discuss briefly with a partner what the missing words could be. Elicit or give the answers (*book* and *most*). Elicit an explanation of the sayings (You can't understand what a person is really like from how they look, speak, dress, etc.; What you think of a person the first time you meet them stays with you for a long time). Ask the class if they agree with the sayings, and whether they have similar expressions in their language(s).

Start up

1 Focus on the picture. Ask the students if they think the people know each other or have just met. Ask them how they know? Give the students time to discuss the questions, then take feedback from the class.

Reading

2 Pre-teach *posture* (the position you hold your body in). Read the questions and give the class five minutes to read the text without looking up words. Allow them time to compare answers in pairs before checking the answers.

ANSWERS

a People with straight teeth are perceived to be happier, more intelligent and more trustworthy than those with crooked teeth.
b Your choice of footwear reveals a lot about you in terms of age, income and personality traits.
c Whether a woman wears a skirt or trousers still has a bearing on how she is perceived in the modern-day workplace.
d Wearing too much or too little make up can tip the balance between being considered competent/likeable and unreliable/dishonest.
e Your posture conveys the strongest impression of you, both positive and negative.

Vocabulary

3 Ask the students to match the highlighted words in the text to the definitions without using dictionaries, using the context to help them. Ask them to compare answers before checking the answers.

23

ANSWERS

1 scruffy 2 capable, competent 3 arrogant 4 aggressive
5 dishonest 6 trustworthy 7 confident 8 conscientious
9 unreliable 10 powerful

4 Ask the students to work in pairs to categorise the adjectives. Ask them which ones could be positive or negative, depending on the context (*confident, powerful*).

ANSWERS

positive: confident, trustworthy, conscientious, capable, competent, powerful
negative: arrogant, aggressive, scruffy, unreliable, dishonest

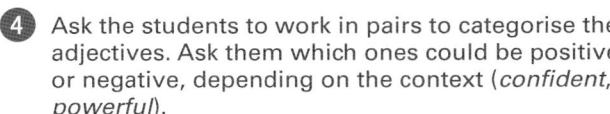 Students can find more activities at www.richmondatwork.net

Listening

5 Elicit or teach verbs that can be used with an adjective to describe first impressions, when seeing a picture of a person (*He/She looks ...*) or actually meeting them (*He/She comes across as / seems ...*). Give the students time to discuss the pictures before taking feedback. Write the four people's names on the whiteboard, with the adjectives students suggest for them underneath.

6 **1.1** Give the students time to read questions 1–5 then play the audio. Check the answers, then write on the whiteboard:

I thought he looked quite friendly, but _____ he came across as a bit aggressive.

Elicit words or phrases that can go in the gap (*in fact / actually*). Allow the students time to talk about the discussion questions before taking feedback.

ANSWERS

1 He has spoken to customers and helped with large projects.
2 She's been in London for nearly four years.
3 He hasn't spoken much English.
4 She's just come back from travelling round the world.
5 She sold timeshare holiday apartments.

 **1.1**

Charlie
Yes, thank you, I'd like a glass of water. As you will see from my CV, I've worked in this sector since I graduated, but in an administrative role. I do have lots of experience, though. I've spoken to customers and I've helped with large projects, for example. Working in sales is my ultimate goal and since I already have a lot of contacts, I don't think it would be very difficult to transfer.

Brigitta
Yes, that's right, Brigitta Klaff – K-L-A-double F.F. Yes, I moved to London from Munich when I got a job with my present employer about three and a half years ago. So, I've been here for nearly four years now. I worked in the sales department at Handler when I was still a student so I have probably about five years' sales experience in total. Having worked in a larger organisation, I'm sure I'd have no problems handling this job. No, thank you. I don't want any coffee.

Didier
Yes, please. Milk with one sugar. So yes, as I was saying, I worked in direct sales for nearly two years when I was with Delcaux in Paris. It was quite an international environment, so we spoke English most of the time. I haven't spoken much English for the last year or so because there wasn't any need for it in my present job. I don't think I've forgotten anything. As you can hear my accent isn't perfect, but I've never had any problems in getting people to understand me.

Sheryl
Oh, is that my coffee ... thank you so much. Oops, sorry ... I'll just ... yes ... there you are ... Sorry, what were you saying? That's right, I've just come back from travelling round the world. I worked selling timeshare holiday apartments in Ibiza for about six months.

Grammar

7 Focus on the **Grammar** box. Ask the students to match the uses of the present perfect to their answers in **6**. Remind them to check the grammar reference on page 109 if necessary. Give the students a few minutes to do the exercise. Check the answers.

ANSWERS

1 She's just come back from travelling around the world.
2 He has spoken to customers and helped with large projects.
3 She's been in London for nearly four years; He hasn't spoken much English.
4 She sold timeshare holiday apartments.

 Students can find more activities at www.richmondatwork.net

Speaking

8 Ask the students to work in pairs to write the questions using the prompts. When one or two pairs are ready, nominate a student to ask you one of the questions. Expand on your answer and encourage questions. Answer two or three questions in this way, then elicit the correct form of the questions for the students to check. Then ask the class to continue in pairs, taking turns to ask each other any of the questions 1–5. After ten minutes, or when one or two pairs have finished, nominate students to report one thing their partner said.

ANSWERS

1 How long have you been in your present job/course? When did you start?
2 Tell me about someone you have always wanted to meet?
3 Have you ever worn the wrong clothes for something? Were you too smart or too scruffy?
4 Tell me about someone who has made a good or bad impression on you recently. Why?
5 How long have you had your favourite pair of shoes? Where and when did you buy them? What impression do you think they make on people?

People 1

Extra activity

Ask the students to look up or work out the opposites of the highlighted adjectives in ❷. Alternatively, write the opposites on the whiteboard, and get the students to match them.

Possible answers:
confident – nervous/lacking in confidence
trustworthy – untrustworthy
conscientious – sloppy/careless
arrogant – modest
aggressive – calm/laid-back
scruffy – smart/smartly-dressed
capable – useless/hopeless
competent – incompetent
powerful – weak/insignificant

Lesson 3: Making contact, page 8

LESSON OBJECTIVES:

Students will learn and practise ...
starting and maintaining conversations
introducing yourself by email

Warm up

Prepare small pieces of paper with the following words: *nice, expensive, beautiful, America, hungry, time, cold, money, airport, sure, really, sound, sky, people, home, green, sun.*

Give each student a piece of paper and tell them that they will have to start a conversation with another member of the class with the aim of making that other person say the word on their piece of paper.

Demonstrate by taking one of the words and starting a conversation with a confident student. For example, if you have the word 'Australia', you could say, 'I saw a really interesting documentary about New Zealand last night. The Sydney Opera House is amazing!' The student might respond, 'But Sydney's in Australia!', and you would be the winner. When you succeed in getting them to say your word, say 'yes!' and show the class the word. Explain that the first person to make their partner say their word wins. After each round, ask the students to swap pieces of paper and partners and repeat the game.

Start up

❶ Start by asking students to guess where the people are in the pictures (a = in a karaoke bar, b = in a restaurant, c = on a plane, d = at a conference, e = in a business meeting). Then ask the students to work in pairs to choose two of the pictures and write down one opening gambit for each situation. Take feedback and write down suggestions on the whiteboard. Then ask pairs to think about the other three situations and for each one to write down three suitable topics to discuss and one not suitable to discuss. Take feedback, and encourage comments and discussion of the suggestions.

POSSIBLE ANSWERS

a Karaoke evening: *So what kind of music do you like / are you into?*
b In a restaurant: *Mm! This is delicious, isn't it?*
c In a plane: *I didn't catch that. Did you hear what that announcement said?*
d Coffee break at a conference: *So what did you think of that last speaker? Did you enjoy the talk?*
e Waiting for a meeting to begin: *How was your journey this morning? Do you know what the first item on the agenda is all about?*

As a rule for small talk, you can comment about what's going on or what you can see around you, e.g. the building, décor, weather, food, etc. – or some aspect of your shared experience, e.g. *How long you have been waiting? What time you are going to arrive? When something is going to finish?*
You can also ask non-invasive general questions about your interlocutor's experience or opinion of what you are doing/observing, e.g. *Did you enjoy the X? What did you think of the last X? So do you often X?*
You could even ask a general information question to which you might actually know the answer, but can use as an excuse for getting a conversation going, e.g. *Do you know what time ... ?*

Listening

❷ 🔊 1.2 Ask the students to write the numbers 1–5 in their books, then play the audio once for students to match pictures a–e with the recordings. Check the answers.

ANSWERS

1 d   2 c   3 b   4 e   5 a

❸ Students listen again and complete the phrases. With weaker classes, you may like to pause the recording after each conversation. Check the answers.

ANSWERS

1 a did you think   b do you fancy
2 a Did you hear   b Do you know
3 a Have you tried   b your first visit
4 a was your journey   b the weather like
5 a come here often   b are you into

🔊 1.2
1
A: So, what did you think of that last speaker?
B: Well, he was obviously trying to be provocative, but at least it was interesting. I didn't really get what he was saying about social media though, did you?
A: No. I think he lost it a bit in the second part. Perhaps he was getting tired and it was just too near the coffee break! Speaking of which, do you fancy a coffee? Can I get you one?
B: On, yes thank you. Black with two sugars, please.
2
C: Excuse me. Did you hear if they said anything about arrival times in the last announcement?
D: I think she said that we'd be landing at around 12.30.

25

C: Thanks … Do you have any idea how long it takes to get from the airport to the city centre by taxi? Do you know Madrid at all?
D: Actually the quickest way to get to the city centre is by metro – you'll only end up sitting in traffic if you take a taxi. Whereabouts are you going?
C: I'm supposed to be in a meeting at 2.00 in … hang on … Calle Serrano … and …

3
E: Have you tried these dumplings, Kasia?
F: Oh no, thank you. They look delicious, but I really can't eat any more! Could you pass me the water, please?
E: Yes, of course, here you are. … So, is this your first visit to Seoul?
F: No, it's actually my third time in Seoul, but I never seem to have any time to visit the city properly. I'd be really interested in seeing the …

4
G: How was your journey, Rafael? I heard you guys got in really late last night.
H: Yes, we didn't have a great trip. We were delayed for three hours in New York, but anyway, we've made it.
G: I'm sorry the weather is so awful. We've had nothing but snow and ice since November. It must be quite a change for you, I'd imagine. What was the weather like in Buenos Aires when you left?
H: Well, warm and sunny, I have to say! But I thought it always snowed here in the winter.

5
I: So, do you come here often, Sergio?
J: Yes, this is one of our favourite places – here, take a song list. What kind of music are you into?
I: I like music, but you have to believe me, Sergio, I really, really can't sing. I sound terrible – just ask my wife! I'll be quite happy just listening.

Fluency

4 **1.3** Write the last phrase from ❸ on the whiteboard: *What kind of music are you into?* Ask the students to work in pairs to decide which three of the words are essential to understand the meaning of the sentence (*what, music, into*). Then elicit which parts of *music* and *into* are stressed (*mu-* and *in*). Underline *What*, *mu-* and *in-* on the whiteboard. Say these syllables as you do three evenly-spaced clicks with your fingers:

What … mu … in

(click … click … click)

Get the students to do it with you a few times, then stop. Signal for the students to listen, then add the rest of the sentence into the rhythm, with the same finger clicks. Exaggerate the *What … mu … in* and make the rest of the sentence faint and less distinct.

Again, get the students to join in with you. Repeat several times so that they can feel the rhythm. Everyone should be smiling!

Now read the rubric. The demonstration should help the students understand 'stress-timed'. Tell the students that most languages are not stress-timed, and elicit or teach 'syllable-timed' (describes a language where each syllable takes approximately the same amount of time).

Ask the students to work in pairs to underline the stressed syllables in each sentence, then play the audio to check answers. When everyone has the correct syllables marked, play the recording again for them to listen and repeat.

ANSWERS
1 Do you <u>fan</u>cy a <u>drink</u>?
2 <u>Black</u> with <u>two</u> <u>sug</u>ars, please.
3 Could you <u>pass</u> me the <u>wa</u>ter, please?
4 We were de<u>layed</u> for <u>three</u> <u>hours</u> in New <u>York</u>.
5 So, do you <u>come</u> here <u>of</u>ten?

 1.3
See Answers above.

Speaking

5 Read the rubric and demonstrate the activity with a confident student. Ask the class to choose one of the situations 1–4 for the two of you to demonstrate, e.g. afternoon coffee break at a conference in London. Have a look with your demonstration partner at the most appropriate opening gambit from ❸, then stand together as if on a coffee break, and get the student to begin the conversation, *e.g. So, what did you think of that last speaker?* Improvise an answer, then add another comment or question that your partner can respond to, *e.g. I thought she made some very good points, but she didn't seem very confident. Did you enjoy the talk?*

Wait for your partner to improvise an answer, and then gesture that he/she needs to add another sentence after the basic answer, to keep the conversation going. Continue like this, taking turns to respond and add a comment or question, until you have each spoken four or five times. Ask the class if they can remember the opening gambit used (*So, what did you think of that last speaker?*) and elicit the four key syllables (*what … think … last … speak-*). Demonstrate this sentence with regular finger clicks, to remind them to try to incorporate the stress-timed feeling when they speak.

Ask the students to continue the exercise in pairs, improvising conversations in the various situations. Monitor as they do this, noting any pronunciation or language issues that you can deal with afterwards with the class.

Reading

6 To link with the previous exercise, write on the whiteboard:

making first contact

conversation   *by email*

Point at *conversation* and elicit/recap the 'rules' (you start with an opening gambit about the context you are both in, and you continue to talk about a range of acceptable topics, taking short turns).

People 1

Point to *by email*, and elicit ways in which this first contact is different (e.g. you have to say why you're contacting the person and explain who you are, then go on to the exact details of what you're writing about; you would stick to business rather than general topics; your language would be more formal; you don't get an immediate response).

Focus attention on the email and read the questions. Pre-teach *computer forensics* (examination of the information on a computer while investigating a crime), *secure a contract* (to successfully arrange a formal agreement) and *training package* (training that includes several different parts). Allow the students time to read the email quickly and answer the questions. Check the answers as a class.

ANSWERS
1 I was given your contact details by my colleague …
2 He's the Managing Director of a private security firm.
3 He wants training for his staff in social network analysis because he has recently secured a number of new contracts where this skill will be required.

 Ask the class to do the first line as an example. Give everyone time to think before eliciting the answer (*Don't … first names*). Give the students time to complete the exercise and compare their answers in pairs before checking the answers as a class.

ANSWERS
1 Don't, first names 2 Do, purpose 3 Do, contacting
4 Don't, attachment 5 Do, position 6 Don't, faithfully
7 Don't, save

Writing

 Ask the students to work on the email in pairs in class, or set the task for homework. If doing it in class, set a time limit, then get pairs to compare their email with other pairs and discuss major differences. Monitor as they do the task, answering any questions and noting language issues to deal with later.

POSSIBLE ANSWER
Dear Ms Price
I was given your contact details by XX who you may remember meeting at the XX conference in Hong Kong last month. My name is XX and I am XX (job) at XX (company) in XX (place). I am contacting you because I feel ready to move on from my present job and I am looking for new opportunities. I understand that you are looking for people with my profile and might be able to put me in touch with companies who have openings available. I attach my CV with full details of my qualifications and experience and would be very happy to meet you for an initial interview or discussion. I will be in London next month if that would be a convenient time to meet up.
Yours sincerely
XX (full name)
XX (job title and company)

Extra activities

a Dictate the sample answer from ❽ for the students to write down, replacing the XX with names. Then give them each a copy to check their version against.

b Prepare twice as many small pieces of paper as there are students in the class. On each piece of paper, write a common word that is not obviously connected to business, e.g. *baby, ball, banana, crossword, fire, hat, hospital, jungle, lion, lipstick, moon, pencil, plastic, sand, shark, soap, storm, tooth, tree, wedding*.

Tell the students that they are at a conference, and they have to start conversations with new people. To make it more difficult, you are going to give them a word, and they have to try and use this in the conversation without the other person guessing what the word on the paper is.

Demonstrate the activity with a student by each taking a piece of paper and looking at it secretly. Then improvise a conversation starting with an opening gambit, and trying to work in your word. After about one minute, stop and ask the class what they think the word written on the paper is. After they have guessed, reveal the answer.

Give each student a piece of paper with a word. Ask the students to stand and pair up with their first partner, and say 'Go'. After about a minute say 'Now guess the word'. Allow time for guesses, then say 'Change partner'.

Scenario: The right judges, page 10

SCENARIO OBJECTIVE:
Students will choose two judges for a literary panel.

Warm up

 Write on the whiteboard:
What is the most prestigious literary prize in your country?
How is the winner decided?
What is the prize? Who provides the prize?
Can you name any famous winners?

Elicit the meaning of *prestigious* (highly respected), then ask the students to discuss the questions before taking feedback. Write any useful vocabulary on the whiteboard, adding *panel of judges* if this doesn't emerge naturally.

Read the questions with the class, then give the students two or three minutes to read the text before comparing answers in pairs. Check the answers.

ANSWERS
1 They had been finding it difficult to finance the prize.
2 Garner Pharmaceuticals, a wealthy pharmaceutical company.
3 three

 Focus on the pictures and elicit who the people are (authors, who are potential panelists). Ask the students what their impression of the first person is, going by the picture.

Elicit *She looks* + adjective. Then ask the class to compare their first impressions of the people in pairs. Take feedback and write up any useful vocabulary on the whiteboard.

Focus attention on the prompts, and elicit which questions would use the present perfect (2, 3 and 4). Quickly elicit the question forms from the class.

Divide the class in two halves, A and B. Tell the students they are going to read about three of the authors, and they can note down three key words for each author to help them remember the key points afterwards. Ask the students on side A to read the texts on page 97, and the students on side B to read the texts on page 102. Set a time limit of six minutes.

When the time is up, ask the students to work with a partner who has read the same texts and compare the keywords they chose, explaining them in context.

Rearrange the students in AB pairs, and get them to ask each other the questions from prompts 1–5, and answer them from memory, only checking information if they can't remember.

ANSWERS

1 What kind of books does he/she write?
2 How many books has he/she written?
3 How long has he/she been an Arbour House author?
4 Has he/she written anything recently?
Jo-Jo Heinz: 1 comic novels   **2** two novels   **3** two years
4 Yes, has written two books recently.
Billy Jansen: 1 writes political biographies   **2** six biographies
3 15 years   **4** Yes, wrote a best-seller last year.
Selina Edgely: 1 historical, romantic fiction   **2** about 20
3 20 years   **4** Yes, publishes a novel a year.
Amrit Singh: 1 a trilogy about a traditional Indian family
2 three novels   **3** 12 years   **4** nothing for ten years
Delia Lane: 1 spy thrillers   **2** 12 novels   **3** 14 years
4 nothing for two years
Fabyan Jackson: 1 poetry   **2** one   **3** one year   **4** a book of poems last year

3 Ask the students to suggest reasons for inviting Jo-Jo Heinz onto the panel (e.g. popular novelist and personality, would make prize more popular). Do the same with reasons against (e.g. not a good writer, maybe doesn't have necessary knowledge and experience). Then ask the students to work in pairs and complete the table for the other authors. When they have finished, ask them to compare their notes with another pair.

POSSIBLE ANSWERS

Name	For	Against
Jo-Jo Heinz	Funny and entertaining. Well-known because on TV a lot. Popular.	Young and inexperienced, not really a very good writer although books have popular appeal.
Billy Jansen	Wrote best-seller last year. Popular and well known. Strong personality and could stand up to Sir James.	Strong personality, but often offends people. Can be arrogant and sarcastic so could cause trouble.
Selina Edgely	Has mass appeal as a best-selling author, but is also considered 'literary' so an ideal candidate.	Political views and particularly attitude regarding animal rights and testing in pharmaceutical labs means unlikely she would get on with Sir James. Politically dangerous and could even result in Arbour House losing the support of Garner Pharmaceuticals.
Amrit Singh	Ideal in many ways because is a gifted author with good standing in the literary world. Shares tastes with Sir James (cricket).	Hasn't written anything new for ten years.
Delia Lane	One of Arbour House's best-selling authors. Sir James is a big fan. Putting her on panel might encourage her to stay with Arbour House.	Quite shy, so may not want to be on panel. Not written anything in last two years.
Fabyan Jackson	Amusing, charming, popular with young people and a strong public profile.	Very different from Sir James and personalities likely to clash.

4 1.4 Elicit what happens at a book festival (e.g. authors talk about their books; readers have a chance to ask authors questions; publishing companies sell books).

Play the audio for students to tick the names of the authors mentioned.

ANSWERS

Billy Jansen, Selina Edgely, Amrit Singh and Fabyan Jackson are mentioned.

5 Give the class time to read the questions. Play the audio again once or twice for them to make notes. Give them time to think about their notes and answer the questions, then ask them to compare their answers in pairs.

ANSWERS

1 Students might decide to eliminate the following candidates:
- Billy Jansen because he is too rude and aggressive and generally doesn't seem to get on well with people. He has offended two other Arbour House authors recently; Amrit Singh by making remarks about him on Twitter and Fabyan Jackson by shouting rude remarks during his talk.
- Fabyan Jackson because he has offended Sir James by making remarks about big corporations. It is Sir James's corporation which is sponsoring the prize and it would be too risky to bring the two of them together.
- Selina Edgely because she has been arrested for breaking into a Garner pharmaceuticals lab with an animal rights group. She needs to be kept away from Sir James.
2 Liz-Anne De Grey is the author of the Inspector Valentine novels about an aristocratic detective. She is similar to Sir James as they both send their children to the same school.
3 Students' own answers. (The authors on the shortlist in **6** are Amrit Singh, Liz-Anne de Grey, Jo-Jo Heinz and Delia Lane).

People 1

 1.4

Conversation 1

A: Did you go to the Fabyan Jackson poetry reading? I heard it was fantastic!

B: Well yes, personally I enjoyed it a lot, but some people were offended by all the political jokes he made. Billy Jansen was there and started shouting rude comments, but Fabyan just made the audience laugh at him, so he left in a rage … serves him right, too, horrible man!

C: Sir James Garner left before the end, too. He really didn't like it when Fabyan started making rude jokes about big corporations. You could tell he was taking it personally.

A: Um, well, considering it's his own big corporation that is financing our prize, I think we're on dangerous ground there. How did Selina Edgely's talk go by the way? I had to go to a meeting so I missed it.

C: Oh, didn't you know? We had to cancel it. We had a call from her agent last night to say that she had been arrested for breaking into a Garner pharmaceuticals lab with an animal rights group and was being held in police custody.

A: Oh no!

Conversation 2

A: Isn't that Amrit Singh over there? One of us needs to go and talk to him. I've heard he's upset about some rude remarks Billy Jansen made about him on Twitter.

B: Billy Jansen again! What's the matter with him? He seems to be getting more aggressive every day. That does it! I don't think we should invite him to do anything else for us. He just can't work with people.

C: I agree! I've got a meeting with Amrit later on, so I'll try to find out exactly what happened. Who is that woman in the corner with Sir James, by the way? They seem to get on very well. They've been talking for ages.

B: That's Liz-Anne de Grey, author of the Inspector Valentine novels – you know, the books about the aristocratic detective. We didn't consider her for the judge's panel because we are worried that she and Sir James are too similar – they send their children to the same expensive private school, for example. So, we thought it might be too much of a good thing.

A: Yes, but our candidates seem to be eliminating themselves rather fast. I think she's worth considering.

6 Read the instructions and explain to the students that they are going to play the role of the authors. Divide the class into pairs, and ask them to read the instructions on this page and their roles on page 97 or 102. Again, ask them to write three key words to help them remember the necessary information for the role. When they are ready, ask the students to perform part 1 of the role play.

When they have finished, give them a few minutes to individually note down any positive and negative points about the authors that have emerged during the interviews, and which could affect who is chosen for the panel. Then follow the same procedure for part 2 of the role play. Once they have made their notes, take feedback from the class.

7 Ask the students to work in pairs and discuss which two authors should be chosen for the panel based on the evidence they have collected, and to reach a joint decision. Ask them to make their decision known in an email to the author, which they should write together. Monitor and answer any questions as they do this.

Ask pairs to read out their emails in turn. Make a note of who the most popular choices are for the panel. Discuss as a class how different pairs reached their decisions, and what evidence they based them on.

Extra activity

Write on the whiteboard:

Who's your favourite author?

Why do you like him/her?

What's your favourite book by this author?

What's it about?

Ask the students to form pairs or small groups and discuss the questions. They can write their answer for homework.

Writing emails

Go to **Writing emails 1** on page 44 and do the exercises. Teacher's Book reference on page 62.

The best way to work

UNIT OBJECTIVES:	Students will practise ...	and they will learn how to ...
	articles	give effective feedback on work
	words that are used before nouns	
	describing a typical day	
	talking about productivity	

Lesson 1: Working too hard?, page 12

LESSON OBJECTIVES:

Students will learn and practise ...
describing a typical day
using articles

Warm up

With books closed, divide the class into AB pairs and ask them to face each other. Tell Student A to open their book on page 12. Give them five minutes to describe one of the pictures at the top of the page (without using gesture). Student B draws the picture in as much detail as possible, asking questions to get it precise.

Reassure the students that this a language exercise, and you do not expect them to be great artists. Afterwards, ask pairs to compare the drawing with the original.

Start up

1 Write on the whiteboard (or dictate the questions and help where there is doubt):

Who ...
1 ... has higher qualifications? (Arnold)
2 ... jointly founded their company? (Emma-Jayne)
3 ... had instant success? (Emma-Jayne)
4 ... is working on new products? (Emma-Jayne)
5 ... uses Facebook and Twitter for marketing? (Arnold)

Set a time limit of three minutes for the students to read the texts and answer the questions. Ask them to compare answers when they've finished, then check as a class.

Ask the students to discuss what they think the product is in each case, but don't offer answers at this stage.

2 **2.1** Play the audio for the students to check their answers. Ask the students to explain what the products do to check they understand (Arnold's product is a golf trolley that carries you and your golf clubs around when you play golf; Emma-Jayne's umbrella changes colour when it rains).

ANSWERS

1 ride-on golf trolley 2 an umbrella
3 changes colour in the rain 4 umbrellas

2.1

My name's Arnold du Toit, and I founded a company called Drive Daddy when I was 21 years old, after studying Design Engineering at university. Then I did a Masters Degree, which teaches you to run your own business, and that's when this concept turned into our first product – it's the world's first ever ride-on golf trolley, and it took two years to bring it to market. We use social media a lot to communicate our brand, and now we're taking it around the world.

My name's Emma-Jayne Parkes. I met my business partner when I was studying Product Design and Development at college, and that's when I came up with the idea of an umbrella which changes colour in the rain. We started our company, Squid London, and we tested the market with just 100 umbrellas, and, fortunately, we had a fantastic response, and sold out in 11 days. Then we started looking for clients who were interested in placing large orders. Now we're adding to our product range.

Listening

3 **2.2** Focus on the timeline and the key to the symbols. Ask the students to listen to the audio while following the timeline, then work in pairs to complete the key with the symbols.

ANSWERS

↗ ↘	get up / go to bed
～～～	desk work
⋀⋀⋀	out-of-the-office work
❙❙❙❙	other activities
- - -	free time
✓	food / drink
ℓℓ	Meetings

2.2
Arnold
I set my alarm for seven every day. When I wake up, I like to take everything very slow – the mornings are my 'me time', so I have a nice long shower, have some coffee, listen to the radio, clean my teeth really properly, then I feel good to go out into the world. On my walk to work I normally listen to something relaxing – a bit of Frank Sinatra maybe. I tend to be at my desk by nine. I start by dealing with emails and returning phone calls. At ten I grab something to eat, and a coffee, then about eleven I head down to the factory until about two, and then we have lunch at the pub. Then there's lots of emailing in the afternoon; responding to customers, taking new orders. I don't really take breaks – just grab a coffee at my desk every now and then. That's till about eight. From eight till ten I often go to networking events, or sometimes there'll be a late-night meeting, or I get together with other entrepreneurs and we help each other, or just go for a drink. So, food is either a buffet or a snack. I try to get eight hours' sleep a night. I spend my weekends promoting the product, so it's seven days a week ... but I don't think of it as work – it's just what I have to do!

4 🔊 **2.2** Play the audio again at least twice for the students to add 'V' symbols at the points on the timeline where Arnold eats and drinks. Give them time to compare answers before checking as a class. If the students do not find this hard, you could ask them to listen again and note down more details about what Arnold eats and drinks.

ANSWERS
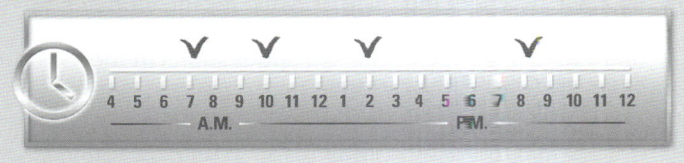

5 🔊 **2.3** Play the audio for the students to complete the timeline.

ANSWERS

2.3
Emma-Jayne
Typically, I wake up between six and seven, and I'm always in the office by eight o'clock, as I'm working on production with China, and that's when they're still at work. My office is in my house, so I have a bowl of cereal and a cup of tea at my desk. Between ten and twelve I'm normally out at the warehouse down the road, doing logistics and sorting out the day's orders.

Between twelve and one I normally do another hour back at the office, working on, maybe, sales or press releases. I have lunch between one and one thirty, and then usually after lunch is when we hold our meetings, until about four, and then it's back to the desk to do more work on the computer. Then I head to the gym at six thirty-ish for an hour, come back and have some dinner. I normally check emails and things around nine, then have some free time, then check emails again around eleven to eleven thirty, then I go to bed about midnight. We work weekends too, but only a few hours – some people do tell me I work too hard, but when it's your company, it doesn't seem like work!

6 Give the students time to compare their symbols, and listen again if they find the exercise difficult. Then play the audio once more for them to write the symbols above the timeline. Check the answers. If the students do not find this hard, you could ask them to listen again and note down more details about what Emma eats and drinks.

ANSWERS
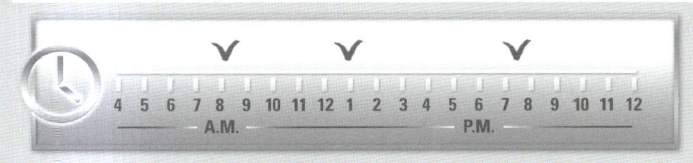

7 Ask the students to discuss the questions in pairs, then take feedback.

Vocabulary

8 Ask the students to complete the phrases with the verbs. When several have finished, ask the class to check their answers with the audioscript on page 119.

ANSWERS
1 set 2 deal with / check 3 return 4 grab 5 go to
6 get together with 7 go for 8 get 9 sort out
10 check / deal with

9 Ask the students to draw two blank timelines, one for themselves, and one for their partner. Then give them time to fill in their own line using the symbols in ❸. When they have finished, ask them to take turns to talk through their day in detail to their partner. As each student listens, they write symbols and notes on the blank timeline. Give them time to compare their days, then take feedback on similarities and differences.

🌐 Students can find more activities at www.richmondatwork.net

Grammar

10 Ask the students to work in pairs to complete the questionnaire with articles or with a dash (–) to indicate no article. Remind them to check the grammar reference on page 110 for help. Check the answers.

ANSWERS
1 – 2 a 3 – 4 the 5 The 6 the 7 a 8 – 9 a
10 the 11 – 12 –

🌐 Students can find more activities at www.richmondatwork.net

Speaking

11 Ask the students to complete the questionnaire for themselves.

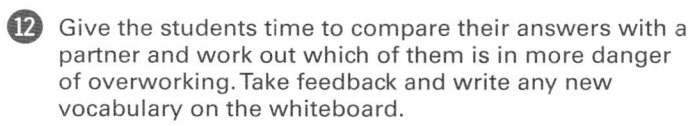

12 Give the students time to compare their answers with a partner and work out which of them is in more danger of overworking. Take feedback and write any new vocabulary on the whiteboard.

Extra activity

Ask the students to work in pairs and look at audioscript 2.3 on page 119. Ask them to mark places where there is *a*, *the* or no article (–) before a noun, and take turns to explain why in each case.

For homework, ask students to write an account of a typical working day.

Lesson 2: How efficient are you?, page 14

LESSON OBJECTIVES:

Students will learn and practise ...

talking about productivity

words that are used before nouns

Warm up

Ask the students if they have any specific techniques for memorising lists. Then teach them this method of memorising lists in the correct order. Write on the whiteboard:

sun, shoe, tree, door, hive, sticks, heaven, gate, line, pen

Elicit or teach *hive* (a place where bees live and make honey). Read the list and asks the class if it sounds familiar (it sounds like the numbers 1–10). Go through the words, checking students understand the meaning of each, and asking them to close their eyes and picture a typical, simple example of each. Then tell them you are going to read them a list of ten everyday tasks, and you want them to remember the list in order. Say: *1 – deal with phone calls*, and ask the students to picture someone checking phone calls, but using a very small sun instead of a phone. Then continue slowly, asking them to form an image for each item:

2 check emails   3 grab something to eat   4 go to a meeting   5 have a drink   6 talk to a client   7 make an important phone call   8 write a report   9 meet a visitor   10 prepare a presentation

Ask the students to work with a partner to try to remember the list in order, without writing, then ask them how successful they were. Ask some students to describe the images they formed.

Start up

1 Write on the whiteboard: *If you have an appointment you mustn't miss, how do you make sure you remember it?* Ask the students to discuss briefly with a partner, then get feedback on the different methods.

Ask the students to complete the sentences with the words in the box. Check the answers.

ANSWERS

1 timetable   2 Take   3 focus   4 Tackle   5 remember
6 Schedule in   7 cross off   8 Do

2 Ask the students to work in pairs and decide on two more tips. Take feedback, helping with the language where necessary, and writing their ideas on the whiteboard.

POSSIBLE ANSWERS

Check emails only at scheduled times.
Make an action programme for each project.
Schedule in time for unexpected events.
Prioritise your to-do- list.
Organise your files carefully and back them up.
Delegate where possible.
Relax when you're away from work.
Get enough sleep.
Eat well.
Keep your desk and work space tidy

3 Ask the students to discuss in pairs which of the tips they do, including the ideas on the whiteboard, and which they think they should do. Take feedback from the class.

Listening

4 ◀)) 2.4 Play the audio once or twice for the students to tick the things that Arnold and Emma-Jayne do. Remind them to include their own two suggestions in the exercise. Check the answers.

ANSWERS

Arnold: 1, 3, 4, 5, 7   **Emma-Jayne:** 1, 2, 4, 6, 8

> ◀)) 2.4
> **Arnold**
> Well, I've certainly got more creative skills than organisational skills! My mind works in lots of different directions at the same time, so I have to force myself not to multitask. If I try to do lots of things at once, I end up doing none of them well. Luckily, I work with someone who's extremely well organised. To keep on top of my schedule, I put everything into the calendar app on my phone, no matter how small, and that calendar's shared with the rest of the team, so all of them know where I am and what I'm doing 24/7. And I set alarms on my phone so that I never forget appointments.
>
> I also write down everything I have to do on paper. If it's a big project, I work out the individual little tasks that are involved and write those down. From that list, I make my to-do list for the day. When I finish something on the list, I cross it off, but I also add things to the list all the time, so I never get to the bottom. You have to prioritise, so I mark the jobs that are most important, and do those first. I try not to fill my time, though, because I like to leave space to deal with things that come up. If there's a crisis, you have to be able to react immediately.

The best way to work 2

Emma Jayne
I'm very organised most of the time – certainly in my working life. The way we organise ourselves in our business is we have a joint calendar. All our business stuff and personal stuff goes in there, so both of us know when the other person is free. What I work on in a day depends on what projects we're working on, and we decide what the priority is. For example, we just had a big delivery yesterday, so sending out umbrellas and doing invoices has to be top priority. Whereas something like an interview, I might say, 'Yes, it's important', but it's not so urgent, so I'll do that next week.' So, each of us has our own schedule, and on Monday we sit down and decide who's focusing on what needs doing that week, so we share out the work like that.

Emails never stop coming in and neither of us likes to leave them too long, or they can be overwhelming. So it's less stressful to deal with them straightaway. Sometimes when I need to focus on something I book an hour in the day when I ask my partner to deal with calls and emails and I shut myself in another room to work.

Work is always on my mind but to unwind and to keep up my energy levels, I go to the gym for an hour most days. That way I can switch off for an hour. I don't like sitting at my desk all day without a break so every hour I either go and make a coffee or go for a five minute walk.

Grammar

5 Write on the whiteboard:

_____ of my colleagues drink coffee in the mornings.

Encourage students to suggest ways of completing the sentence (e.g. *All, Both*) and how different words change the meaning of the sentence.

Give the students a few minutes to read the grammar reference on page 110. Then ask them to work in pairs to complete the sentences with the words in the box.

6 Ask the students to check their answers in the audioscript on page 119. The purpose of getting them to check rather than give them the answers is to encourage them to use the audioscripts as an additional language resource.

ANSWERS
1 that **2** all **3** both **4** each **5** neither **6** most, that
7 all, every

Students can find more activities at www.richmondatwork.net

Reading

7 Focus on the word *procrastinate* in the Help box. Ask the students if they procrastinate. If anyone does, ask them why they think they do so, and what they do to avoid it. Ask the students to read the article quickly and add sentences a–f in the correct positions. Check the answers.

ANSWERS
1 e **2** c **3** d **4** f **5** a **6** b

8 Write *burn out* and *trigger* on the whiteboard. Ask the students to find them in the text and suggest what they could mean (*burn out* = to become so tired that you can't work any more, *trigger* = to cause something to happen). Ask the students to look through the text again to find the words to fill the gaps in sentences 1–5. Check the answers.

ANSWERS
1 never-ending **2** immune system **3** good ideas
4 thinking time **5** too busy

Speaking

9 Ask the students to work in pairs or small groups and discuss whether the advice in the text would work for them before discussing the other questions. Take feedback from the class and write any useful vocabulary on the whiteboard.

Extra activity

Ask the students to work in pairs and spend five minutes chatting to find out what they have in common. Ask them to note down key words, then write on the board:

Neither of us ...   *Neither X nor I ...*
Both of us ...   *We both ... / We're both ...*

Ask pairs to report to the class what they have in common, using these forms.

Lesson 3: How have I done?, page 16

LESSON OBJECTIVES:

Students will learn and practise ...
giving effective feedback on work

Warm up

Write on the whiteboard:
When did you last praise/criticise someone?
What was their reaction?
How did they receive the praise/criticism?
How did you feel?

Elicit an explanation of *praise* (verb = to tell someone that they have done something well; noun = something you say to tell someone that they have done something well), *criticise* (to tell someone that they have done something badly) and *criticism* (something you say to tell someone that they have done something badly). Give the students time to discuss the questions, then take feedback from the class.

33

Start up

1 Focus on the quotes. Elicit what each quote is saying and ask the students what they know about the people who said them. Ask the students to work in pairs and discuss questions 1–3, making very brief notes to remind them of what they discussed. Take feedback from the class and write useful vocabulary on the whiteboard. (Note: LeBron James is a basketball player; Frankl P. Jones was a journalist; Elbert Hubbard was a writer.)

Reading

2 Pre-teach *performance review* (a report about how well a company employee has worked in the past year, written by his/her manager and based on facts collected by the manager and an interview) and *feedback* (a short spoken or written report on what someone has done). If appropriate, ask if anyone in the class has experienced a performance review (either as an employee or a manager), and what happened. Be aware that this could be a sensitive subject if people from the same company are in your class. Focus on the pictures, and ask the students which part of the text reports positive effects of performance reviews (the left-hand side), and which side negative (the right). Ask the students to answer questions 1 and 2 individually.

3 Ask the students to discuss their answers with a partner, then take feedback from the class.

Speaking

4 Arrange the students in groups of three or four to discuss the questions. If you think some students might find it difficult to come up with ideas, brainstorm different types of feedback, e.g. informal spoken comments at any time, self-assessment, peer review (comments or assessment done by people at the same level as you, a test on the knowledge you should have at your level. Nominate a student in each group to take notes on the discussion. Set a time limit of 5–10 minutes for the activity. When the time is up, take feedback from each group and write any useful vocabulary on the whiteboard.

Functional language

5 Focus on the first item, and ask which option students think is better. Emphasise that there is no 'correct' answer, and accept any suggestion. Encourage discussion and don't offer any suggestions at this stage. Ask the students to work in pairs to discuss the other items. Tell them that the reason for choosing one option over another can be different in each case.

6 ◁)) **2.5** Play the audio once for the students to tick Donna Webb's choices, then again for them to note down the reasons she gives. Ask the students to compare their answers in pairs before checking as a class.

ANSWERS

1 B – it's specific
2 B – it's gentler
3 A – it's more effective to describe behaviour rather than give it a name
4 A – it talks about improvement, rather than criticising and generalising
5 A – contains action points and has a positive message
6 B – it's more specific
7 B – unlike A, it doesn't contain assumptions

◁)) 2.5

Well, for number 1, the more effective feedback is certainly B, because it's specific. A is very positive, but it's too vague to be useful. B is also my choice for number 2, because it's gentler. It's best to avoid 'you should' where possible. I also think the personal example sounds helpful, not critical. The problem with B in number 3 is that the speaker uses the word 'socialising'. The person receiving the feedback might think 'it's not socialising – I'm talking about work!' So it's much more effective to describe the behaviour, not to give it a name, especially one with a negative feeling. For number 4, I think B is ineffective for two reasons – it's a generalisation, and it's expressed in a very negative way. A is much better – it talks about improvement rather than criticising. Asking for the person's own opinion is also good, it makes the appraisal a two-way process. Number 5 would definitely be A: the summary needs to consist of action points, and should have a positive message; B is just a repetition of the criticism. Again in 6, the more specific point is better, so that would be B. What I don't like about A in number 7 is, firstly, the word 'forget'; the speaker is making assumptions – maybe the person didn't forget, but had another reason for missing the meeting. Also, asking 'why did you …?' in a critical way is sure to make the listener feel defensive, and negative about the feedback received.

7 Ask the students to agree with their partner on three rules for giving feedback, using their own ideas in **5**, and Donna Webb's in **6**. Write each pair's suggestions on the whiteboard, and decide on the class's overall top three.

POSSIBLE ANSWERS

Express feedback in positive rather than negative way.
Sandwich negative comments between positives.
Comment on the work, not the person.
Be specific.
Allow the person to put forward their own opinions, suggestions, etc.
Never argue.
Remain unemotional.
Give your own behaviour as an example.
Avoid 'You should …'
Suggest specific steps for improvement.
Don't accuse the person of something.

Speaking

8 Allow the pairs time to write their sentences. Monitor as they write and help with any language problems.

The best way to work 2

Write these suggestions on the board if the students are struggling for ideas:

Your assistant …
- arrived 15 minutes late again today – typical!
- did a fantastic sales presentation last week, as always.
- forgets to put his/her appointments on the shared calendar.
- forgot to return a phone call to a client this week.
- comes up with great ideas in meetings.

Then ask each pair to join with another pair, and read their sentences so that the other pair can identify the one that doesn't follow the rules. When the pairs have finished, ask some pairs to read out 'good' or 'bad' sentences for the class to identify, and encourage discussion of the reasons for this.

Extra activity

Write the following verbs on the whiteboard, and ask the students to write the related noun next to each, using the unit, a dictionary or their shared knowledge to help them:

appraise (appraisal)   help (help)
criticise (criticism)   improve (improvement)
develop (development)   judge (judgement)
encourage (encouragement)   motivate (motivation)
evaluate (evaluation)   perform (performance)
focus (focus)   review (review)

For homework, students could write a sentence using each of these nouns, which refers to their own work or study.

Scenario: Downsizing, page 18

SCENARIO OBJECTIVE:

Students will decide, of four employees, who to let go, who to keep and who to promote.

Warm up

With books closed, write the word *helmet* on the whiteboard. Ask the students to name a few sports or activities where people wear helmets (e.g. motorcycling, cycling, skiing, kayaking, motor-racing). Write these model sentences on the whiteboard:

A _____ helmet needs to be _____ so that _____ .
It also needs to be _____ so that _____ .

Ask the students to work in pairs and to choose one of the activities. Give them five minutes to write two or more sentences to describe the design features of the helmet they would need, using their dictionaries to help them. Then take feedback from the class, and write any new words on the whiteboard. Possible words that may come up include: light, tough, durable, impact-resistant, streamlined, wind-resistance, protect/injure/hit/bang your head.

 Elicit or pre-teach the meaning of *keep* (continue to employ), *let go* (ask to leave the company – point out that this is a euphemism; you are not really letting them go, but in fact you are ending their contract), *promote* (move up to a more important position in the company). Write on the whiteboard: *money, design, selling*. Give the students one minute to read about the people and link a name or names to each word (money = Fatima, design = Montse and Joseph, selling = Tomek). Check the answers, then ask a different student to paraphrase the information on each person for the class. Point out to the students that they should write their positive comments in the table on the next page. As they will need to add quite a lot of information to this table, suggest the students copy it into their notebooks.

POSSIBLE ANSWERS

Tomek: has run a successful business, has strong marketing skills
Montse: has done top level quality control, has a successful website
Joseph: top design skills, sports specialist
Fatima: reliable fundraiser

 2.6 Tell the students that each voicemail is about a different employee. Ask them to listen and complete the table. Play the audio once for them to write the names, and again for them to write the message.

ANSWERS

1 Fatima, praising her for helping sort out a problem
2 Montse, she isn't returning calls or emails and the customer needs information urgently
3 Joseph, repeated missing of deadlines
4 Tomek, complimenting excellent sales presentation and subsequent interest in products
5 Fatima, sent the wrong order again

🔊 2.6
1
Hi, this is Stefan Klammer – I'm a customer of Fatima. Just wanted to thank her for all her help and the time she spent sorting out my problem. Everyone I know who buys your products says she's always helpful like that – you don't find that with many companies! So, pass on my thanks to her, please. Bye.

2
Erm, hello, this is Monica from SportsXtra. Montse's not returning my calls or emails. Can you tell her I need that information urgently, please? This isn't the first time I've had to chase her. It would be great if she could, you know, just let me know what's happening! Thanks.

3
This is Henry Lee from the factory. I've got an urgent message for Joseph – so … I was expecting the drawings for the new design by five last night, your time. I have a meeting in an hour and I need them then, or it's too late. The same thing happened last month, and, I mean, a deadline is a deadline. So, I'm waiting.

4
Oh, er, message for Tomek. This is Viviane from SportsTech. Just to say, thanks Tomek for coming to the conference. Your sales presentation was just brilliant as always – we've had a lot of interest here in your products, and I'm sure you will too. So thanks and, erm, well done again!

35

5
Er … my name's Alan Jeffries and this message is for Fatima. I'm afraid you've sent us the wrong order again. I spent a long time giving you the exact order after the mistake last time so I'm surprised … Actually, I'm not surprised, because it happened last year too. You're great in most ways, Fatima, but please try to get our order right.

3 Ask the students to compare their information, and to discuss what positive and/or negative qualities the voicemails reveal about each employee. Ask them to add these qualities to the table.

POSSIBLE ANSWERS

Tomek: excellent sales presenter
Montse: doesn't return phone calls or emails
Joseph: bad at meeting deadlines
Fatima: helpful, good at sorting out problems, makes mistakes with orders

4 Ask the students to read the emails and to add any further qualities they reveal about the employees to the table.

POSSIBLE ANSWERS

Tomek: talks too much, doesn't always do necessary admin
Montse: argumentative, lacks tact and creates bad atmosphere, good at planning
Joseph: doesn't check figures
Fatima: doesn't work hard enough, doesn't check work

5 Ask the students to read the information on page 97 and make notes on each employee. Students can compare their notes and explain how they decided.

POSSIBLE ANSWERS

Tomek: focuses on detail but doesn't see the big picture, poor on routine administrative tasks and record-keeping
Montse: always produces high-quality work, attention to detail, efficient
Joseph: creative and innovative, however poor scheduling
Fatima: understands customers' needs, however often keeps people waiting

6 Give the students, in their pairs, time to discuss all the information they have collected in their tables, and agree on which employees to keep, which to promote and which to let go. Then ask them to agree on an action plan for the employee who will be kept but not promoted.

7 Split the pairs of students to form two groups in the class, and ask each group to compare and explain their decisions. Take feedback from the class.

8 Ask the students, either back in their pairs or individually for homework, to write an email to the employee who will be kept, telling them the news and explaining the action plan. Remind the students of the tips for giving feedback in the previous lesson.

Extra activity

Write *sort out* on the whiteboard. Ask the students if they can remember which noun went together with this verb in the lesson (*problem*). Then ask them to look back through the unit and the audioscripts, and list ten verb + noun collocations (words that are commonly used together) that they want to add to their repertoire. Give the students a chance to compare their lists. Ask several students for their favourite in their list.

Writing emails

Go to **Writing emails 2** on page 45 and do the exercises. Teacher's Book reference on pages 62–63.

3 The future

UNIT OBJECTIVES:	Students will practise ...	and they will learn how to ...
	using *be going to* and present continuous for future arrangements	plan and manage change talk about social media and digital communications
	making predictions	

Lesson 1: Planning ahead, page 20

LESSON OBJECTIVES:

Students will learn and practise ...

be going to and present continuous for future arrangements
planning and managing change

Warm up

Tell the students: *You and your partner have won £1,000 to spend on a week's holiday. You both have a week next week free. Agree on a plan.*

Set a ten-minute time-limit, then take feedback from different pairs. Point out the difference between pairs who want each detail planned in advance (e.g. a package holiday or a cruise), and those who prefer to improvise once on holiday (e.g. buying a plane ticket to a destination, then deciding once they are there). Ask if any pairs had to negotiate because one person likes to plan more.

Monitor as the students speak and note down problems expressing future plans, to deal with later.

Arrange the students in different pairs for the Start up.

Start up

1. Elicit or pre-teach *plan ahead* (to make plans in advance), *be spontaneous* (to decide in the moment, without planning in advance), *long-term/short-term plan* (a plan for action over a long/short period of time) and *contingency plan* (a reserve plan, in case the main plan isn't possible; a 'plan B').

   Ask the students to discuss the two questions, then take feedback from a few students. Write up any useful vocabulary on the whiteboard. Make a note of inappropriate tenses that students use, but don't correct them at this stage.

Listening

2. Point out the **Help** box that explains *control freak*. Ask the students to read the profiles, then explain to their partner which person they are most like. Take feedback from the class.

3. ◀))) **3.1** Play the audio once or twice for the students to complete the tables. Check the answers.

ANSWERS

Henrik Peterson
birthday: in six months' time so no plans yet, but it's his 50th so perhaps will have a party
holiday: going to cycle round the coast of north Germany with family
retirement: doesn't think he'll ever retire as can't afford to

Mercedes da Silva
birthday: quite soon so knows exactly what she's doing – is taking the day off and going shopping with her daughters
holiday: several holidays, all planned and booked
retirement: planning to retire at 60 and travel the world or start an internet business

◀))) **3.1**

Henrik Peterson
I'm reasonably organised at work – you have to be if you run your own business – but I'm not naturally someone who likes to plan their life down to the last detail. My birthday isn't for another six months and I certainly don't tend to plan that far ahead; besides at my age, I think I prefer to forget about them! But since I'm going to be 50 this year, perhaps I'll have a party and celebrate for a change. I'll invite all my 50-year-old friends and have a last big bash before old age sets in ... but I'll have to get my wife to agree. We usually plan my summer holiday at the beginning of the year because I have to organise work commitments around it. This year, we haven't worked out all the details yet, but we're going to cycle round the coast of north Germany with our two teenage sons. We need to sort everything out and book soon though or the campsites will be full. As for retirement plans ... I don't think I'm ever going to retire, I can't afford to!

Mercedes da Silva
I have a very busy work schedule as well as a young family with kids so I need to be very disciplined about planning my time or everything would just fall to pieces. I plan my family time with as much care and attention as I do my work, so we all know what we're doing. This year for example, we're having a week's family holiday together in Miami in the last week of July and we're going skiing for four days at Thanksgiving. My birthday, well, that's actually quite soon, so I can tell you exactly what I'm doing: I'm taking a day off and I'm going shopping with my daughters. As far as retirement is concerned, well, that seems a long way off, but the plan is that my husband and I are both going to retire at 60 and move to our place in the mountains, but I don't know, I might go crazy doing nothing. Maybe we'll travel the world or start an internet business or something. We'll see when the time comes.

4. Ask the students to work individually to try to complete the sentences from memory and their grammatical knowledge, then compare with a partner. Play the audio again to check the answers. Ask the students to name the future forms used.

37

ANSWERS

a 'll have (= future with *will*) **b** 're going to cycle (= *be going to* future) **c** 're having (= present continuous for future)

Grammar

5 Ask the students to read the rules and write a, b or c next to each one. Check the answers.

Point out how Henrik uses perhaps to show the plan is possible, not definite. Elicit other adverbs that show a degree of possibility (*maybe*, *probably*). Point out that *probably* is used in a different position by writing on the whiteboard:

Maybe/Perhaps I'll go.

I'll probably go.

ANSWERS

1 c **2** b **3** a

Students can find more activities at www.richmondatwork.net

Speaking

6 Demonstrate the activity by writing three dates and times on the whiteboard that are important to you, e.g. *tomorrow / next Saturday / 28th November*. Make sure that one represents a definite activity that is in your diary or calendar (present continuous), and one is a definite intention, but as yet unscheduled plan (*be going to*). Describe each plan to the class. Expand on each plan, and encourage questions (but don't focus on the grammar of the questions).

Ask the students to do the same in pairs or small groups. Monitor as they talk, and note down any problems with future tenses to deal with later.

Reading

7 Write on the whiteboard:

How far ahead do you plan?

How far ahead does your company plan?

Elicit what type of answer is required (a period of time, e.g. a month, ten years), then ask the students to discuss the questions in pairs. Take feedback from the class.

Pre-teach *snapshot* (literally, a photo, but used to refer to anything that gives us a picture of life at a particular moment in history). Read the questions with the class, then ask the students to read the text quickly and answer the questions. Allow the students to compare answers in pairs before checking the answers as a class.

ANSWERS

1. Because unlike small immediate decisions which are easy to make, people find it difficult and frightening to think about their long-term future.
2. They need to consider the consequence their drilling will have on the environment.
3. Possible answer: Most of a shop's revenue tends to be centred around Christmas sales. Restaurants use a more immediate timescale for feedback on how their business is doing.
4. Creating 'snapshots' for different lengths of time in the future so that you can plan for each of these times.

8 Ask the students to use the context, not dictionaries, to match the highlighted words and definitions. Check the answers.

ANSWERS

1 consequences **2** eventualities **3** be highly resistant
4 far-reaching **5** shape, plan ahead **6** procrastinate

9 Elicit or pre-teach *worst case scenario* (the worst way you can imagine a situation developing) and *best case scenario*. Elicit the question that would produce the answer in the example, and write it on the whiteboard: *What will you do if the/your company relocates to New York?*

Ask a strong student who works for a company to complete the example with a spontaneous decision. If no one works for a company, choose a different example. Ask the students to take it in turns to choose a situation from the box to ask their partner. Monitor as they talk and note down any problems using *will* or the present tense after *if* appropriately. Take feedback from the class.

Extra activity

Play audioscript 3.1 as far as *our two teenage sons* as a dictation, pausing after each sentence for the students to write. Play it a second time for them to fill in any gaps. Then ask them to look at the audioscript on page 120 to check.

Lesson 2: The uncertain future, page 22

LESSON OBJECTIVES:

Students will learn and practise …

making predictions

talking about future challenges

Warm up

Write on the whiteboard:

_ _ *the future* (in)

_ _ *50 years' time* (in)

_ _ _ *day* (one)

20 years _ _ _ _ *now* (from)

_ _ _ _ *the next 10 years* (over)

Tell the students that these are phrases for referring to a time in the future. Ask pairs to use their dictionaries and share their knowledge to complete the phrases. In some cases, there is more than one possible answer. After a few minutes, check the answers.

Write a prediction of your own on the whiteboard about a change using one of the future timeframes above, e.g. *In the future, there won't be so many young people*. Ask the students to discuss their own predictions about the view in pairs, and to write five sentences together. Listen as they talk, and note down any problems expressing predictions, to deal with later. Take feedback from the class on their predictions.

The future 3

Start up

Focus on the box. Tell the students you are going to read the names of the industries, and you want them to underline the main stressed syllable. Read, including *the*:

the <u>auto</u>mobile industry ... the <u>food</u> production industry ... the <u>pub</u>lishing industry ... the telecommu<u>ni</u>cations industry

Check the answers. Point out that you need to use *the* /ðə/ in each case, but that it is pronounced /ðiː/ in the *automobile industry*, because that begins with a vowel sound.

Ask the students to work in pairs to match the pictures with the names of the industries, then quickly check the answers.

Write on the whiteboard: *... demand for food will rise.* Elicit what can go at the start to show you are stating your own opinion and not a definite fact. Write good suggestions on the board, adding *I think* and *I have a feeling* if these aren't suggested.

Then ask the students to discuss possible future problems and challenges for the industry and briefly note down their ideas. Take feedback from the class and write any new vocabulary on the whiteboard.

ANSWERS
a automobile industry b publishing industry
c telecommunications industry d food production industry

Reading

2 Ask the students to read the text quickly, filling in the names of the industries, and comparing the ideas in the text against their own ideas in **1**. Check the answers.

ANSWERS
1 publishing industry 2 food production industry
3 automobile industry 4 telecommunications industry

3 Ask the students to read the text again and answer the questions. Allow them time to compare their answers in pairs before checking the answers as a class.

As an extra activity, write the following words and phrases on the white board, and ask the students to find words with those meanings in the text: *1 old-fashioned and no longer used* (obsolete), *2 stop* (cease), *3 plants farmers grow* (crops), *4 stop growing or developing* (stagnate), *5 speed* (pace).

ANSWERS
1 a food production industry b telecommunications industry
  c publishing industry d automobile industry
2 a food b petroleum c BRIC

Grammar

4 Read the **Grammar** box with the class. Elicit the opposite of *tentative* (confident/sure) when it occurs, and check that the students understand *about to* (happening extremely soon). Ask the students to work in pairs to write sentences from prompts 1–6, using a different future form in each case. Take feedback from the class, and write one suggestion for each prompt on the whiteboard, using a different form of the future for each one.

ANSWERS
1 The publishing industry is bound to / will definitely / is sure to / is certain to change a lot.
2 Writers might/may no longer need publishers.
3 The industry is on the verge of / the brink of disappearing.
4 The oil industry is bound to / will definitely / is sure to / is certain to grow substantially in Asia.
5 The market is unlikely to / probably won't expand in Europe.
6 The telecoms industry will probably / is likely to continue to diversify.

Students can find more activities at www.richmondatwork.net

Listening

5 Ask the students to work in pairs to match the words and pictures, using dictionaries and sharing their knowledge. Check the answers. Pronounce the words for the students to repeat, pointing out the pronunciation of *exhaust* and *heartbeat* in particular, as these are likely to be mispronounced.

ANSWERS
a locust b algae c seaweed d heartbeat
e exhaust fumes f beetle
Students' own answers.

6))) 3.2 Play the audio for the students to write the numbers 1 to 4 next to the industries, then check answers.

ANSWERS
1 publishing 2 food production 3 automobiles
4 telecommunications

))) **3.2**
1
Personally, I can't see us disappearing because this wouldn't ultimately be in the interests of either readers or writers. Publishers exist to create value at both ends of the system – by polishing, presenting and promoting writers' work and making it accessible to readers. The models for doing this have changed and so have the media we work in, but the need for high-quality content is unchanged. Print media may become obsolete, but we'll definitely continue to find new ways to produce and sell content for the new communication devices as they emerge – e-book readers, smartphone apps, whatever comes up next!
2
I predict that we'll definitely see an increase in 'micro livestock' farming, for example, raising insects such as locusts and beetles for food since they are very nutritious, but don't need much space or resources to breed. In fact they are already widely eaten in some countries. It's also likely that seaweeds and algae will become part of our diet since they are an excellent source of oils, fats and sugars, and algae can grow very rapidly at sea, in polluted water and under conditions that would normally kill many other food crops.

3
It's predicted that the world's oil reserves will not last much longer than the next 40 years and already the damage to the environment from CO_2 emissions, from exhaust fumes as such, that car-manufacturing companies worldwide are under pressure from governments to evolve in a more ecologically friendly way. R&D costs in the industry will continue to rise as manufacturers compete to develop a cheap and practical alternative to the petroleum-fuelled engine.

4
Well, we expect that all the different purposes and uses of mobile phones will evolve to the point where we might even forget that the original function of these mobile devices was to make phone calls. In the future, they're likely to replace credit cards as the way we pay for things, and passports for identification purposes as well as becoming an important tool for monitoring our blood sugar levels, heartbeat and general health. We'll probably start wearing these devices rather than carrying them or we might even have a mobile device implanted directly into our bodies.

7 Read the questions with the class. Elicit or pre-teach the meaning of *R&D* (Research and Development). Play the audio again once or twice for the students to answer the questions. Allow the students to compare answers in pairs before checking as a class.

ANSWERS

1 Publishers will always be necessary to help improve and promote writers' work.
2 locusts, beetles, algae and seaweed – because they are nutritious and easy to breed/grow in difficult environments, e.g. lack of space or polluted waters.
3 to develop more ecologically-friendly engines
4 They are competing to invent cheap and practical alternatives to the petrol-driven engine.
5 that they were originally designed to make phone calls

8 Ask the students to make sentences about the things mentioned in 1–6. They can use the audioscript on page 121 and the grammar reference on page 112 to help them. Monitor and help as the students write, then take feedback from the class and write one or two successful versions for each prompt on the whiteboard.

POSSIBLE ANSWERS

1 Print media is likely to become obsolete.
2 Publishers are bound to find new ways to produce and sell content.
3 There is certain to be an increase in 'micro-livestock' farming.
4 Oil reserves are unlikely to last more then 40 years.
5 Mobile phones might replace passports and credit cards.
6 We may wear mobile devices or have implants.

Speaking

9 Read through the question with the class. Elicit or pre-teach *obsolete* (no longer useful or necessary). Give the students 10–15 minutes to discuss their ideas. Monitor and note down any problems with future tenses to deal with later. Take feedback from the class, then go through some of the problems you have noted with the class.

Extra activity

a In a monolingual class, ask half the students to translate audioscript 3.2 number 3 into their own language, and the other half of the class to translate number 4. Then ask them to swap translations with a student from the other half, and translate the text they receive back into English. At the end, pairs can compare their final version against the audioscript on page 121.

b In a multilingual class, ask the students to underline all the verb forms and expressions that are used to express predictions in audioscript 3.2. Then ask them to write a text expressing their predictions for their own industry, or about an area of business that interests them, including some of the same verb forms and expressions.

Lesson 3: The future of communication, page 24

LESSON OBJECTIVES:

Students will learn and practise ...
talking about social media
talking about digital communication

Warm up

With books closed, brainstorm social media sites and write them on the whiteboard. Then write on the whiteboard:
Which are becoming more/less popular?
Which are in the news at the moment?
Allow the students 5–10 minutes, depending on the amount of discussion generated, then take feedback from the class.

Start up

1 Write on the whiteboard: *How often ...?* Elicit and write up a range of possible answers (e.g. *not very often, rarely, every day, once a month, once every two weeks*). Read the question and the items in the box with the class. Allow the students five minutes to discuss the question before taking feedback on each form of communication.

2 Ask the students to change partners to discuss the questions. Take feedback from a few students and write any useful vocabulary on the whiteboard.

Reading

3 Ask the students to complete the texts with the words in the boxes. Allow them to compare answers with a partner before checking as a class. Clarify any words whose meaning they were uncertain of (e.g. *screening* – checking a person's background to help decide if they are suitable for something; *trolls* – people who enjoy posting negative, critical or insulting comments anonymously on the Internet).

40

The future 3

> **ANSWERS**
> 1 social networking 2 settings 3 profiles 4 screening
> 5 search engine 6 hits 7 accessing 8 trolls 9 platforms
> 10 integrate 11 cross post 12 follow

4 Ask the students to read the texts again and find the information for questions 1–3. When they have finished ask them to compare their answers with a partner and together note down two positive and two negative points for each type of media. Take feedback from the class, writing any useful vocabulary on the whiteboard.

> **ANSWERS**
> 1 a) For individuals, prospective employers sometimes use it as part of the screening process.
> b) For companies, people can post untrue, negative reviews about you.
> 2 You need to update the contents frequently, to make sure it can be viewed properly on a mobile phone.
> 3 You need to integrate everything, and make sure you always cross post your updates.

Vocabulary

5 Write on the whiteboard:

What annoying technical problems have you experienced with your mobile phone?

Give the students a few minutes to discuss the question in pairs before taking feedback. Write any useful vocabulary on the whiteboard.

Ask the students to read sentences 1–10 and write *I* or *S* next to each one. When they have finished, they can compare answers with a partner and together discuss what equipment each could refer to. Check the answers, and ask volunteers to clarify the meanings of *breaking up, fuzzy, frozen, blank, jerky* and *out of sync*, using voice, gesture or paraphrase.

> **ANSWERS**
> 1 S 2 I 3 I 4 I 5 S 6 S 7 I 8 S 9 S/I 10 S

Students can find more activities at www.richmondatwork.net

Listening

6 🔊 **3.3** Play the audio for the students to tick the sentences from **5** that they hear. Check the answers.

> **ANSWERS**
> 1, 4, 5, 6, 7, 8, 9, 10

> 🔊 **3.3**
> **1**
> **A:** OK so, Khalid, can you hear us OK?
> **B:** You're rather quiet. Just a minute. I'll turn the volume up. Can you hear me? Do … to discuss the systems review …
> **A:** No, I'm sorry, I didn't catch that. You're breaking up. Could you say that again?
> **B:** Oh, so … be a good idea to consider …
> **A:** Oh no, here we go again. We had these problems last time. Anne, could you try moving the microphone? … No, it's no good, we'll have to call technical support. Khalid, I'm afraid the image and sound seem to be out of sync again. We're going to log out of the system and try logging in again to see if that improves things.
> **2**
> **C:** Yes, and I think you've really hit the nail on the head with what you were just saying about delivery times. That this is precisely the problem that we've been facing and … but we think we've come up with a solution. We've been … a developing a way to … I'm sorry, could you excuse me for a moment? There's a lot of noise outside … Sorry about that. Yes, as I was saying, we've developed a new system. It's not a radical departure from the kind of thing you're probably using already, but there are significant improvements which allow the user to … which allow the user to keep track of orders as they're coming in in real time and …
> **3**
> **D:** Sorry, I still didn't get that. Could you repeat it one last time?
> **E:** We're also requesting a 10% discount on the second order.
> **D:** Ah, 10% did you say, rather than 5% as last time?
> **E:** Yes, well, we are ordering almost double the amount and we're likely to need more stock this autumn.
> **D:** That's certainly something that we're prepared to consider. We'll discuss it during the break if that's OK and get back to you. It's 10.30 now. Shall we reconvene at say 11.15?
> **E:** That would be fine. OK, so we'll sign off for now … Federico …
> **F:** Would you like a coffee, Dave?
> **E:** I think they are really pushing it with the 10% discount request, don't you? I mean they are still fairly new customers and there's no guarantee of a new order in the autumn. I think …
> **F:** Hey, be careful! You haven't turned …
> **4**
> **G:** Shall we make a start? Can you see us OK?
> **H:** We can hear you, but you're a bit jerky when you move. I think we just need to adjust … Oh no, the screen's gone blank …
> **G:** We can't see you either now, but we can still hear you. Shall we go ahead anyway?
> **I:** Yes, we wanted to discuss the fact that we're still worried about the development time.
> **H:** But I think we went through that very thoroughly at our meeting in Seoul last month, didn't we?
> **I:** I think you are talking about the meeting you had with Mr Kim, Mr Gonzalez.
> **H:** Oh, yes, sorry, … er, is that Mr Park?
> **I:** No, Mr Park couldn't be at the meeting, this is Mr Kim, Mr Park's Deputy Manager speaking, not Mr Kim from Production.
> **H:** Yes, of course, Mr Kim … Er, so, as far as the development times are concerned …
> **J:** I wasn't aware that development times were ever a concern, José?
> **H:** … Er, our CEO Kate Lavery has joined us, Mr Park, I mean Mr Kim. So as you heard, we …

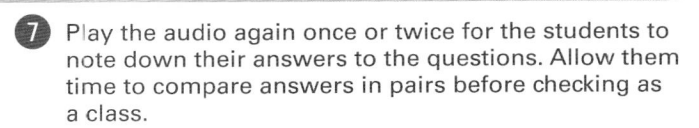

7 Play the audio again once or twice for the students to note down their answers to the questions. Allow them time to compare answers in pairs before checking as a class.

41

ANSWERS

Conversation 1
1 There are problems with the sound – the volume is too low, then speaker is breaking up.
2 It's a recurring problem so asking technical support to check the equipment before the call might have avoided it. They could also arrange for a technician to be in the room during the meeting to help things go smoothly.

Conversation 2
1 The speaker is obviously working from home, and home life and members of his family.
2 He needs to take steps, for example, arranging childcare, to separate his home life from his professional activity and ensure that he is not disturbed during meetings.

Conversation 3
1 They didn't disconnect the call / switch off the microphone.
2 They need to pay more attention to what they are doing and have a procedure for taking breaks so that they always remember to switch off equipment.

Conversation 4
1 The screen has gone blank, so meeting participants don't know who they are speaking to.
2 Technical problems of this sort can't always be avoided or planned for, but the speakers on both sides could begin the meeting by introducing who is in the room, giving name and job title. A protocol for speaking could be introduced whereby each speaker has to give their name when they are contributing/making a comment.

Speaking

8 Read the task with the class, eliciting the meaning of phrases such as *dial-in instructions* (the number you have to use to join the conference), *turn-taking* (a system for making sure that participants take turns to speak rather than trying to speak at the same time) and *minutes* (a written record of what was discussed and decided at the meeting). Give the students about ten minutes to discuss and note down their list of dos and don'ts. Then ask each pair in turn to read out their list.

POSSIBLE ANSWERS

Before the meeting
Do: Send a full list of joining instructions to the participants regarding, time, date and purpose of meeting and how to dial in. For international meetings, remember to adjust the times in relation to the time zone(s) the different participants are working in.
Circulate an agenda.
Prepare some back-up or alternative ways to join the meeting (e.g. alternative telephone numbers) in case those given don't work.
Have a technician check the equipment is functioning and set up properly.
Take steps to ensure that you will not be disturbed during the meeting except in an emergency.
Don't: Assume the equipment will work. Always check.
Forget to accommodate time zones in other parts of the world.
Try to arrange a meeting at a time that falls within all participants' normal working hours.
Keep the other participants waiting if you are the hosts. Switch on your equipment and dial in slightly early so are waiting for them when they arrive.

During the meeting
Do: Ensure there is a technician on hand in the room to help with technical problems, particularly for important meetings.
Make sure everyone introduces themselves at the beginning of the meeting, giving name and job title.
For a teleconference, require participants to have clear name cards on the desk in front of them.
If people can't see each other or if name cards aren't possible, ask participants to give their name before they speak or make a contribution.
Ensure there is a strict protocol for turn-taking and making contributions.
Speak slightly more slowly, loudly and clearly than you might do at a face-to-face meeting.
Take regular breaks at agreed times.
Don't: Allow people to talk over each other or interrupt.
Forget to turn off the equipment during breaks, especially microphones.
Talk about or criticise the other participants whilst you are still in the teleconference room.

After the meeting
Do: Write and circulate minutes and action points as soon as possible.
Follow-up immediately on any technical problems you experienced.
Behave as though the other participants are still present.

Extra activity

Write on the whiteboard:
1 _____ material _____ Facebook (post, on)
2 _____ complete control _____ (have, over)
3 _____ decisions _____ _____ (made, based, on)
4 _____ routine use _____ (making, of)

Ask the students, without looking at their books, to guess/remember what verbs and prepositions are missing. Then ask them to look at the first reading text on page 24 (Marisa Burch) and complete the expressions. Elicit or teach *collocation* (words that are commonly used together). Ask the students to look back at the lesson, including audioscript 3.3 on page 121, and write down ten collocations, that they would like to have in their repertoire.

Scenario: Facing the future, page 26

SCENARIO OBJECTIVE:

Students will decide how to spend their budget to save an arts centre.

Warm up

With books closed, write on the whiteboard:
What was the last show/play/concert you went to?
What was the best show/play/concert you've ever been to?
Allow the students a few minutes to discuss the questions in pairs or small groups, then take feedback from the class.

The future 3

1 Focus on the two pictures at the top of the page. Elicit or teach *run down* to describe the state of the building. Ask the students if they know the name of the bridge, and where it is (the Golden Gate Bridge, in San Francisco). Ask the students what they associate with San Francisco, and whether anyone has been there.

Give the students a few minutes to read the text and discuss the answers in pairs before checking as a class.

ANSWERS
1 Milly Street, Orange Bay, San Francisco. Set up in 1955.
2 plays, shows, concerts, exhibitions, café, children's play area
3 There has been a cut in funding for community arts, and with a fall in visitor numbers, the centre finds itself in debt.

2 🔊 **3.4** Read the rubric and list of speakers a–f with the class, then play the audio for the students to write 1–6 in the boxes. Check the answers.

ANSWERS
1 b 2 c 3 a 4 e 5 d 6 f

🔊 **3.4**

1
A: Over the past few years, we've had to let go nearly all the staff – there's only four of us left now including Wanda, she's the director and I'm the assistant director, but I only work part-time, or at least I'm supposed to. But we're going to have to lose the facilities manager as well and I just don't know how we're going to continue paying the salaries of the café and the play area people – which is ridiculous because actually the café and the play area are the only things that make any money.
B: So, isn't Wanda going to retire soon? I think it might be a good idea to … er, get some new blood in.
A: Not on your life, she isn't! She just loves the centre, you know. She couldn't bear the idea of moving on.

2
C: The website said to take the first left after the traffic circle, but there it's all one-way.
D: Yes, I think the centre is over there somewhere, but I'm not sure how we get there. Try turning right here and perhaps we can double back. Let me have a look at the map now … Oh no, the one-way system is going to take us past the entrance to the Milly Street without us being able to turn into it. Help!

3
E: I'm sorry to tell you this, Wanda, but if you can't find the money to pay for the maintenance work soon, health and safety regulations are going to force you to close the building. You've got some serious structural problems with the glass roof on the ground floor. It's about to fall in and I'm afraid you're going to have to close the café whilst you get it repaired. In fact, the whole place looks as if it's about to collapse at any moment. When was it built anyway?
F: 1963. The architect won a design award at the time.

4
G: What shall we do this weekend? I'd like to go out for a change.
H: OK, why don't you look and see what's on at the arts centre?
G: I already tried, but there seems to be a problem with their website. You can only access the programme for last month and next month, but not this month.

5
I: What a great place! It's really ugly from the outside, but this play area is fantastic – all the glass and light. I can't believe it! I never even knew it was here.
J: Yes, what with the new traffic system and all those new office buildings that have gone up, the centre has got completely hidden away. It's a shame.
I: It certainly is.

6
K: Well, I know we should encourage local artists, but most of that was terrible!
L: Yes, you wonder how people get away with calling themselves 'artists' … Anyway, how about a cup of coffee? The cappuccino here is great and really cheap and their carrot cake is fantastic.
K: Good idea. Oh. It says the café closes at three. We'll have to go somewhere else.

3 Play the audio again for the students to complete the sentences in their own words, then again for them to note down any additional problems mentioned. Allow them time to compare their answers in pairs before checking as a class.

POSSIBLE ANSWERS
1 More of the staff is probably going to be made redundant.
2 The present manager of the centre, Wanda, is unlikely to retire.
3 Even though the café is very popular, it may be necessary to close it.
4 The glass roof on the ground is on the verge of collapse.
5 The whole building looks as if it might fall down.
6 The centre is bound to continue losing customers unless the website is updated more frequently.

4 Elicit what the two documents are (a review of a play in a newspaper, and an email to the group of people – the 'Friends of Milly Street' – who support the theatre). Ask the students to quickly read the texts, then work in pairs to discuss and note down answers to the questions. Then ask the students to form one group and discuss their answers together.

ANSWERS
1 No. Because it's boring and pretentious and doesn't appeal to the local community.
2 a The production has been cancelled and the centre is closed.
   b Wanda has resigned. It is likely that the Friends of Milly Street asked her to do so.
   c Milo has been promoted to the post of Director
3 Possible answers:
   a The glass roof of the building will definitely be replaced.
   b The Friends of Milly Street society will probably take a more active role in running the centre.
   c Future productions at the centre are likely to be less pretentious and more suitable for the local community.

43

5 Arrange the class into groups of three: A, B or C. (If the number isn't divisible by three, ask a pair or pairs of students to work as if they were one person.)

Ask Student A to turn to page 98, Student B to page 102 and Student C to page 106.

Allow the students time to read their information and make notes (suggested time ten minutes), then bring them together in their groups of three to hold their meeting and decide how to spend funds, and to write their action plan (15–20 minutes) listing the five steps that will be taken.

Ask one or two groups to present their action plan to the class. Take feedback from the class and find out what groups agreed about. Encourage discussion, and note down any useful vocabulary and/or language problems to deal with later.

ANSWERS

Email A is from a social media consultant who makes recommendations for how to develop a social media presence for the centre so it can market itself effectively to the local community. She recommends employing a part-time social media manager to set everything up and then write posts and maintain it all.

Email B is from a designer and she recommends rebranding the centre – giving a new logo, a totally new website and overall new look to all its communications with the outside world.

Email C is about the results of the Friends of Milly Street research questionnaire when they asked what the local community wanted from the centre, different suggested possible ways of spending the budget to repair the building and ideas for future events/performance that will attract locals.

Extra activity

Write on the whiteboard:
DOMESTIC NEWS   SPORT
INTERNATIONAL NEWS   WEATHER

Ask the students to work together to write four real-life predictions about these areas. Encourage them to use the expressions in the **Grammar** box on page 23. Write one or two predictions of your own and read them out (e.g. *It's likely that the Minister of Education will resign. The situation in [name of country] might start to improve. Manchester United are bound to beat Barcelona. It probably won't rain at the weekend*). Ask the students to write their names on their piece of paper. Collect them in to check which predictions were correct in the next lesson.

Writing emails

Go to **Writing emails 3** on page 46 and do the exercises. Teacher's Book reference on page 63.

4 Getting a job

UNIT OBJECTIVES:

Students will practise ...	and they will learn how to ...
forming questions	improve their interview technique
forming word families	deal with difficult interview questions
describing jobs	
describing positive professional qualities	

Lesson 1: Career jumpers, page 28

LESSON OBJECTIVES:
Students will learn and practise ...
describing jobs
forming questions

Warm up
Tell the class you will leave the room for a minute or two, and you want them to agree on a well-known job, which you will try to guess. When you come back in, ask yes/no questions, and make a mark on the whiteboard each time you ask a question in order to count how many questions it takes you to guess. Possible questions would include:

Do you work regular hours / shifts / outdoors / at a desk / for an organisation / at weekends?

Does your job involve selling / animals / children / driving / making something?

Do you have to wear a uniform / have a degree / speak another language / have a specialist skill?

Once you have guessed the job, ask the students to work in pairs, taking turns to think of a job. Tell them to count their questions (an unsuccessful guess counts as a question), and see who guesses in the least number of goes.

Start up

1 Focus on the pictures and give the students time to speculate in pairs before taking suggestions.

ANSWERS
A woman is making a film – the same woman is speaking to a group of elderly people; A man is looking at plans on a construction site – the same man is teaching a class of teenagers. The connection is that the pictures show a woman and a man who have both changed jobs.

Reading

2 Elicit or pre-teach *commercial* (a television advertisement) and *choir* (a group of people who sing together). Allow the students time to read the texts, then ask them to discuss their answers to the questions. Take feedback from the class.

ANSWERS
1 Possible answer: feeling they wanted to 'give back' to society / do something more worthwhile/fulfilling
2 Students' own answers.

Listening

3 Ask the students to work in pairs and read through the questions together. They predict who each option is likely to apply to, Libby or Victor.

4 🔊 4.1 Play the audio for the students to write *L* or *V*. Allow them to compare answers, and play the audio again if necessary. Check the answers.

ANSWERS
1 a V c L
2 a V b L c L
3 a V b L&V
4 a L b L V c V (at first)
5 a V b L c V
6 a L&V

🔊 **4.1**
Libby
I = interviewer, L = Libby
I: Why did you decide to change career?
L: Well, advertising is an extremely competitive industry, and it, erm ... I started to feel that some of the companies I was working with were unethical, and I was just a small part in a huge, money-making machine. It's all about the bottom line, really, and it felt a bit ... meaningless. It sounds like a cliché, but I wanted to 'give something back' and do something for society rather than just for big corporations.
I: What does your current job involve?
L: Well ... everything! I have to plan the fundraising strategy and recruit the team, and ... generally handle the financial side – it's been a steep learning curve! But the core of my job is running projects with our clients. We get them doing lots of art, and have exhibitions, and for the last year I've run the choir, which has been a great success.
I: What do you like about your job?
L: Working with elderly people is just brilliant – they're real characters. It's incredibly fulfilling to see them come to life when they sing a song from when they were young – you can see it bring some kind of memory alive. And all in all, I've just loved the new challenge – it's so different from 'my old world'.
I: Are there any downsides?
L: Yes, there are. The constant need for money – I have to spend so much of my time fundraising. And also it can be quite emotionally demanding at times working with our clients – when you learn their stories, you want to cry sometimes, but you can't.
I: Is there anything you miss from your old life?

45

L: Well, I got to go to some amazing places, and to work with same amazingly talented people. Mostly, though, I miss eating out at a really good restaurant – that was one of the perks of the job, but I can't afford to any more.
I: Would you say you did the right thing?
L: Yes, I would, definitely. I wouldn't go back.

Victor
I = interviewer, V = Victor
I: What made you change jobs?
V: My job became more and more office-based. I guess I wanted a more people-orientated job as a change from making things. I've always had a secret desire to teach, and I thought I might be a good teacher, because I've got the life experience and ... I'm a good talker!
I: What is involved in your job?
V: I teach Maths, so that involves lessons, obviously, but also you have your own group who you're responsible for – so you hear about whatever worries they have in and out of school, and help if you can. And I teach art, too.
I: What makes you smile at work?
V: The kids are fantastic, although, of course, some of them can be ... er ... challenging! But those moments when they finally understand something and you see a light go on in their head – that's the most fulfilling part of the job. I get on well with my colleagues too – we have a good laugh.
I: Are you less keen on certain aspects of the job?
V: It can get quite stressful – you work long hours, and that's exhausting at times, but of course, there's a lot of holiday. And the pay is low at first, but you do go up the pay scale ... slowly!
I: Surely you miss your old life, don't you?
V: Well, I do miss being part of a team – you're on your own in the classroom. It was also immensely satisfying to see a building go up, and become real, and you're part of that. And I suppose I miss being able to do something really, really well – I'm still learning this job.
I: So, changing career was the right thing to do, was it?
V: Yeah, I'm so glad – best decision I've ever made.

Vocabulary

5 Ask the students to find the words and phrases in the audioscript on page 122. Allow them time to compare their answers in pairs before checking the answers as a class.

ANSWERS
1 it's all about the bottom line   2 give something back
3 steep learning curve   4 perks   5 have a good laugh
6 pay scale

6 Read the adjectives and ask the students to underline the stressed syllable (cha<u>ll</u>enging, com<u>pe</u>titive, de<u>man</u>ding, ex<u>haus</u>ting, ful<u>fi</u>lling, <u>high</u>-status, <u>off</u>ice-based, <u>peo</u>ple-oriented, pre<u>ssur</u>ised, re<u>spon</u>sible, re<u>war</u>ding, <u>sat</u>isfying, <u>stim</u>ulating, <u>stress</u>ful, worth<u>while</u>). Then ask the students to work in pairs, using their dictionaries and sharing their knowledge, to decide if each word is positive, negative or neutral. Take feedback, and encourage discussion if there is disagreement, but accept any answer that is justified.

POSSIBLE ANSWERS
Opinions will probably vary for *competitive*, and possibly *demanding*.
positive: challenging, (competitive), fulfilling, high status, responsible, rewarding, satisfying, stimulating, worthwhile
negative: (competitive), demanding, exhausting, pressurised, stressful
neutral: office-based, people-oriented

7 Play audio 4.1 again for the students to tick the adjectives used. Check the answers.

ANSWERS
Libby: competitive, fulfilling, demanding
Victor: office-based, people-oriented, responsible, challenging, fulfilling, stressful, exhausting, satisfying

Students can find more activities at www.richmondatwork.net

Grammar

8 Ask the students to work individually to complete the questions, then check their answers with a partner.

ANSWERS
1 did you   2 What does   3 do you   4 Are there
5 Is there   6 Would you   7 made you   8 What is
9 makes you   10 Are you   11 don't you   12 was it

9 4.1 Play the audio again for the students to check their answers.

ANSWERS
See 8 in the Student's Book.

10 Ask the students to work in pairs to complete the rules for forming questions. Remind them to use the grammar reference on page 112 if they need help. Check the answers.

ANSWERS
a auxiliary   **b** short   **c** negative   **d** question   **e** subject

11 Ask the students to match the questions in 8 to the rules in 10. Check the answers.

ANSWERS
1 d   2 d   3 d   4 a/b   5 a   6 a   7 e   8 d   9 e
10 a   11 c   12 c

Students can find more activities at www.richmondatwork.net

Speaking

12 Elicit or pre-teach the meaning of any unknown vocabulary in the boxes. Give the students a time limit of ten minutes, to prepare their answers about their imaginary job change, and to practise the questions in 8 to ask their partner.

Getting a job 4

Then ask the students to take turns interviewing each other and making notes. Monitor as they talk, and note down any problems with question forms to deal with later. Take feedback from the class, and write up any useful vocabulary on the white board.

13 For homework or in class, ask the students to write a profile of their partner's career jump, or of a real-life career jump if they prefer.

Extra activity

On the whiteboard, write five lines (representing missing words, repeated 14 times):

1	2	3	4	5
6	7	8	9	10
11	12	13	14	15
16	17	18	19	20
21	22	23	44	25
26	27	28	29	30
31	32	33	34	35
36	37	38	39	40
41	42	43	44	45
46	47	48	49	50
51	52	53	54	55
56	57	58	59	60
61	62	63	64	65
66	67	68	69	70

Tell the students that this is the first thing Libby Walker-Reid said about her 'career-jump', and they have to try to reconstruct it. Pairs of students take it in turns to guess a word, and they get a point for each time the word appears. Tell them that contractions such as *it's* count as two words. Ask the first pair to guess, and you write their guess in the position(s) it appears, and mark up however many points they earn. If the word is not in the text, ask the next pair to guess. They should realise themselves that it is better to start with common words such as *and, is, so, I, etc*. As more and more words are filled in, it will become easier to guess the 'content' words.

Here are the correct guesses, and the positions to write them in:

a (26, 30, 45, 51) felt (44) really (41)
about (37) for (63, 68) small (27)
advertising (1) give (57) society (64)
all (36) huge (31) some (12)
an (3) I (8, 16, 23, 54) something (58, 62)
and (22, 42, 60) in (29) sounds (49)
back (59) industry (6) started (7)
big (69) is (2, 35) than (66)
bit (46) It (34, 43, 48) that (11)
bottom (39) just (25, 67) the (14, 38)
but (53) like (50) to (9, 56)
cliché (52) line (40) unethical (21)
companies (15) machine (33) wanted (55)
competitive (5) meaningless (47) was (17, 24)
corporations (70) money-making (32) were (20)
do (61) of (13) with (19)
extremely (4) part (28) working (18)
feel (10) rather (65)

Here is the complete text:
1–5 Advertising is an extremely competitive
6–10 industry – I started to feel
11–15 that some of the companies
16–20 I was working with were
21–25 unethical, and I was just
26–30 a small part in a
31–35 huge, money-making machine. It's
36–40 all about the bottom line,
41–45 really, and it felt a
46–50 bit meaningless. It sounds like
51–55 a cliché, but I wanted
56–60 to 'give something back' and
61–65 do something for society rather
66–70 than just for big corporations.

Lesson 2: What employers look for in you, page 30

LESSON OBJECTIVES:

Students will learn and practise ...

describing positive professional qualities
forming word families

Warm up

With books closed, write on the whiteboard:

a positive characteristic I have

a special ability I have

Demonstrate the activity by talking about these two things for yourself. Describe your most positive character feature and back this up with examples or an anecdote, and do the same for a special ability (e.g. *I'm very easy to get on with, and I think that's probably my most positive character feature. I never seem to argue with anyone, and I've always seemed to make friends easily ...*). Encourage questions, then ask the students to do the same in pairs. Take feedback from the class.

Start up

1 Ask the students to discuss briefly in pairs what jobs are pictured (airline pilot, stockbroker / stock trader, TV news reporter, athlete, receptionist, police officer).

Read the qualities, and ask the students to underline the stressed syllable (<u>cool</u>ness under <u>press</u>ure, a<u>bil</u>ity to see the big <u>pic</u>ture, commu<u>ni</u>cation skills, an <u>eye</u> for detail, <u>prob</u>lem-solving skills, <u>lead</u>ership qualities, in<u>i</u>tiative, quick <u>think</u>ing, crea<u>tiv</u>ity, total re<u>li</u>ability).

Ask each pair to choose a job, or designate a job to each pair. Ask the students to discuss the qualities needed for that job on the scale of 0–5. Take feedback from the class, and encourage any discussion.

2 Tell the class your own answers to the questions. Encourage questions, and write any useful vocabulary on the whiteboard. Then allow the students time to discuss the questions in pairs. Take feedback from the class.

Listening

3 Arrange the students in different pairs. Elicit a description of what a *personality test* is (a series of multiple-choice questions about your preferences and habits, how you see yourself, etc.; the results are analysed to test whether you are suitable for a particular job), and the meaning of *recruitment process* (the series of things that happen in order for a new person to be employed by a company, e.g. advertising the job, people applying for the job, candidates being chosen for interviews, tests). Focus on the first statement in the picture (*I feel confident about making decisions*). Ask the students what answer – 'true' or 'false', it would be better to give in a personality test if you wanted to get the job, and why. (It would probably be to say 'true', as most jobs need you to be able to make some decisions independently.) Take feedback, then ask the students to carry on discussing the other statements in the same way in pairs. Accept any answer that is justified, and encourage discussion.

Then ask the students to discuss questions 1–3, before taking feedback from the class.

4 ◀)) **4.2** Play the audio for the students to listen and answer the question. Allow the students time to discuss the question in pairs, then check the answers.

ANSWERS
They're good for checking someone's basic suitability for a job type, so are a good way to cut down a large number of applicants.

◀)) **4.2**
I = interviewer, S = Sarah Patterson
I: And here to give her opinion on personality tests is Human Resources consultant Sarah Patterson. So, do personality tests actually help companies recruit the right person?
S: Well, as far as selecting job candidates goes, I'd say they're good for checking someone's basic suitability for a job type. It's a good way to cut down a large number of applicants because it's quite inexpensive, but it's less reliable as a way of finding the best person for a particular job. I mean, if you're advertising a specific job, say an administrator, a personality test would show you whether they had the basic requirements – extremely well organised, of course, and as they're, kind of, at the centre of a team, they'd obviously need to be a natural communicator. And have good teamworking skills as well as the ability to work on their own initiative without needing instruction all the time. And they'd need to be meticulous about checking their work so that it's accurate. So, you can make sure an applicant is more or less the right kind of person.
I: Whereas an administrator wouldn't need excellent analytical skills or a creative approach, for example?
S: That's right, but if you're looking for someone with, let's see, management potential, then you'd need someone with strong strategic skills, who could analyse the situation and form a plan, you know, be proactive rather than just, sort of, reacting to events. And they'd need the flexibility to deal with new situations that came up. So you're looking for different qualities. An applicant's CV, of course, gives you some indication of the work they're suited to, but a personality test can sometimes reveal qualities that you can't see in the CV.
I: What do you see as the limitations of personality tests?
S: Well, of course it's often possible to guess the answer that the employer wants, so people may not answer honestly. Actually, the same is true of the interview, of course – candidates give the answer that the interviewer wants to hear. But then an interview can reveal things that a personality test can't, such as whether a person really has excellent communication skills, and erm... a person's dynamism – their level of drive and enthusiasm.
I: So, is it worth using personality tests at all?
S: Good question. Well, where I think it has value is in directing someone towards a field of work, for example, someone who's still studying, and wants to know what kind of work they'd be suitable for. Or, you know, someone who's lost their job or wants to change. They would certainly give honest answers, and so a good-quality test would be able to give them an idea of the types of work that would be suitable. And as far as finding the right candidate is concerned, they are useful for adding information to the CV and covering letter for selecting candidates for interview.
I: Sarah Patterson, thank you.

5 Allow the students a few minutes to read the questions. Then play the audio again for them to choose the correct option for each. Check the answers.

ANSWERS
1 cheap **2** who to interview **3** check their work carefully / be well organised **4** make plans **5** not always answer truthfully **6** driven **7** still studying

Fluency

6 Read the rubric with the class. Emphasise that 'fillers' are commonly-used words or expressions that add little or nothing to the sense of a sentence. Play audio 4.2 again for the students to complete what Sarah said with the 'fillers' she used. Check the answers.

ANSWERS
1 Well **2** quite **3** I mean **4** kind of **5** let's see
6 sort of **7** Actually **8** Good question

7 Ask the students to work in pairs and take turns to speak for one minute about what they do. Tell them to count how many of Sarah's 'fillers' their partner manages to use, and ask who used the most.

Vocabulary

8 Focus on number 1. Elicit what could be added to complete the word (*-ness*). Ask the students to try to complete the words and expressions using their own knowledge first, before using the words in **1** and the audioscript for help. Allow the students to compare their answers in pairs before checking as a class.

Getting a job 4

ANSWERS

1. coolness under pressure (noun phrase)
2. an eye for detail (noun phrase)
3. excellent leadership qualities (adjectival phrase)
4. able to work on your own initiative (adjectival phrase)
5. creativity (noun)
6. a creative approach (adjectival phrase)
7. dynamism (noun)
8. total reliability (noun phrase)
9. a natural communicator (adjectival phrase)
10. meticulous (adjective)
11. excellent analytical skills (adjectival phrase)
12. strong strategic skills (adjectival phrase)
13. proactive (adjective)
14. good problem-solving skills (adjectival phrase)
15. good teamworking skills (adjectival phrase)
16. flexibility (noun)

Students can find more activities at www.richmondatwork.net

9 Arrange the students in AB pairs, and ask a Student B to ask you the first question from the test on page 103 as an example (*Can you hold people's attention when you speak?*). Answer with *Definitely*, *To some extent* or *Not at all*, and give an example of why this is the case. Encourage any questions. Elicit what positive characteristic your answer reveals (e.g. a good/natural communicator / good communication skills).

Ask the students to continue in a similar way, taking turns to ask questions and encourage their partner to give details, and note down any positive characteristics suggested by the answers.

Speaking

10 Ask the students to tell their partner the adjectives they wrote, with a brief explanation. Encourage them to focus on the positive. Invite some students to give the class a summary of what they found out about their partner.

11 Ask pairs to discuss the questions, then take feedback from the class.

Extra activity

Ask the students to think of a job, and write a description of the characteristics and natural strengths this person would need. Tell them that other students will have to guess the job, so they should give just enough information to make it guessable, but not too easy, e.g. *This person needs to be a natural leader and have fantastic communication skills in a range of different situations. Their analytical and strategic skills need to be top class. They need to be able to work as part of a team, and to form strong relationships. They should also be flexible, as their resources will keep changing. They have to be able to work under constant media pressure.* (Answer: football / sports manager)

Set a ten-minute time-limit, then ask the students to take turns reading out their description for the class to guess.

Lesson 3: Getting the job, page 32

LESSON OBJECTIVES:
Students will learn and practise ...
improving your interview technique
dealing with difficult interview questions

Warm up

With books closed, write on the whiteboard:

confident	lacking in confidence

Ask the students to imagine a very confident person in their mind's eye. Ask, 'What is it about the person that shows they are confident?' Brainstorm aspects of behaviour, movement, etc. that show confidence, and write them in the left-hand column, helping students to express them in English where necessary. Then do the same *for lacking in confidence*. Some suggestions that may come up are:

- confident: *upright posture, decisive movements, good eye contact, a strong voice, hand gestures, physical contact with others, takes up a central position, opens conversations, a confident smile*
- lacking in confidence: *a stooping/slouching posture, slow/uncertain movements, a lack of eye contact, displacement behaviour (unnecessary fiddling with objects, scratching head, etc.), a quiet voice, awkwardness about what to do with hands, stands at the side or back of the room, reactive rather than proactive in conversations, a serious expression or nervous smile*

Start up

1 Focus on the pictures, and allow the students a few minutes to discuss the questions. Take feedback from the class, and write any useful vocabulary on the whiteboard. Encourage the students to try and match vocabulary from the **Warm up** to the pictures.

POSSIBLE ANSWERS
a defensive **b** overly-relaxed **c** confused/perplexed
d stressed **e** confident

2 Allow the students time to read the statements and decide whether or not they agree.

ANSWERS
See **3**

3 Ask the students to discuss, justify and argue for their answers. Take feedback from the class.

POSSIBLE ANSWERS

(Some may differ in different cultures.)
1 No – a good CV may get you an interview, but is not enough to get you a job.
2 No suggestion – it depends.
3 Usually yes – find out as much as possible by researching the company before the interview, and focus on the quality of questions, not the quantity.
4 No – they have invited you to hear how you communicate, so expand on your answers, but keep everything relevant.
5 Yes – most questions are predictable, and this will help you think about your answers.
6 It depends – you will naturally do most of the talking, but remember that communication is a two-way process, so demonstrate your listening skills too, and make sure you stay relevant.
7 No – it's safer to look as if you will fit in with a team, and with the employers' expectations of dress

Reading

4 Pre-teach *references* (letters written usually written by respected people you know, mentioning your positive qualities), *pose* (a particular way in which you hold your body and facial expression, for example when someone is taking your photo) and *struggle* (to have difficulty with something). Ask the students to read the texts about Omar and Akram, underlining the factors in favour of each one being chosen for the job, and then to discuss and justify their answers. Take feedback from the class, and encourage discussion.

POSSIBLE ANSWERS

Omar: two years' relevant experience, good references, strong handshake, long eye contact, starts nervously then does very well
Akram: last interviewee, no experience but great potential, makes himself appear confident, normal handshake and eye contact, starts and ends well, but struggles in the middle, spills coffee

5 Ask the students to read the study and discuss the questions. Take feedback from the class, and encourage discussion.

POSSIBLE ANSWERS

According to the study, Akram would be more likely to get the job, because he: 'power poses' to appear confident; has great potential, which is preferred to experience; is interviewed last; shows confident eye contact while recognising the interviewer's dominance; avoids an extreme handshake; does very well at the beginning, rather than improving later in the interview; makes himself seem likeable by spilling his drink (this only helps him because the interview went well).

6 Ask the students to discuss the questions in pairs, then take feedback from the class. Ask the class if anyone has heard any other psychological tips for interviews.

Functional language

7 Write on the board:

Why have you changed jobs so many times?

Ask the students what would be the best way to answer this interview question. Take feedback, then ask students to read the interview questions and discuss the questions in the rubric with their partner. Discuss their answers as a class. You could extend the activity if your class have a lot of interview experience by asking what other difficult questions people have faced, and how they answered. Write any useful vocabulary on the whiteboard.

ANSWERS

All these questions have difficulties, but 5 would be especially hard as it involves explaining a negative situation, and 6 because you have to answer the question without making yourself sound weak in any way.

8 4.3 Play the audio for the students to write a–f next to the questions in **7**. Check the answers.

ANSWERS

1 d 2 b 3 a 4 e 5 f 6 c

4.3

a   I feel that my skills and experience are a perfect match for this post, and I would hit the ground running because of my experience using the same software.
b   The company is a leader in the industry, with 40% market share. My research has convinced me that it would be very rewarding to be part of this company.
c   I'm not a natural public speaker, so in my last job I asked to do a public speaking course, and now I'd count it as a strength.
d   I want to leave my job because I'm getting bored with doing the same work all the time. Plus, I don't really get on with my colleagues or my boss.
e   I think in five years' time I should have gained enough experience here to be in a position to start my own business, which is my ultimate aim.
f   My work is important to me, so I've been selective in the jobs I've applied for, to make sure my next role is the right one for me.

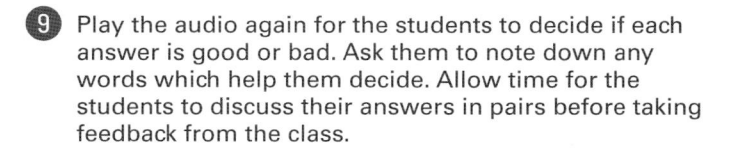

9 Play the audio again for the students to decide if each answer is good or bad. Ask them to note down any words which help them decide. Allow time for the students to discuss their answers in pairs before taking feedback from the class.

POSSIBLE ANSWERS

a   good – shows knowledge of software used and matches it to own experience
b   good – knowledge of market share shows research and therefore interest
c   good – demonstrates awareness of own performance and initiative in turning a weakness into a strength
d   bad – suggests negative attitude: boredom and poor relationships can be a problem in any job if you have the wrong attitude

- e bad – suggests that the company is being used just as a stepping stone; companies tend to invest in people for the long term
- f good – a difficult question to answer is expressed in a very positive way

10 Ask the students to discuss appropriate and inappropriate things to say in answer to each question. Ask each pair to join with another pair to discuss their answers, then take feedback from the class.

POSSIBLE ANSWERS

1 **mention:** looking for new challenges, responsibilities, skills not offered by previous job; your good performance and relations in previous job
   don't mention: boredom, bad relations, bad boss – be positive and specific about previous job and this one
2 **mention:** possibility of new responsibilities and skills, long-term career goals and how this job meets them; specific aspects of job or projects that attracted you (show evidence of research); company's success and reputation for quality
   don't mention: good pay and conditions
3 **mention:** specific qualities that would be especially valuable in this job (show research and thought)
   don't mention: being a hard worker (they assume this); vague, unsupported statements such as 'I'm a good fit for the job'
4 **mention:** building a career within this company (show research); specific and realistic responsibilities and skills you hope to have, or projects you would like to be involved in
   don't mention: working for another company or yourself; unrealistic goals; having the interviewer's job
5 **mention:** specific qualities you have been looking for in a job, and how this job finally matches them; evidence of constructive use of time; details of reasons expressed in as positive way as possible, e.g. conditions have been challenging in this industry
   don't mention: inability to get interviews, bad luck stories
6 **mention:** specific examples of how you identified weaknesses and made them strengths, e.g. improved your English level, took training course, etc.
   don't mention: weaknesses you have done nothing about

Speaking

11 Arrange the students into AB pairs. Give the students time to read the information on page 98 or 103 and note down key words to help them remember the main points. Elicit the meaning of *put a positive spin on* (present something so that it focuses on the good aspects). Then ask the students to take turns asking their partner an interview question from **7**, and noting down positive points about their answers. Take feedback from the class.

Extra activity

Tell the students you are going to play them one of the recordings from the lesson again for them to reconstruct. Play audio 4.3 answer (a) twice, then ask the students to work in pairs to try to reconstruct as much as possible of what is said. Encourage them to compare with other pairs to try to fill in gaps. Do the same with answer (b), and then with answer (c), then finally tell the students to look at the audioscript on page 123 to check their answers.

Getting a job 4

Scenario: Arctic venture, page 34

SCENARIO OBJECTIVE:
Students will decide which of four candidates should be given the role of manager for an outdoor clothing superstore.

Warm up

Focus on the pictures. Tell the students you're going to give them a test, and that they have one minute to study the pictures (but not the map). After one minute, tell them to close their books, and work in pairs to agree on and write down the answers to your questions. Read out these questions:

1 What does the third picture show? (houses)
2 What's the man with the dog wearing on his body? (a fur coat / an animal-skin coat)
3 Does he have a moustache? (yes)
4 What's he wearing on his head? (a white headband)
5 There's a picture of a man on his own. What colour is his coat? (yellow)
6 What's the weather like in the picture? (sunny)
7 There's a picture of houses. What colours are the houses? (red, yellow, green and blue)
8 What's in the background of the picture? (sea and ice/icebergs)
9 There's a picture of an oil drill. What colour is it? (green)
10 What's in the background? (mountains)

Check the answers, and get each pair to add up their scores. Congratulate the winners!

1 Ask the students to discuss the two questions in their pairs, noting down three points for each question. Take feedback from the class, and write any useful vocabulary on the whiteboard.

POSSIBLE ANSWERS

1 The lives of indigenous people would have become more 'Western'. Traditional clothes and food would have gradually been mixed with or supplemented by mass-produced, and traditional forms of transport by modern, e.g. 4x4s and snowmobiles. Exposure to global media through TV and Internet would have made everyone aware of global brands and culture, and increased the use of English at the expense of indigenous languages.
2 Recent warmer temperatures would have made expansion of towns possible, and made the area easier for outsiders to settle in, bringing in new types of business and consumer goods. It has also made oil and mineral speculation easier.

2 Ask the students to read the scenario and then compare their understanding of the basic facts with their partner before discussing the two questions. Take feedback from the class and encourage discussion.

ANSWERS

1 The population is rising so there's an increased number of consumers. There's political unrest on the island between the native population and 'outsiders', and Eklund Outdoors would be an 'outsider' company.
2 Suggested answer: The person would ideally be willing to take risks, adaptable to any kind of situation, able to 'think on their feet', good at problem-solving, calm and good at forming relationships with all kinds of people. They would ideally have experience of building a company or branch in a new place, of building a team, of marketing to a new market, and of living in a different culture, with a willingness to learn a new language.

3 Ask the students to read about the four candidates and underline the strengths of each one before comparing their answers in pairs. Take feedback.

4 ◀)) 4.4 Play the audio for the students to number the order of the candidates. Check the answers.

ANSWERS

1 Renée   2 Dan   3 Karen   4 Ranjit

◀)) **4.4**

1
I would have to say my strength is my ability to keep a cool head. I've experienced a wide variety of unusual, often dangerous situations, and have always managed to react in a calm and logical way. I feel there is nothing that I wouldn't be able to deal with.

If I have a weakness, it's possibly that I joined the army at 18. I left at 30 and set up a business where my supplier is the army, so all my experience is connected to that, and, you could say, slightly limited in that way.

2
I think the fact that I didn't go to business college is possibly my greatest strength. I rely on instinct, and my instinct has been pretty good so far. I take decisions which other people would see as too risky, or would not think of, and I've found they usually work.

As for a weakness, that's easy – I spent six years working in Norway and Denmark, and I think I have a good feeling for the culture – I can sense the right way to talk to people, to behave with people to make them feel comfortable. But in all that time ... I'm not proud of this ... I must admit I haven't learned to say a thing in any other language. It just doesn't come naturally to me, I'm afraid.

3
Well, I'm known for my ability to stand back from a situation – it could be a business situation, or the economic state of a country – and read it. So, I can instantly see what's happening and why, what's going to happen, and what needs to be done.

And weaknesses ... erm ... well, not so much a weakness, but an area I haven't touched yet, is management. I've always worked alone – not by choice especially. But I do feel I would be very good at management given the chance, because ... I think I read people well, and I get on well with everyone, just about.

4
It's very hard to pick out a main strength – perhaps presenting is something my colleagues would mention. I seem to able to grab an audience's attention, and be very persuasive. I suppose it's a key skill in sales, and it's been very useful all through my career.

And if I had to choose a weak area, maybe it's that I work myself too hard. But, I don't know, perhaps an employer wouldn't see that as a weakness! I've had to work under extreme pressure for long periods, and dealing with such an enormous sales region was too much for me at times – the workload was just unbelievable.

5 Allow the students time to copy the table into their notebooks, in landscape format (i.e. turning the notebook sideways) to make the columns wide enough to write notes in. Play the audio again once or twice for the students to make notes in their table about the strengths and weaknesses of each candidate.

POSSIBLE ANSWERS

Ranjit
- strengths: long experience as Head of Sales, experience in clothing industry, has led company into new market, good at learning languages, experience working under great pressure
- weakness: experience mainly in Sales, pressure has been 'too much' at times

Renée
- strengths: probably adaptable and a good leader, runs own company, experience in clothing industry, good at languages, experience in unusual and dangerous situations, ability to keep a cool head
- weakness: experience all connected with the military

Dan
- strengths: experience managing large store in a different culture, some experience in clothing industry, probably very dedicated and driven, trusts his instincts and willing to take risks, finds creative solutions, good feeling for culture
- weakness: only speaks English, despite having lived in Norway

Karen
- strengths: expert on all aspects of the region and speaks language fluently, runs own (small) company, experience in clothing industry, good at analysing situations on a big scale
- weakness: no experience running large-scale business, no management experience

6 Ask the students to compare their answers and discuss who they think is/are the favourite(s), but don't take feedback at this stage.

7 Check that the students remember the meaning of *references* (letters usually written by respected people who you know which mention your positive qualities), and elicit or pre-teach *tact* (the ability to deal with difficult situations or people in a calm way without upsetting anyone). Ask the students to read the texts and answer the questions, using their dictionary if necessary. Allow them time to compare their answers in pairs before checking as a class. For each answer, ask the students what clue led them to the answer.

ANSWERS

1 Renée   2 Dan   3 Ranjit   4 Ranjit and Karen   5 Ranjit
6 Karen   7 Dan   8 Renée

Getting a job 4

8 Allow the students time to write notes into their table and discuss their current thoughts in pairs.

POSSIBLE ANSWERS
Ranjit: adaptable, good at working in different culture, popular with team
Renée: adaptable to different cultures and situations, good in crisis (but not so good when there's no crisis)
Dan: proven success in building a store in a different culture, a talented, charismatic leader (but can upset people with criticism)
Karen: great with new challenges, great understanding of economy (but not tested under pressure, and seems to prefer working alone)

9 Give the students one minute to read the texts and match them with the candidates, then check the answers quickly. Ask them to read the extracts again and underline any relevant information before adding to the notes in their tables.

ANSWERS
a Dan **b** Ranjit **c** Renée **d** Karen

10 🔊 **4.5** Read the questions with the class, and deal with any unfamiliar vocabulary. Play the audio for the students to choose the correct option. Allow them time to compare their answers in pairs before checking as a class.

ANSWERS
1 going well **2** unstable **3** difficult at first **4** isn't
5 the team **6** dynamic

🔊 **4.5**

Just to update you on the situation here. Building is going according to plan, so that's fine. The situation in the country, though, is changing day to day – things are quite uncertain at the moment. The one thing that's sure is that we'll need someone with a cool head – you know, who can react to situations as they come up, and make sensible decisions. Not just day to day, of course, because we'll need to start developing our strategy for the long term, so seeing the big picture is absolutely essential. They're certainly going to face lots of problems – we just don't know what yet!

It would be very important, I'd say, for the person to make a big effort from the start to learn the local language. It's become a very political thing, so, you know, for outsiders it's important to show an interest in the culture and the language – that would really help. Yes, the culture ... erm ... getting a feel for how people think here is really key, because I can say it's quite different from Europe.

And because of the sensitive situation at the moment, we really need a great communicator – someone who always says the right thing and keeps all sides happy. Their team will have a mixture of people, both native Kinavut-speakers and people from outside, so some great management skills will be needed to keep them working as a team. And ... erm ... there's so much happening here, and it's happening so fast, that, of course, we need someone who likes that environment, and has the energy to deal with it. OK, so good luck finding the person with all that!

11 Arrange the students in new groups of three or four, in a different group from their previous partner if possible. Ask each group to nominate a secretary and spokesperson to note down and report to the class the points made in the discussion. Set a time-limit of ten minutes for the discussion. If a group finishes early, ask them to rank the candidates in order from strongest to weakest.

12 Ask the spokesperson of each group in turn to report their decision, explaining how the decision was reached. Encourage discussion, and work out who the most popular candidate was overall. If there is time, you could then ask each student individually to rank the candidates from 1 to 4 (strongest to weakest), and work out the overall ranking.

Extra activity

Give out ten very small pieces of paper to each student, and ask them to look back through the unit and write ten useful nouns, adjectives or verbs. Then pass around a bag or other container and ask the students to fold up each piece of paper and put them all in.

Divide the class into two teams and toss a coin to see which team goes first. Ask who is going first on that team, and tell them they have one minute to take one word at a time from the bag and explain it for their team to guess (without using gestures!). When it's guessed, they put it aside and quickly go on to the next one. If they think the team can't guess, they can fold up the word and put it back in the bag. Tell them to start, then after one minute say 'stop' and add up their points for correctly guessed words. Then the other team does the same with the remaining words for one minute. Carry on like this until everyone has had a turn (or two in a small class). If all the words have been guessed before everyone has had a turn (or two in a small class), put all the words back in and continue as before – this will speed the game up as the students have heard all the words, so just a reminder is necessary. The team with the most points after everyone has played is the winner.

Writing emails

Go to **Writing emails 4** on page 46 and do the exercises. Teacher's Book reference on page 63.

Start up

1 Focus on the picture. Give the students a couple of minutes to discuss the questions, then take feedback from the class, and encourage discussion.

Reading

2 Write on the whiteboard:

Do you use travel review websites (e.g. tripadvisor) when planning a trip?

If so, how useful is it?

Have you ever posted a review on it?

Ask the students to discuss these questions briefly, then take feedback from the class.

Focus attention on the reviews, and tell students they are reviews of the accommodation in the photo. Ask what the average rating is (2 stars). Then ask the students to read the *Who ...?* questions 1–6 and match each one with a name. Check the answers.

ANSWERS

1 Paul 2 Gina, Tori 3 Hussein 4 Astrid 5 Stef
6 Andy

3 Focus on Andy's review. Elicit what improvement could be made based on his suggestion, then write at the top of the whiteboard: *cut the grass*. Ask the students to continue in pairs, agreeing on a list of improvements based on the reviews. Each student should write down the list, as they will need it for the next task.

POSSIBLE ANSWERS

parking closer to the cabins, some heating and lighting in the cabins, a shop selling basics, bikes for hire that have been serviced properly, better security, storage space and a table/chairs, all repairs to be carried out, e.g. fixing the roof

Listening

4 🔊 5.2 Read the rubric with the class, then play the audio once or twice for the students to tick any improvements on the list they wrote in **3** that she mentions. Allow them time to compare answers in pairs before checking answers. Note that students' lists will not all be exactly the same.

ANSWERS

See **5**

🔊 **5.2**

Well, we've learned a lot since last year, and we're getting much better comments these days.

The field has been made into a car park. We cut the grass, and took off the gate ... so that was simple.

And erm ... the roofs have been repaired – Martin did that – and we had the doors replaced by our friend who's a carpenter. All the buildings needed making more secure, so we got all the locks changed.

So, yeah, shelves and cupboards have been put up in every cabin. We had them made especially by our friend again but we put them up ourselves. That was hard work.

Nowadays we put basics like milk and coffee in the cabins, and people can buy more if they need to, from us when we're there or from the farm nearby.

Then we er ... we put gas lamps in each cabin – the type you hold in your hand – they last a long time, and they're completely safe.

The bikes needed servicing, so that's being done now by the local bike shop. We're going to get them checked more regularly from now on.

And what else ... erm, oh yes, we had gas heaters put in each cabin – we got a professional to do it as we're not trained to do that.

And so, erm, now there are still a few little things that need doing, but we've done the main jobs, and our guests are a lot happier.

5 🔊 5.2 Play the first three sentences of the audio up to *... so that was simple*. Elicit the two tasks Maya mentioned (cutting the grass, taking off the gate) and ask whether they did it themselves or a professional did it (they did it themselves). Maya says *We cut the grass, and took off the gate*, so ask the students what they should write next to those tasks in their lists (O).

Play the audio for the students to continue in the same way. Allow them time to compare answers in pairs before checking answers.

ANSWERS

Students' own answers. (She mentions: the field has been made into a car park – O; roofs have been repaired – O; doors have been replaced and locks have been changed – P; shelves and cupboards have been put in each cabin – P for the making, O for installing; basics such as milk and coffee are supplied in each cabin – O; basic are available to buy from Maya and Martin or the nearby farm – O; gas lamps and heaters have been added to each cabin – O; the bikes are being serviced – P)

Grammar

6 Play the audio again, pausing after the sentences in the exercise for the students to write in the missing words. Allow the students to compare their answers in pairs before checking as a class.

ANSWERS

1 has been made 2 cut, took off 3 had, replaced
4 got, changed 5 servicing

7 Ask the students to work in pairs to match questions 1–4 with the sentences in **6**. Remind them that they can use the grammar reference as well as the **Grammar** box if they need help. Check the answers.

56

New products and services 5

ANSWERS
a 5   b 3, 4   c 2   d 1, 3, 4, 5

8 Allow the students time to underline the verb forms in the audioscript on page 124, then check the answers.

POSSIBLE ANSWERS
We had them made especially.
All the buildings needed making more secure.

Students can find more activities at www.richmondatwork.net

Speaking

9 Arrange the students in pairs, and set a time limit of 15–20 minutes for them to plan their project. Tell them to sketch their ideas on the plan of the railway carriage, with labels if they like. Remind them to think about the verbs they will need as well as the nouns. Encourage them to have fun being imaginative. Monitor and help as they prepare their projects.

10 Remind the students to use the grammar of the lesson when presenting their ideas to another pair. Set a time limit of ten minutes for the activity. Monitor as they do the activity, and note down any problems with the grammar of the lesson or with vocabulary to deal with later. Ask each pair to make positive comments on the other pair's plans. Encourage questions and discussion.

Extra activity
Play audio 5.2 a chunk at a time as a dictation. Pause after ... these days / ... that was simple / ... who's a carpenter / ... all the locks changed / ... in every cabin / ... hard work / ... the farm nearby / ... completely safe / ... from now on / ... not trained to do that / ... a lot happier.
Allow the students to compare what they've got, then play the audio again, pausing in the same places, for them to fill in any gaps. Finally, ask them to look at the audioscript on page 124 and check their answers.

Lesson 3: Presenting, page 40

LESSON OBJECTIVES:

Students will learn and practise ...
tips on effective presenting
key presentation phrases
planning a presentation

Warm up

Write the following lists on the whiteboard, and elicit which item in the right hand list collocates with *try not to get* (too nervous). Tell the students that all the collocations relate to preparing for a presentation. Ask them to work together to join the beginnings and endings of the collocations.

1 try not to get	a memory stick (6)
2 memorise	a run-through (7)
3 reduce your script to	bullet points (3)
4 copy	cue cards (8)
5 prepare for	handouts (4)
6 put everything on	questions (5)
7 do	the equipment (10)
8 prepare	too nervous (1)
9 research	your audience (9)
10 test	your intro (2)

Start up

1 Ask the students to focus on the quotes. Read them with the class, and ask for volunteers to paraphrase them (e.g. *I hate presentations. I get so nervous in front of an audience, I can't think or speak; I like performing for people, so presenting is something I enjoy and am good at*). Ask the students to discuss the questions, then take feedback from the class, writing any useful vocabulary on the whiteboard.

2 Arrange the students in groups of three or four. Ask each group to nominate a secretary to note down the ideas for question 1, then ask groups to discuss the questions. You may want to set a time limit of 10–15 minutes. Take feedback from each group, and again write any useful vocabulary on the whiteboard.

POSSIBLE ANSWERS
technology: projector or computer may not work, file may not open, memory stick may not work or get lost, software could be incompatible, could be problems with audio
organisation: you or audience could be late, you could forget or not have time to make handouts, preparation time could be too short, may not be enough chairs
performance: could be insufficiently practised or affected by nerves
audience: may have problems understanding, could ask difficult questions, could be too few or too many
other: finding the venue, unexpected events, incorrect information, etc.

Listening

3 5.3 Play the audio for the students to listen for the numbers. Tell them to note down a key word so they can remember what each number refers to. Check the answers.

ANSWERS
50: number of slides in the presentation
20: time spent waiting for speaker to learn how to use the projector
1: rule number 1 is K(eep) I(t) S(imple) S(illy)

ANSWERS

1 and 2: Students' own ideas.
3 outdoor activities include: watersports (e.g. canoeing, kayaking, white-water rafting, sailing, jet-skiing, waterskiing, windsurfing, sailboarding, diving), mountain-climbing, rock-climbing, abseiling, caving / potholing; hiking, skiing, snowboarding, hang-gliding, kiteboarding, mountain-biking, etc.
4 They would probably attract young, active, sporty people, possibly school, work or social groups or young families, depending on what activities were offered and at what price.

2 Allow the students time to read the texts and match each one with one of the picture sets a–c in **1**. Check the answers.

ANSWERS

1 c 2 b 3 a

3 Ask the students to copy the table as large as possible in their notebooks. Tell them to reread the texts in **2**, underlining advantages and disadvantages of each site, then noting these points in the table. Allow the students time to compare their answers, but there is no need to take feedback at this stage.

POSSIBLE ANSWERS

Site 1 (Photo c)
- advantages: beautiful location, simple design, possibly cheaper to renovate
- disadvantages: It's been empty a long time, may need work to make it suitable for accommodation.

Site 2 (Photo b)
- advantages: beautiful location, most buildings would be designed for habitation, probably has water pipes in place
- disadvantages: so many buildings would be expensive to renovate

Site 3 (photo a)
- advantages: spectacular buildings and location, high capacity so high potential profits
- disadvantages: complex, industrial building would be expensive to turn into habitable building, location would add to cost

4 ◀)) **5.5** Elicit what kind of agent the rubric refers to (a real-estate / property agent). Play the audio for the students to match the speakers with the sites, then check the answers.

ANSWERS

Speaker 1 – Photo a (Site 3)
Speaker 2 – Photo c (Site 1)
Speaker 3 – Photo b (Site 2)

◀)) **5.5**

1
Well, this place presents unusual challenges. One or two of the smaller buildings are clearly unsafe, and will have to be pulled down, but the whole place was inspected a couple of years ago, and all the larger structures were found to be completely solid and safe, which is surprising, really.

The main expense here is the conversion of the inside of the buildings to suitable accommodation and facilities. This used to be an industrial site, so to change it to comfortable rooms and so on will be complicated. And the fact it's in the mountains will double that cost. You'd be looking at $2.2 million, we think, to make the conversion, and possibly more if there are any more safety issues.

2
The basic structure's in surprisingly good condition. The outside wall's very unusual because it's made of metal! They obviously knew when they built it that it would survive, because the climate in this part of the country is fairly dry. So only small parts of the wall will have to be replaced, but that shouldn't be too expensive. And the roof is in amazing condition. One section of it was destroyed in a storm, but most of it's in an excellent state.

The main expense with this building is that the inside would need to be rebuilt to accommodate guests. Currently it has large open areas where patients were treated, and a number of smaller rooms, for example, where operations took place – obviously that's not suitable for a hotel or leisure facility. Our estimate for turning this into rooms, with a restaurant, gym and car-parking would be $1.8 million.

3
These buildings are still here because they're built of stone. All the walls are in almost perfect condition, but all the roofs will need replacing entirely. Also, plants and trees have grown inside some of the buildings, so they'll need removing. Apart from that, most of the buildings just need to be decorated on the inside and furnished. There are houses of every size, and a few larger buildings, so they're perfect for a range of accommodation and for a gym, restaurant, etc. without needing to be changed.

Some of the people who lived in the village were pretty rich, so there are some really fantastic and luxurious buildings here. That makes the cost of building materials a bit higher, of course. But we've worked out that it would cost about $1.2 million to make the village into an activity centre.

5 Play the audio again once or twice for the students to note down further advantages and disadvantages for each site. Allow them time to compare their answers, and to write in their tables.

New products and services 5

POSSIBLE ANSWERS

Site 1
- advantages: in surprisingly good basic condition, relatively cheap to replace one section of roof and parts of wall
- disadvantages: expensive to convert interior to leisure facility ($1.8 million)

Site 2
- advantages: walls in perfect condition, good range of buildings for accommodation and leisure, some buildings are beautiful
- disadvantages: roofs need replacing, just need furnishing and decorating, luxurious buildings are more expensive to repair ($1.2 million)

Site 3
- advantages: surprisingly solid (although some smaller buildings unsafe)
- disadvantages: complicated and expensive job ($2.2 million), possibly more safety issues

6 Arrange the students in groups of three: A, B, C. Read the rubric, then allow the students five minutes to read about their site and note down key words in their notebook. Ask Student A to read about photo A, Student B about photo B and Student C about photo C.

7 Ask the students to share their information as a group, and to write in their tables.

8 Ask the groups to discuss the advantages and disadvantages of each site, and to agree on one to develop. Set a time-limit of five minutes for groups to aim for, but be flexible if groups can't agree easily. Ask groups to explain which site they chose.

9 Read the rubric and the table with the class, then set a time-limit of 15 minutes for groups to discuss and note down details of their plan.

POSSIBLE ANSWER

Example table for Site 1 (photo c):

target market	young professionals – couples, singles or groups, young families
activities offered	watersports: windsurfing, sailing, canoeing, kayaking; hiking; mountain biking; horseriding; 'zorbing'; sea-fishing
accommodation	30 double and 20 single rooms, each with own bathroom
eco features	energy from solar panels and heat exchange from the sea; recyclable materials; discounts for arriving by boat; rainwater saving; recycling, re-use and waste control systems
style of décor	ultra-modern, cutting-edge technology
food	healthy and high quality; 'standard' and 'gourmet' menus; luxury packed lunches
facilities	wi-fi in all rooms; gym; sauna; pool; restaurant and bar with terrace; games room; TV room
staff and service	young, sporty, friendly, very well trained, well paid; we want staff to stay and customers to return year after year
five main things you will do to the site	convert inside to rooms put in water and electrical supply install solar panels and heat exchange system put in gym, pool and sauna build kitchen, bar and terrace

10 Set a time-limit of 15–20 minutes for groups to prepare their presentation. Tell them to share out the presentation so that each group member does part of it, and remind them to use some of the presentation language they learnt in lesson 3. Monitor and help as they prepare.

Ask groups to take turns to stand up and make their presentation. Ask the students who are listening to make notes on the presentations.

When all groups have finished, give the students a little time to decide individually which project to vote for – tell them they can't vote for their own.

11 Take a vote on which project will get the investment, and congratulate the winners. Then take feedback on who people voted for, and why.

Extra activity

Ask the students to look back through the unit and choose two expressions from each lesson (eight in total) that they would like to add to their repertoire. Then ask them to compare and explain their choices to a partner.

Writing emails

Go to **Writing emails 5** on page 48 and do the exercises. Teacher's Book reference on page 64.

Writing emails

1 Introducing yourself, page 44

Warm up

Write on the whiteboard:

work / education   current / previous

Give the students two minutes to write sentences about their current and previous work and education. You do the same. Change the information in two of your sentences so that they are false, then read out your sentences and ask the students to discuss in pairs which they think are false. Take feedback and reveal the answers. Ask the students to make two of their sentences false. Then ask them to stand up and find a partner. Ask pairs to read their sentences and guess the false sentences, then change partners. After a few minutes, ask the students to sit down. As an ice-breaker with a new class, you could then ask the class what facts they remember about each student in turn.

Reading

Focus on the questions, then ask the students to read all the emails quickly to answer the questions. Check the answers. Ask the students which sentence led them to the answers.

ANSWERS

1 F (... Daniel Powter, who you recently helped to find a post in the UK ...)   2 T (... especially keen to work in sales outside the clothing industry ...)   3 T (Please find my CV with names of referees attached.)   4 F (I'd be happy to circulate your CV around my contacts, although of course I can't promise any results)

Focus on

Read the **Focus on** box with the class and encourage any comments or questions. Ask the students which of the sentences are asking a favour (the first and third). Ask what the function of the other sentence is (making a suggestion). Ask the students if they would ask these questions more directly if writing a formal email in their language.

Style tip

Read the **Style tip** with the class. Ask the students to underline examples of the last three bullet points (greeting: *Dear Mr Reid, Dear Paul*; signoff: *Yours sincerely, Best wishes*; informal expressions after first email: *I'll give you a call, Look forward to speaking to you then*; contractions after first email: *I'll, I'd, you'd* – note that *don't* and *aren't* would be perfectly acceptable in a formal email these days).

Language tip

Read the **Language tip** with the class. In a monolingual class, ask the students how they would translate these sentences. In a multilingual class, ask if the students can say what typical mistake someone from their country could make with these sentences.

Task

Draw the students' attention to the **Phrasebank** on page 54, which they can use as a reference for writing emails. Then read the **Task** with the class and ask the students to write an email of introduction individually in class or for homework.

Extra activity

Write on the whiteboard: _____ *a favour* and ask the students, without looking at their books, to try to remember the missing verb (*request*). Ask the students to find another collocation in the emails that combines a verb and a noun and that would be useful to learn (e.g. *circulate my CV*). Ask the students individually to underline three more collocations in the emails that contain a verb and a noun, and possibly other words too. When they are ready, ask them to work in pairs and test their partner. They have to take turns to say only the noun of a collocation, and their partner should try to remember to rest. Possible examples are: *find a post, look for a position, have a degree, broaden/expand my experience, let me know a suitable time, require further information, give me a call.*

2 Evaluating performance, page 45

Warm up

Tell the class about a time when you received written feedback, for example, on school or college work or relating to your work, in a way that made you feel sensitive or annoyed. Encourage any comments or stories from students, but remember it can be a sensitive area. Write on the whiteboard: *What would be your golden rule for giving feedback on someone's work?*

Give the students a chance to discuss their golden rule in pairs before taking feedback from the class. Write up suggestions and take a vote on the best.

Reading

Focus on the questions, then ask the students to read the email quickly to answer the questions. Check the answers. Ask the students which sentence led them to the answers.

ANSWERS

1 more (... we're up on our target ...)   2 Aisha (... Aisha's done extremely well ...)   3 Jacob (...he's only given out a couple of business cards ...)   4 being in the office (He's always so lively around the office ... He's been chatting to people a bit ...)   5 selling (He needs to focus on developing some basic sales techniques)

Focus on

Read the **Focus on** box with the class and encourage any comments or questions. Ask the students to write five sentences about their actions and activities today using the present perfect simple and continuous. Give the students the chance to read their sentences in pairs before taking feedback.

Writing emails

Style tip
Read the **Style tip** with the class. Point out that these expressions can also be used to close an informal phone call.

Language tip
Read the **Language tip** with the class. Ask the students to write three sentences evaluating the performance of a real-life person or group. This could be a sports team, the current government or the student him/herself. Give the students the chance to read their sentences in pairs before taking feedback.

Task
Read the **Task** with the class and ask the students to write an email reporting on performance so far, individually in class or for homework.

Extra activity
Ask the students in pairs to choose five expressions from this email lesson that they want to learn, and then, write and perform a short conversation in which someone is evaluating another person's performance, which includes the five expressions.

3 Making arrangements, page 46

Warm up
Write the following questions on the whiteboard:
When's your busiest time of the week/month/year, and why?
How busy are you over the next week? What are your most important things to remember?
Ask students to discuss the questions in pairs before taking feedback.

Reading
Focus on the questions, then ask the students to read all the emails quickly to answer the questions. Ask the students which sentence led them to the answers.

ANSWERS
1 R (I'm leaving at 3 on Monday!)
2 P (... I'll join you guys after an hour)
3 D (I may be able to do Thursday if we start later) and P (I guess I could join the conference from home after three ... I'll check that and get back to you)
4 I (...I'm going to be at a conference from Wednesday to Friday)
5 R (For us all to meet face-to-face ... is ... an unnecessary expense)
6 I (It's called Livespeak)
7 R (Tuesday isn't possible for me – I'm in an all-day meeting ...)
8 D (I may be able to do Thursday if we start later)

Focus on
Read the **Focus on** box with the class and encourage any comments or questions. Ask the students in pairs to write and perform a six-line dialogue, using as many expressions as they can from **Focus on**, in which they arrange to meet next week.

Task
Read the **Task** with the class and ask the students to write an email arranging a time for a meeting, individually in class or for homework.

Extra activity
Ask the students to take a piece of paper and divide it into Monday, Tuesday, Wednesday, Thursday, Friday. Ask them to fill half the time with invented appointments – at least one on each day. When the students are ready, ask them to stand up and find a partner. They have to arrange a meeting time with their partner, then move on to someone else without a partner. Set a time limit of ten minutes for the activity. The aim is for the students to arrange meetings with as many students as possible.

4 Applying for a job, page 47

Warm up
Ask the students to look at the job advert for one minute and try to remember the key details. After one minute, ask the students to close their books and work in pairs to try to write down as much of the ad as they can in two minutes. After this time, tell them they can open their books and see how well they did.

Reading
Focus on the questions, then ask the students to read the email quickly to answer the questions. Check the answers. Ask the students which sentence led them to the answers.

ANSWERS
1 second (... an MBA, with a speciality in Human Resources ...)
2 find suitable work (... giving them advice ... that will help them find the job they want)
3 spent time at (... and have visited your manufacturing plant)
4 research psychometric testing (In my current post I have developed methodological research methods)

Focus on
Read the **Focus on** box with the class and encourage any comments or questions. Ask students to circle the prepositions *in*, *for* and *as* and notice how they are used in this context.

Task
Read the **Task** with the class and ask the students to write the email of application individually in class or for homework.

Extra activity
Ask the students to underline five phrases in the email that they would like to add to their repertoire, and share their choices with a partner.

5 Enquiring about a product or service, page 48

Warm up
With books closed, write *3D printers* on the whiteboard. Give the students one minute to work with a partner and quickly write down anything they know about 3D printers. If they don't know anything, ask them to write some questions they would like answered about 3D printers. Take feedback and note down what they know on the whiteboard. If anyone wrote questions, ask if they have been answered by the brainstorm.

Reading
Focus on the picture. Elicit what it is (a replacement hip joint – see the **Help** box). Then focus on the questions, and ask the students to read the email quickly to answer the questions. Check the answers. Ask the students which sentence led them to the answers.

> **ANSWERS**
> 1 F (We currently hand-shape the joints …)
> 2 T (…in case we introduce new materials)
> 3 F (I need to know … how much it would cost to print … one hip joint … in titanium)
> 4 T (…possible to have a rep visit and demonstrate the printer?)

Focus on
Read the **Focus on** box with the class and encourage any comments or questions. Ask the students to discuss briefly in pairs what happens to the grammar of the original question when *I need to know …, Do you know …,* etc. is used. (It no longer uses the question form, so *would it* changes to the normal word order, *it would*.) Point out that question forms using *do* also change – this will be practised in the extra activity below.

Style tip
Read the **Style tip** with the class. Write on the board: *further information > contact me* and ask the students to write a formal sentence using *should* instead of *if* (*Should you require further information, please do not hesitate to contact me*).

Task
Read the **Task** with the class and ask the students to write the email requesting information individually in class (if the students can access the internet) or for homework.

> **Extra activity**
> Ask the students to show their phone to their partner, or write down the make and model if they don't have it with them. Tell the students they have five minutes to write down as many questions as possible about the phone, using the 'softer style' described in the lesson. They then swap questions and write answers to their partner's questions.

6 Updating people on plans, page 49

Warm up
With books closed, write on the whiteboard:
SHOES
Who are the top designers?
Why will people pay a lot of money for them?
What's the most you would pay for a pair of shoes?
Arrange the students in small groups and ask them to discuss the questions. When you sense that the first groups has finished, take feedback from the class.

Reading
Focus on the questions, then ask the students to read all the emails quickly to answer the questions. Check the answers. Ask students which sentence led them to the answers.

> **ANSWERS**
> 1 d (Rino … won't be able to do the interview … I've asked Arantxa to take Rino's place)
> 2 b, c (Jelena will be going over to do the QC … / Jelena will be back in the office with Mandi dealing with orders)
> 3 c, f (… I'll be helping Mandi … / I'm meeting the Corte Inglés buyer …)
> 4 e (Marcus, you'll have to pick up the ones you need … on your way to the exhibition centre. You've put up this display before
> 5 g (… Arantxa won't be able to do the shoot, but Mina says she feels confident to handle it …)
> 6 a (Rino didn't feel so good this morning, and he's accepted he won't be able to do the interview)
> 7 c (see 2)

Focus on
Read the **Focus on** box with the class and encourage any comments or questions. Ask the students to think of a recent occasion where their plans changed, and write two sentences to describe what happened, using *meant/supposed* and *which/this meant* (point out that *meant* is the past simple and past participle of *mean*).

Style tip
Read the **Style tip** with the class. Ask the students to write two sentences about something that is going to happen that they are optimistic about, using some of the language here.

Task
Read the **Task** with the class and ask the students to write an email with their schedule followed by one containing updates, individually in class or for homework.

> **Extra activity**
> Ask the students to underline useful verb + noun collocations in the emails. Then ask them to compare answers with a partner, and agree together on the two most useful ones (Possible answers: *make it to a meeting, do the QC, do a TV interview, do a photoshoot, deal with orders, put up a display*).

Writing emails

7 Apologising, page 50

Warm up
Write on the whiteboard:
When did someone last apologise to you?
When did you last apologise to someone?
Answer the questions yourself first, and encourage questions and comments. Then ask the students to discuss the questions in pairs. Check the answers.

Reading
Focus on the questions, then ask the students to read all the emails quickly to answer the questions. Check the answers.

ANSWERS
1 C–F 2 A–E 3 D–G 4 B–H

Focus on
Read the **Focus on** box with the class and encourage any comments or questions. Ask the students to pay attention to the preposition used after *apologise/apologies* and *sorry* (*for*, but note that *sorry about* ... is also correct) and the form of the verb that follows (*-ing*, but note that *sorry* can be followed by a complete verb clause, e.g. *I'm sorry I forgot*).

Task
Read the **Task** with the class and ask the students to write an apologetic email individually in class or for homework.

Extra activity
Ask the students in pairs to choose a typical scenario at work where someone has made a mistake, and write two very short conversations – one formal and one informal – in which an apology is made and accepted.

8 Sending an email newsletter, page 51

Warm up
Write *email newsletter* on the board and elicit or explain what it is (a regular email that updates people who choose to receive it on a company's special offers, latest news, etc.). Ask the students if anyone subscribes to one or more, and why, and if anyone works for a company that uses these as part of its marketing.

Reading
Focus on the questions, then ask the students to read the newsletter quickly to answer the questions. Check the answers. Ask the students which sentence led them to the answers.

ANSWERS
1 F (From a light lunch to a romantic dinner ...)
2 T (... our award-winning chef ...)
3 F (...book a room before 30 July to claim your meal)
4 T (... relaxing in the evening sun on our terrace)
5 T (Cooking demonstration by Marco)

Focus on
Read the **Focus on** box with the class and elicit or explain any unknown words. Encourage any comments or questions. You may also choose to do the extra activity below at this point.

Task
Read the **Task** with the class and ask the students to work in pairs to help each other write an email newsletter for their own company or possible future company. They could prepare the newsletter in class, and write it for homework.

Extra activity
Ask the students to work in pairs to link each bullet point in **Focus on** to that feature in the example email newsletter
Answers:
- Tell subscribers what's in the newsletter: chef's secrets + summer offer)
- Offer some exclusive knowledge: Learn our chef's secrets
- Link it to time: summer offer
- Put important text at the top to grab attention: info about new summer menu
- Use short sentences and short sections: most sentences are short
- Use sub-headings: New menu / Enjoy a meal on us / Join us)
- Tell the recipient about the benefits of your product or service: recharge your batteries / enjoy a meal
- Get your readers to imagine themselves experiencing the product or service: imagine yourself relaxing ...
- Tell them what action to take, and what benefits they'll receive: download the voucher and book a room to claim your meal

9 Putting forward suggestions, page 52

Warm up
Write on the whiteboard:
Think of a company website whose design you think is effective. List some of the features that make it effective.
Give the students five minutes to make their list of features, then ask them to talk to their partner about it. At this point, allow the students to use the language they already know to describe the features rather than pre-teaching any. Take feedback from the class and write their ideas on the whiteboard, helping now with any unknown language.

Reading

Read the **Help** box with the class. Then focus on the questions, and ask the students to read the email quickly to answer the questions. Check the answers. Ask the students which sentence led them to the answers.

> **ANSWERS**
> 1 reflects (... the design captures the feel of our company well)
> 2 unclear (It needs to draw the user's eye to the important things)
> 3 fewer (... a single striking image rather than the three ...)
> 4 text (make the ... copy colours a touch more subtle)
> 5 is too much information (the copy needs editing down by 50%)
> 6 old-fashioned-looking (I'm not sure about the retro font ...)

Focus on

Read the **Focus on** box. Check the students can pronounce *enough* and *a touch* correctly. Ask them to study the box for two minutes, then take turns to test each other in pairs by reading one of the examples, but missing out a word, e.g. *It needs [pause] a little*. Get a student to demonstrate by testing you first.

Style tip

Read the **Style tip**. Emphasise that these expressions are very similar in meaning. Pronounce the sentences for the students to repeat, so that they can practise getting their tongue round the long phrases.

Language tip

Read the **Language tip**. Again, these expressions have more or less the same meaning. Ask some students which of these expressions they can already use, and challenge them to add one or two more of them to their repertoire.

Task

Read the **Task** with the class and ask the students to write a feedback email individually in class or for homework.

> **Extra activity**
>
> Ask the students to work in pairs to design a logo for an imaginary company called 'Kan-dee'. Ask them to design it so that is not very good, and has obvious faults. Then ask pairs to stand up and pair up with two other students, and give each other feedback on the logo using language from this lesson.

10 Making a complaint, page 53

Warm up

Write on the whiteboard:
When did you last make a complaint?
What was the result?

Answer the questions yourself first, and encourage questions and comments. Then ask the students to discuss the questions in pairs.

Reading

Read the **Help** box with the class. Focus on the questions, then ask the students to read the email quickly to answer the questions. Check the answers. Ask the students which sentence led them to the answers.

> **ANSWERS**
> 1 F (... a vehicle we are developing)
> 2 T (... the higher than permitted amounts of organic solvents in the paint)
> 3 T (... the paint is described in the catalogue as meeting the latest safety standards)
> 4 F (... we have had to remove your paint from our prototypes)
> 5 F (no mention)
> 6 T (... unless you fulfil my conditions above, we will be forced to take legal action)

Focus on

Read the **Focus on** box. Ask the students to underline examples of the words and phrases from the bullet points in the email (*furthermore, as a result, because of, to, despite the fact that, unless*).

Style tip

Read the **style tip**. In a monolingual class, ask what the equivalent would be to *To whom it may concern* in students' language.

Language tip

Read the **Language tip**. Point out that the formal examples are normally used in the context of a complaint, as they could seem too aggressive otherwise.

Task

Read the **Task** with the class and ask the students to write an email of complaint individually in class or for homework.

> **Extra activity**
>
> Ask the students to work in pairs to write a reply to Enver Beqiri's letter, referring to Unit 7 of Writing emails for ways of apologising.

6 Meetings

UNIT OBJECTIVES:

Students will practise ...	and they will learn how to ...
reported speech and reporting verbs	conduct meetings efficiently
	communicate assertively
describing and organising meetings	write minutes
	contribute to a discussion

Lesson 1: My worst meeting, page 56

LESSON OBJECTIVES:

Students will learn and practise ...
describing and organising meetings
best practice for meetings

Warm up

Write on the whiteboard:

People who enjoy meetings should not be ...

Meetings are indispensable when you don't want to ...

Tell the students that these are the beginnings of quotes by famous people (US writer Thomas Lowell, and Canadian economist John Kenneth Galbraith) about meetings. Ask the students to agree in pairs how they would finish the quotes. Allow them some time, then write their suggestions on the whiteboard. Then write up the original endings (*... in charge of anything, ... do anything*). Ask the students to discuss with their partner to what extent they agree with the quotes, then take feedback from the class.

Start up

1 Ask the students to study the pictures for one minute, then tell them to close their books. Ask the students to work in pairs to describe the pictures in as much detail as possible from memory. After a few minutes, ask them to open their books and comment on what they got right and what they missed. Read the rubric and questions with the class. Allow the students time to discuss the questions (depending on the experience of the students, they may have a lot to say). Take feedback from the class, and write any useful vocabulary on the whiteboard.

Listening

2 Focus on the pictures. Read the names of the objects for the students to underline the stressed syllable (*a squeeze ball, a talking stick, an empty chair, a wind-up robot*). Remind the students that the *l* in talking is *silent*, and point out that *wind* (verb) is pronounced /waɪnd/. Ask the students to listen to their partner pronounce the words, then allow pairs time to discuss the question. Encourage the students to think creatively!

3 🔊 **6.1** Allow the students time to read the ideas, then play the audio for them to number the ideas in order. Check the answers.

ANSWERS

1 f   2 d   3 e   4 c   5 a   6 b

🔊 **6.1**

OK, so the first problem with meetings, when they start being a waste of time, is when they don't start on time, right? One solution is to always have one less chair than there are people at the meeting, so the last person to arrive knows that he or she will have to stand. This is an added incentive to arrive on time, especially if the last person to arrive also has to write the minutes! Alternatively, remove chairs from the meeting room altogether and hold meetings standing up. This prevents people from getting too comfortable and encourages shorter meetings. Some companies have special standing-only meeting rooms which they use for certain types of meeting, for example. quick updates at the beginning of the day. According to recent research, a quarter of US workers would rather go to the dentist than attend a dull meeting, so clearly, if you are trying to improve your meetings, it's essential to make them less boring! Recently, companies have been experimenting with using toys in meetings. The theory is that when people have something to play with, they involve more of their brain and body in what they're doing and so become more creative. Using a squeeze ball – a soft ball you can squeeze in your hand – is helpful because it gives the brain a break and so improves concentration: half of the brain rests squeezing the ball, while the other half attends to business. Not only that but, if participants are allowed to throw the ball at a person they disagree with, this can relieve their stress and frustration and prevent arguments! 'Creative' companies like advertising agencies take it a step further by using wind-up toys to send across the table in the direction of the quietest participants to get them to talk more, or towards the wafflers and people who love the sound of their own voice to encourage them to stop talking. Finally, the use of a talking stick is an excellent way of getting people to take turns to speak and listen to each other properly. Only the person holding the stick is allowed to speak. When they've finished speaking, the stick is put back in the middle of the table and anyone else who wants to contribute must take it, or ask for it, to be allowed to speak.

4 Focus on the **Help** box, and read the definition of *waffle*. Elicit what a *waffler* is (a person who talks a lot about nothing in particular). Play the audio for them to match the ideas with the objects. Allow the students to compare their answers, then play the audio again for the students to note down how the objects (or lack of chairs) do the things mentioned. Check the answers.

67

ANSWERS

1 using a soft ball – half of the brain rests squeezing the ball
2 having one less chair – the last person to arrive would have to stand
3 throwing a ball at someone you disagree with – relieves stress and frustration
4 using toys – theory is that when people have something to play with, more of their brain is active, making them more creative
5 not having chairs – people don't get too comfortable
6 wind up toy – send toy in direction of quiet person to encourage them to add their opinions
7 wind-up toy – to make it clear they are talking too much or for too long
8 talking stick – only the person holding the stick can talk

5 Give the students time to discuss the question, then take feedback from the class.

Reading

6 Focus on the text. Elicit what kind of a web page it is (a forum) and ask where the contributors are from (Brazil, China, the USA, Australia and France). Ask the students to read the text and underline what was bad about each meeting. Allow the students to compare their answers in pairs before checking as a class. Then allow the students time to talk about any bad experiences they have had with their partner, before inviting volunteers to share their experience with the class.

ANSWERS

Olivia.R: The meetings were very long and the chairperson didn't keep people to a time limit or to the agenda. People interrupted each other, and no decisions were made.
MeiMei: The meeting was much longer than it should have been. And in the end, she didn't get her chance to speak.
Office Guy: They had to write down what they hated about each other and then talk about it.
Rudi Roo: They had to talk to a puppet on the consultant's hand.
Anais: She was the only person phoning in to a conference call. They kept forgetting about her and putting their phone on mute so she couldn't hear.

7 Pronounce the four adjectives for the students to repeat. Ask them to discuss with their partner which adjective applies to each contributor to the forum. Take feedback from the class.

POSSIBLE ANSWERS

Olivia.R: bored (because people were allowed to 'waffle' on) annoyed (that the meeting was so badly managed) and frustrated (by her inability to control events)
MeiMei: bored (since she had to sit there for five hours without saying anything); annoyed and frustrated (when her one chance to speak was taken away from her)
OfficeGuy and Ruid Roo: embarrassed (at being put into such a difficult position) and possibly annoyed as well (depending on their personalities)
Anais: bored (because it was so long), annoyed (at being forgotten and having to ask them to take their phone off mute)

Vocabulary

8 Elicit the meaning of *collocate with* (commonly go together with). Give the students time to add headings and the bold words from the text to the table, using their dictionary to help them, then check the answers. The word you can use twice is *update*. Elicit the difference in pronunciation between *update* meeting and to *update* an agenda.

ANSWERS

1 verbs that collocate with *agenda*: stick to, update
2 verbs that collocate with *meeting*: schedule
3 phone meetings: take the phone off mute, dial in
4 roles in a meeting: chairperson, delegates
5 types of meeting: strategy, conference call, update
6 meeting equipment: PowerPoint slides

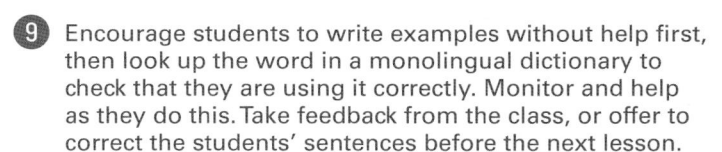

9 Encourage students to write examples without help first, then look up the word in a monolingual dictionary to check that they are using it correctly. Monitor and help as they do this. Take feedback from the class, or offer to correct the students' sentences before the next lesson.

Students can find more activities at www.richmondatwork.net

Speaking

10 Arrange the students in groups of three or four. Ask groups to nominate a secretary, who should draw a table to record the group's dos and don'ts, like this:

	Do ...	Don't ...
before	• • •	• • •
during	• • •	• • •
after	• • •	• • •

Set a time-limit of 15–20 minutes for groups to decide on their best practice tips, then take feedback from the class.

POSSIBLE ANSWERS

Before a meeting
- Do: book venue and refreshments well in advance; make sure you reserve any equipment you are going to need and that it is in good working order; prepare an circulate and agenda; check that the key people you need to be there are going to attend; have clear aims for the meeting and a set time for it to begin and end
- Don't: assume people can come if you haven't heard back from them; keep changing the date, time or venue

During a meeting
- Do: appoint a chair to manage the meeting and a secretary to take notes; insist that people take turns to speak; stick to the agenda; in a long meeting, have regular breaks so that people don't lose concentration; try and agree on and set a date for the next meeting, if needed, whilst everyone is present

Meetings 6

- Don't: tolerate waffling, shouting people down, interrupting or any other bad behaviour; run over time; reschedule difficult decisions to be discussed again at another meeting, deal with them now.

After a meeting
- Do: write and circulate minutes; make it clear what the action points are for each person
- Don't: take too long to write up the minutes or write minutes that are very long and detailed; Stick to the main points

Extra activity
Divide the class into two teams. Two students, one from each team, should sit with their backs to the whiteboard. Tell the class you are going to write a word on the whiteboard, which the teams have to explain/define to their person at the board. Each team member can contribute, and they can say complete definitions or individual words. The first person at the board to guess the word wins a point for their team, and two new students take the seats facing away from the board. Keep the game moving fast. Here are some words to use:

attend	schedule	delegate	interrupt
chairperson	present	strategy	attendee
item	team-building	update	project
agenda	budget	consultant	cancel

Lesson 2: He said, she said, page 58

LESSON OBJECTIVES:
Students will learn and practise ...
reported speech and reporting verbs
writing minutes

Warm up
With books closed, write on the board:
l ___ your tem ___ (lose your temper)
manage to k ___ your co ___ (keep your cool)
bot ___ ___ your ang ___ (bottle up your anger)
get shou ___ ___ (get shouted at)
___ an argu ___ ___ someone (have an argument with)
be ang ___ ___ someone (be angry with)

Tell the students these expressions are all related to feeling angry. Ask them to work in pairs to complete the expressions, using their dictionaries and sharing their knowledge. Check the answers with the class, and ask volunteers to explain the meaning of the expressions in their own words. Write on the whiteboard: *When did you last ...?* and ask a student to ask you the question using one of the expressions (e.g. *When did you last lose your temper?*) Answer the question, and encourage questions. Then ask the students to take turns asking their partner the question with one of the expressions.

Start up

1 Focus on the pictures. Ask the students what's happening in each and encourage them to use the expressions from the **Warm up** (e.g. An airline worker is getting shouted at, but she's managing to keep her cool; A man is having an argument with a police officer; A man has lost his temper and is shouting at a colleague). Allow the students time to discuss the questions, then take feedback from the class, and write any useful vocabulary on the whiteboard.

ANSWERS
1 Suggested answer: Getting angry at work could be justified if it related to unethical behaviour such as cheating, lying, bullying, harassment, breaking rules in such a way as to endanger life or other types of unacceptable risk.
2 Students' own answers.

Listening

2 Draw the students' attention to the definition of *trade union* in the **Help** box. Allow the students time to discuss the questions, then take feedback from the class.

POSSSIBLE ANSWERS
1 A flight attendant's job is all about customer service so it might become stressful in situations where customers behave unreasonably. Since a flight attendant is very much concerned with flight safety, situations in which passengers are in real or perceived danger (in which case they might become panicky) might also be a cause of stress.
2 Difficult passenger behaviour might include rudeness and aggressiveness, making unreasonable demands, becoming irrational through fear of flying, ignoring safety requirements and thereby putting themselves and others at risk, drunken and rowdy behaviour.

3 🔊 **6.2** Pre-teach or elicit the meaning of *crew* (the pilots and flight attendants who work on a plane), *resign* (to leave your job), *spoilt* (behaving badly because parents are not strict – usually used about children) and *sue* (to take legal action to try to get money from someone in court because you think they have done something to harm you). Allow the students time to read the questions, then ask them to note down answers as you play the audio twice. Allow the students to compare their answers in pairs before checking as a class.

ANSWERS
1 Martin says he was trying to protect a colleague. We know he lost his temper with a passenger but he might have done any number of things – he could have hit the passenger, shouted at the passenger, thrown something at the passenger, ...
2 Diana is his colleague. Karen is his boss. Diana is very supportive (he did what he did to protect her); Karen says his behaviour was unprofessional.
3 There's going to be a full investigation.

🔊 6.2
M = Martin, T = Tomas

M: I must admit that I lost my temper, Tomas, but I acted the way I did to protect a colleague.
T: Yes, I know, Martin. The rest of the crew all agree that the passenger was behaving in an unreasonable way and that you were justified in responding how you did. Your colleague, Diana, says that that if you get fired because of what happened, she will resign as well. She knows you did it for her. We're all going to support you because in the end, this situation is about all of us. It isn't part of our job description to be abused by passengers behaving like spoilt children.
M: But Karen, my boss, says that there is no excuse for my behaviour. She says that I 'acted unprofessionally' and that's the end of it.
T: Yes, but Karen wasn't actually there at the time, was she? So, I don't think her opinion counts for anything.
M: Well, that depends … Karen has never liked me and if HR ask for her opinion, I know she's going to give it. Apparently the passenger is threatening to sue the airline and says that he is going to get me sent to prison.
T: That may well all turn out to be empty threats. It's an expensive business. He isn't going to look good and – from what I understand of what happened, he wouldn't win anyway.
M: Well, Karen says that they haven't heard anything from him so far. She says that she doesn't know what will happen next and we'll have to wait to hear from HR.
T: Don't worry Martin, there's going to be a full investigation into the incident and I'm sure we'll hear from HR soon.

4 Ask the students to match the two parts of the sentences, then play the audio again to check the answers.

ANSWERS
1 b **2** d **3** f **4** a **5** c **6** e

Grammar

5 Allow the students time to compare the words in the audioscript on page 126 with the reported speech in **4**, and to complete the **Grammar** box. Allow the students to compare their answers in pairs before checking as a class.

ANSWERS
1 I admit that I lost my temper.
2 The rest of the crew all agree that the passenger was behaving in unreasonable way.
3 Diana says that if you get fired because of what happened, she will resign as well.
4 Karen says that there is no excuse for my behaviour.
5 The passenger is threatening to sue the airline and says that he is going to get me sent to prison.
6 There's going to be a full investigation into the incident.
Grammar summary: 1 third **2** present continuous – past continuous, past simple – past perfect, *will* future – *would*

Students can find more activities at www.richmondatwork.net

Listening

6 🔊 **6.3** Write *aisle* and *luggage* locker on the whiteboard, and elicit their meaning and pronunciation. Allow the students time to read the questions and options before playing the audio for them to choose the correct options. Allow the students to compare their answers in pairs, and play the audio again if necessary. Check the answers.

ANSWERS
1 b **2** c **3** a **4** b **5** c **6** b **7** c **8** a

🔊 6.3
H = HR officer, M = Martin

H: So Martin, the purpose of this meeting is to investigate the complaint made against you and hear your side of the story. The passenger, a Mr Robert Miller, claims that you insulted him, calling him an 'idiot', and he also complains that you attacked him physically. Is this true?
M: It's true that I pushed the passenger hard when he was trying to get out of his seat and this made him fall sideways and hit his head against the luggage locker. I also admit that I called him an idiot. My colleague, Diana Mores, and I had asked him several times to stay in his seat. We were clearing up the mess in the aisle this passenger had made earlier when he threw his meal on the floor. The floor was slippery and dangerous there, but after a while Mr Miller wanted to go to the bathroom and became angry at having to wait and kept trying to get out of his seat. He tried to push past Diana who was cleaning the floor. He pushed her really hard, so I pushed him hard to make him sit down again.
H: And was this when you called him an idiot?
M: Yes, I think I said, 'Sit down, you idiot' or something like that. I admit I was really angry at this point. The passenger's behaviour had been consistently rude from the beginning of the flight. When we were welcoming the passengers on board, he threw his coat onto Diana's shoulder, and said, 'Take care of it.' This was already very rude, but she simply smiled, folded the coat and placed it in the luggage locker. The passenger then angrily turned around and shouted, 'I told you to take care of it.' From then on, he consistently criticised Diana. He told her she didn't know what she was doing when she checked his seatbelt, said she hadn't listened properly when she took his drinks order, and finally he pushed his entire meal on the floor because he said he 'didn't like the look of it'.
H: I see. OK, throwing his meal on the floor definitely constitutes unreasonable behaviour, which Mr Miller, not surprisingly, didn't mention in his complaint.

7 Allow the students time to discuss the question in pairs, then take feedback from the class. Encourage discussion, and write any useful vocabulary on the whiteboard.

Grammar

8 Allow the students time to complete the **Grammar** box with the bold verbs from **4** and **6** and compare with a partner before checking the answers as a class.

70

Meetings 6

ANSWERS

criticise someone for + *ing*
claim, admit, agree, explain that
accuse someone of + *ing*
threaten to + infinitive

Students can find more activities at www.richmondatwork.net

Speaking

9 Arrange the students into AB pairs and ask them to go to page 99 or 107 and read what Mr Miller's lawyer and Martin's trade union representative said. Ask them to note down some key words to help them report to their partner afterwards. Allow them time to prepare, then ask them to take turns to report what their person said. Ask the students to work in pairs to write the statements for the minutes, or you can give this as individual homework.

Allow the students time to discuss question 2, and take feedback from the class. Encourage discussion, and write any useful vocabulary on the whiteboard.

POSSIBLE ANSWERS

1
Lawyer
He explained that his client had a fear of flying/was afraid of flying.
His client admits/admitted that he had thrown his meal on the floor, which was unacceptable.
He apologised to Diana Mores for his bad behaviour.
He threatened to take legal action.
He demanded that Martin resign from his post.
Martin's representative
Martin admits/admitted that he hadn't acted in a professional way.
He apologised for injuring Mr Miller.
He explained that he was concerned for his colleague.
He accuses Mr Miller of bullying and criticising Diana Mores.
He doesn't agree that his reaction to Mr Miller's behaviour was unacceptable.
He refused to resign.
2 Action points could include:
ML's representative to request ML to write an apology to Mr Miller; Airline to forward the apology to ML's lawyer but inform him that they consider his behaviour in defence of his colleague to be justified; Airline to engage lawyer to defend them in case Mr Miller takes legal action.
OR
ML's representative to request ML to write an apology to Mr Miller; Airline to discipline ML for his behaviour – suspend from duty, fire him, fine him, transfer him; Airline to request that ML resign.

Extra activity

Write the following prompts on two pieces of paper:

A	B
Accuse B of something ↘	
	↙ Deny it!
Give evidence ↘	
	↙ Admit it and apologise
Forgive B ↙	

A	B
	Criticise B for something ↙
Agree, but make an excuse ↘	
	↙ Refuse to accept explanation
Complain about B's attitude ↘	
	↙ Accept complaint and apologise

Arrange the students in AB pairs and give out one of the cards to half the pairs, and the other card to the other pairs. Set a time-limit of ten minutes for students to write a short dialogue based on the prompts. They have to invent the details of the situation themselves. Then allow five minutes for pairs to practise and memorise their dialogue. Ask the pairs to join to form groups of four, and ask the pairs to take turns to perform their dialogue. The other pair should listen and take notes. When all the pairs have performed, ask them to report what happened in the other pair's dialogue. Finally, ask one or two pairs to read their report of the dialogue they listened to, followed by a performance of the original dialogue their report is based on.

Lesson 3: Getting heard, page 60

LESSON OBJECTIVES:

Students will learn and practise ...
contributing to a discussion
assertive communication

Warm up

Make or photocopy cue cards with the words on the next page. Divide the class into two teams. Explain that a person from each team will try to explain a word without using certain 'taboo' words. Write on the board: *BED, night, sleep* and then elicit attempts to explain *bed* without using *night* or *sleep*. Explain that the game starts with one person from each team taking a piece of paper each and starting to explain their word at the same time to their team. When their word has been guessed, a new team member takes another word and continues in the same way. When all the words have been taken, add up the scores for each team.

CLAIM	say, right
ADMIT	say, accuse
ASK	say, question
EXPLAIN	say, why
ACCUSE	say, do
TELL	say, speak
CRITICISE	say, bad
AGREE	say, same

INTERRUPT	say, stop
WAFFLE	say, continue
REFUSE	say, accept
SPEAK	say, talk
PRESENT (verb)	say, talk
DISCUSS	say, talk
POSTPONE	say, later
CHAIR (verb)	say, lead

Start up

1 Ask the students to study the picture in **2** for one minute, and tell them they will have a memory test. Then ask them to close their books and try to write the answers to the following questions in pairs (the answers are in brackets):

1 What's the woman with dark hair doing? (talking on the phone)
2 One man is reading a book. What colour is it? (green)
3 What has the man with glasses just done? (thrown a paper aeroplane)
4 One man has his hand in the air. Is it his left or right hand? (right)
5 How many cups of coffee are on the table? (two)
6 How many people are in the picture? (eight)
7 A man and a woman are talking. What colours is she wearing? (green and white)
8 What's the man in the top-left doing? (typing on a laptop)

Ask how many questions pairs got right, and congratulate the winners.

Allow the students time to discuss the questions. Take feedback from the class and write any useful vocabulary on the whiteboard.

Reading

2 Write on the whiteboard: *get a word in edgeways, speak over someone, despair*. Ask the students to read the introduction quickly and guess the meaning of these words and expressions. Give them time to compare their guesses in pairs before checking the answers (*get a word in edgeways* = to manage to speak when there are almost no pauses in the conversation; *speak over someone* = start talking loudly when someone else is talking, so that people stop listening to them; *despair* = give up hope of something). Ask the students to read the text and underline each technique for getting heard, then look back at these to discuss their opinion on questions a) and b) with a partner. Take feedback from the class.

ANSWERS

a (the most passive): wait until the end of the conversation and say 'Is it my turn to contribute?'
b (the most assertive): own your ideas

3 Elicit or teach the literal meaning of *hijack* (to take control of a plane or other vehicle by force), and explain that the word is used with a different meaning in this context. Allow the students time to read the text again, answer the questions and compare their answers before checking the answers as a class.

ANSWERS

1 create a diversion = to do something to take someone's attention away from something that you don't want them to concentrate on or notice
Suggested answers for ways you could do this: have a coughing fit, knock something over, let your mobile phone go off, 'accidentally' turn on or off lights, projector or other equipment, arrange for someone to come into the meeting room at a certain point, set off the fire alarm
2 hijacking ideas = taking someone's idea and pretending it is your own. Avoid by: circulating new ideas in advance of a meeting, and if someone tries to hijack the idea, reminding them of the email you sent round earlier with the same idea.
3 shout someone down = to silence someone by talking louder than them
wear someone down = to get someone to agree by asking the same question or repeating the same thing until they are tired of it

Listening

4))) 6.4 Focus on the questions and tell the students to write a, b or c for the four extracts. Play the audio for the students to match the extracts with the descriptions. Allow the students to compare thier answers in pairs, and play the audio again if necessary.

ANSWERS

a 2   b 1,3   c 4

))) 6.4
R = Rosa, A = Andrei, B = Becky, N = Nils
1
R: OK, so we need to find ways to get more hits on our websites and increase our general web visibility. I've got Caz's report here and she says that the way to do this is by increasing our activity on social media. So, I think –
A: Yeah, yeah, we already spend too much time on that stuff. I can't see it helping much. In any case, what we need to do is look into search engine optimisation. We need to create more links to our main page, for example.
R: But don't you think that Caz already –
B: Yes, good idea, Andrei, we need to make sure that the content includes enough key words, do a bit of rewriting.
2
B: So does anyone have any other suggestions?
N: Well, I still think that spending more on web advertising is the best idea.
R: What about –?
B: It might be, Nils, but we just don't have the budget …

Meetings 6

R: No, but –
A: It doesn't have to be about budget, Becky. There are lots of things we can do without spending a penny more.
B: We are absolutely up to the limit on the marketing budget until the end of the year.
N: I'm talking about taking the long view here, guys, OK, and I think that with advertising we at least are guaranteed a result and it's something we can measure.
R: But –
A: But even in the long term, we still don't have to spend that type of money, it just …
3
R: … Now that I've got your attention, I just wanted to say that if we can ensure that all our existing social media output is linked more effectively than it is at the moment, for example by linking our Tweets to our Facebook posts, that alone will …
A: Yes, yes, OK, but we don't have enough resources to increase our social media. It would take up too much time. What do you think, Nils?
N: Well, you might have a point there, but as far as budget is concerned …
4
A: Look, we don't have to spend more money. All we have to do is make sure that all our existing social media activity is cross linked more effectively than it is at the moment.
R: Yes! That's exactly –
B: What do you mean? Linking our Tweets to our Facebook posts, that sort of thing?
N: That's good thinking. And what about tagging our Facebook photos more?
R: I don't believe this! This is exactly what I've been saying for the last half an hour and now it's Andrei's idea.

5 Play the audio again for the students to make notes to answer the questions. Allow the students to compare their answers in pairs before checking as a class.

ANSWERS

1 It is about how to make the company's website more visible and get more hits. Rosa is trying to suggest that the company doesn't need to spend any money in order to do this but by increasing social media activity and linking all their social media updates, this will happen automatically.
2 Suggested answer: Rosa could try raising her hand to indicate when she wants to speak or when the others are interrupting her. Since she can't talk over them, this is a visible sign she wants to speak which they will eventually have to notice. Waiting until the end of the conversation or a pause might be more problematic because if the other's reach agreement on something before she has had a chance to interject, they will be reluctant to reconsider it, but it is worth trying. She could point out, when they finally are listening to her, how difficult it has been to get their attention and how often they have spoken over or interrupted her.

Functional language

6 ◁)) **6.5** Allow the students time to complete the dialogues, then play the audio for them to check their answers. Play the audio again for the students to repeat.

ANSWERS

1 come **2** case **3** ask **4** point **5** back

◁)) **6.5**
See page **6** in the Student's Book.

7 ◁)) **6.6** Tell the students they are going to hear what would have happened in the meeting if Rosa had used some of these techniques to get heard. Play the audio for the students to tick the expressions in **6** that she uses. Check the answers.

ANSWERS

Excuse me for interrupting.
If I could just finish what I was saying about …
I'm afraid I can't agree.
To get back to what I was saying, …

◁)) **6.6**
R = Rosa, A = Andrei, B = Becky
R: OK, so I've got Caz's report here and she's suggesting that we increase our activity on various social media to get more hits on our websites and increase our general web visibility so, I thought that we should –
A: Yeah, yeah, we already spend too much time on that stuff. I can't see it helping much. In any case, what we need to do is look into search engine optimisation. We need to create more links to our main page, for example.
B: Yes, good idea, Andrei, we need to make sure …
R: Excuse me, for interrupting Becky, but I hadn't finished –
B: … that content includes enough key words, do a bit of –
R: Excuse me. If I could just finish what I was saying – I wanted to point out that we don't necessarily have to invest time and money in a major revamp of our website. If we learn to use our social media links better, including those to our main page, everything else will follow.
B: Well, maybe but I agree with Andrei, that if we make sure that the content includes enough key words and do a bit of rewriting, we don't need to bother with all that social media stuff. It's a lot of work that we frankly haven't time for and search engine optimisation …
R: I'm afraid I can't agree with either of you there. To get back to what I was saying, effective social media use is an integral part of search-engine optimisation and we can't afford to ignore it.

8 Ask the students to work in pairs to rewrite two extracts from the audioscripts, using expressions and techniques from the lesson. Monitor and help as they do so.

When most have finished, allow them time to rehearse, and preferably memorise their extracts or use key word cues, before taking turns to perform their dialogues for the class.

Speaking

9 Arrange the students in groups of four. Allow the students time to choose and think about what they are going to say before asking them to take turns to talk about their topic. Monitor as they talk, and note down any language problems to deal with later.

When most groups have finished, ask each group to recreate one of their conversations for the whole class.

Extra activity

Ask the students to look back through the lesson and choose three verb + noun collocations that they would like to add to their repertoire. Then ask them to stand up and mingle, and find a partner. The students take it in turns to test their partner on the collocations, saying, for example, 'Mmmm' your ideas (communicate) or 'Mmmm' your hand (raise). When you see a pair has finished, say 'Change' for the students to change partners.

Scenario: Meeting mayhem, page 62

SCENARIO OBJECTIVE:
Students will decide how a corporation should conduct its meetings more effectively.

Warm up

Prepare pieces of paper with the following verbs written on them: *claim, admit, ask, refuse, explain, accuse, criticise, agree, apologise, deny, threaten*. Ask the students to work in pairs and give each pair a piece of paper. Tell them to prepare a short dialogue demonstrating these verbs and explain that the rest of the class will have to guess their word. Demonstrate the activity with a strong student (e.g. say 'You broke that window, didn't you?' Ask the rest of the class to describe what happened and elicit the response 'You accused [student's name] of breaking the window). Ask pairs to act out their dialogues and elicit responses from the rest of the class.

1 Ask the students to read the scenario and underline three key words in each profile to remember that person. When they have done so, allow them to compare their words with another student. Then allow the students time to read the questions, and reread the text to answer them. Allow them to compare their answers with their partner before taking feedback from the class.

ANSWERS

1 He was a billionaire banker.
2 health and education projects
3 the surviving members of his family
4 Not everyone shares the same ideas about how the company should be run. Suggested answers for what they might disagree about: Mike Zhou, the youngest director wants to change and modernise and to take a more active role. He is likely to disagree with Betty who is in favour of tradition and, as a strong personality, likes to be in charge of things.

2 🔊 **6.7** Read the rubric with the class, then play the audio for the students to answer the questions. Take feedback and check the answers.

ANSWERS

The meeting lasted the entire day (although Lisa didn't stay for the whole meeting). She didn't think the chair did a very good job because: she got distracted by also taking the minutes, she tried to cover too much in one meeting and she allowed some people to sit throughout the entire meeting without making a single contribution.

🔊 **6.7**

L = Lisa, M = Mike

L: I found that exhausting, Mike, and I didn't even stay to the end! Do you regularly have meetings that last for an entire day?
M: Um, well, this was worse than usual, but I have to admit that we often overrun – there's always just so much to get through.
L: Mmm, I could see you had a long agenda, but could you clarify what exactly the purpose of this meeting was? That wasn't clear to me.
M: Well, it's our monthly team update: the main purpose is to review the new applications for funding. Karl and Mei Ling who I introduced you to earlier, deal with those and we use the meeting to decide which ones are suitable to take to the next stage. We also review our finances, and Rita and Pearl, the fundraising managers, update us on what their teams have been doing.
L: OK, well, that sounds like a lot to cover in a single meeting. Maybe you could consider holding several shorter meetings instead, with a clearer focus for each? You seemed to spend an awful lot of time on discussion about the investment fund.
M: Yes, well, Betty is very interested in the financial side of things.
L: Yes, Betty … was she, er, supposed to be chairing the meeting? I wasn't quite sure. It looked like she was at the beginning, but then she got very involved in writing things down.
M: She tries to take minutes as she goes along – she says it's more efficient that way.
L: Well, not if it distracts her from chairing, it isn't. It was really annoying the way that man Karl kept interrupting people and talking over them. Do you realise that some people sat through the whole meeting without making a single contribution? It's the Chair's job to manage all that.

3 Play the audio for students to match the two parts of the sentences, then check the answers.

ANSWERS

1 d 2 f 3 e 4 c 5 a 6 b

4 🔊 **6.8** Allow the students time to read the questions, then play the audio once or twice for them to answer. Allow the students to compare their answers with their partner before taking feedback from the class.

ANSWERS

1 Karl 2 Wayne 3 Pearl and Rita 4 Mike
5 Pearl and Rita 6 Betty 7 Mei Ling

🔊 **6.8**

M = Mei Ling, L = Lisa

M: Yes, those meetings are terrible – I hate them! It means I lose practically a day's work just to sit there and be bored.
L: So, why don't you contribute more? I thought the aim of the meeting was for you and Karl to present the new applications from people asking for money from the foundation.
M: Well, so did I at first, but that never happens. It would be really great to be able to use the meeting to discuss the

Meetings 6

more complicated or problematic applications, but that would only work if people were familiar with the details and have read the information in advance. I used to email all the information before the meeting, but I don't bother now.

L: Erm, I noticed that your colleague Karl does a lot of talking.

M: Yes, Karl has an opinion about everything, which is really annoying. He interrupts people and talks over them when he's really excited about something, which is rude and awful. But I think he's nearly as frustrated as I am about all the time we waste listening to Betty asking Wayne lots of financial questions. Of course, the banking side of things provides a large proportion of the foundation's funds, but that's not what the meeting is for. What would be really useful would be to get Wayne's input on the financial aspects of the projects applying for funds, but apart from answering Betty's questions, he never says anything either.

L: So if you had to choose one single thing to be improved for these meetings, what would that be?

M: Um … actually what annoys me most is the way that Pearl and Rita, the two fundraising managers, hijack the discussion every time Betty is trying to write the minutes. They don't seem to take the meeting seriously at all and spend their time making jokes and trying to impress Mike. I think he likes the attention so he never does anything to stop it or get the meeting back on course.

5 Ask the students to read the email and underline the suggestions that Karl makes, then compare their answers with a partner. Check the answers as a class.

ANSWERS

Karl thinks that Mike should discipline those who don't take the meetings seriously enough. He thinks people should come to the meetings better prepared. He suggests that they hold team meetings more frequently. He thinks it's important to hear all the financial information.

6 Arrange the students into AB pairs, and allow the students time to read their email on page 99 or page 104 and make notes. Then ask them to share information with their partner before taking feedback from the class.

ANSWERS

Betty: Overall she agrees with Karl. She's also most annoyed by the lack of preparation and the joking and flirting. The change she suggests is that Karl should help her chair the meeting

Pearl and Rita: Overall, they disagree with Karl. What annoys them most about the meetings is how badly run they are and that the chair is incompetent. That's why they don't take them seriously. The changes they suggest are that there are fewer update meetings, quarterly only, and that Betty takes the minutes instead of chairing.

Mike: Overall he seems to disagree with Karl. What frustrates him most about the meeting is his inability to behave assertively with regard to Betty. He doesn't know what changes to suggest, but he knows that changes need to be made.

Wayne: Overall he disagrees with Karl, Karl's behaviour in meetings, interrupting and being rude, is one of the things that frustrates him the most. He suggests that there should be fewer meetings involving the whole team, once or twice yearly only and these should be strategy meetings rather than financial updates. He also suggests that Karl should take minutes.

7 Set a time-limit of 20 minutes for pairs to work together to draft their plan. Then put pairs together in groups of four or six to compare their plans, before taking feedback from the class.

Extra activity

Arrange the students in A and B pairs. Give each student a copy of the crossword, and tell them not to show it to their partner. They have to take turns explaining their words for their partner to guess, until they have both completed the whole crossword.

Writing emails

Go to **Writing emails 6** on page 49 and do the exercises. Teacher's Book reference on page 64.

7 Culture

UNIT OBJECTIVES: Students will practise ...
the second and third conditional
communication styles

and they will learn how to ...
avoid cross-cultural misunderstandings
apologise
discuss cultural values
discuss mistakes

Lesson 1: Culture shock in California, page 64

LESSON OBJECTIVES:
Students will learn and practise ...
exploring cultural values
examining communication styles

Warm up

With books closed, write *culture shock* on the whiteboard. Ask the students to discuss with a partner what the phrase means. Take feedback from the class.

Start up

1 Focus on the pictures and elicit what they show. Ask the students to discuss whether these scenes would be typical in business in their country. Take feedback from the class, and write any useful vocabulary on the whiteboard.

ANSWERS
working late, shouting and aggression in meetings, team-building exercises

Reading

2 Ask the students to read the text quickly to get the gist and answer the questions in the rubric.

ANSWERS
He's from the UK, working in the USA. He's a scientist.

3 Elicit or pre-teach *go with your ...* (to look good because it is the same colour as something else), *tell us straight* (tell us in a simple and direct way), *self put-down* (a negative comment you make about yourself). Ask the students to read the sentences and place them in the numbered spaces in the text. Check the answers.

ANSWERS
1 d 2 a 3 f 4 b 5 c

4 Ask the students to read the text again and note down keywords in answer to the questions. Allow the students time to discuss their answers with a partner before taking feedback from the class.

ANSWERS
1 His American colleagues spoke more directly than he was used to.
2 The company didn't have as much of a hierarchical structure as his previous job.
3 His American colleagues were positive about everything.
4 His American boss worked under intense pressure to get results.
5 His American colleagues were very competitive compared to his previous job.
6 His colleagues resented him taking 15 minute's break for a tea break in the afternoon.
7 He wasn't used to people making personal remarks, e.g. about what he was wearing.
8 There wasn't the same team spirit and people were reluctant to share information.

Vocabulary

5 Ask the students to discuss the answer to number 1 in pairs as an example. Check the answer (*evasive*), then ask the class to continue with 2–6. Check the answers.

ANSWERS
1 evasive 2 aggressive 3 hierarchical 4 deferential
5 diplomatic 6 individualistic

6 Ask the students to discuss the answer to number 7 in pairs. Check the answer (*direct*), then ask the students to continue with 8–12. Check the answers.

ANSWERS
7 direct 8 gentle/polite 9 egalitarian 10 disrespectful
11 tactless 12 collectivist

7 Allow the students time to answers the questions with a partner, then take feedback from the class. Point out that *screw up* is considered impolite in the UK.

ANSWERS
1 a mistake: blunder
made a mistake: screwed up
2 to talk something up = to promote it, and make it seem better than it actually is
put-down = an unkind or critical remark, meant to make someone feel stupid
3 self-deprecation = making yourself or your abilities sound unimportant or not very good

Students can find more activities at www.richmondatwork.net

Speaking

8 Allow the students five minutes to complete the questions, then check the answers. Set a time-limit of 15 minutes for the students to discuss the questions, then take feedback from the class.

ANSWERS

1 hierarchical, egalitarian   2 diplomatic, diplomacy   3 direct
4 aggressive   5 collectivist, individualistic   6 deference
7 evasive

Extra activity

Write *culture* on the whiteboard and elicit how many syllables it has (two) and which one is stressed (the first). Draw a big and small circle next to the word to represent the stress pattern: Oo. Ask the same question about *reaction* and draw circles: oOo. Also draw up the patterns oO, Ooo, and ooO. Ask the students to look back through the lesson and find examples of two and three-syllable nouns with the stress in these different positions. (Possible answers: Oo – *person, sweater, comment, mother, colleague, stranger, meeting, people, weather, toilet, power, distance, pressure, ethic, faux pas, treatment, rescue, blunder, minutes, bathroom, rest room, spirit, put-down, message, question*; oO – *response, remark, mistake*; Ooo – *modesty, attitude, circumstance*; oOo – *achievement, reluctance, aggression*; ooO – *afternoon*)

Lesson 2: Cultural sensitivity, page 66

LESSON OBJECTIVES:

Students will learn and practise ...
avoiding cross-cultural misunderstandings
the second and third conditional

Warm up

Read these sentences to the class one at a time:

1 *Thai business meetings often sound like a serious argument to Westerners.* (F)
2 *Scandinavians will typically start negotiations by offering what they believe is the fair price.* (T)
3 *It's normal to sit on a table rather than a chair in Japan.* (F)
4 *The thumbs-up sign in Argentina is impolite.* (T)
5 *In Turkey, people like to get straight to business, without any social talk.* (F)
6 *Westerners usually find negotiations in China finish surprisingly quickly.* (F)
7 *In Mexico, try to give a quick and decisive answer to all questions.* (F)
8 *A man should not shake an Indian woman's hand.* (T)
9 *In the US, a strong handshake is considered rude.* (F)
10 *If invited to someone's house in the UK, it's acceptable to arrive ten minutes late.* (T)

Ask the students to work in pairs and agree on whether each statement is true or false. Check the answers.

Start up

1 Ask the students to guess where the picture was taken (China). Ask if anyone has seen this or any other tea ceremony take place. In a multilingual class, ask the students if their country has a drink with its own culture or rituals. Allow the students time to discuss the questions in pairs, then take feedback from the class, and write any useful vocabulary on the whiteboard.

Listening

2 Ask the students to read the text, then discuss the questions with a partner. Take feedback from the class but don't confirm answers at this stage.

POSSIBLE ANSWERS

dealing with people who spoke different languages and had different work practices

3 🔊 **7.1** Read the rubric with the class, then play the audio for the students to answer the question. Allow them to compare their answers before taking feedback from the class.

ANSWERS

It launched four months late and was a commercial failure. Akrun nearly went out of business and were forced to sell the satellite system.

🔊 **7.1**

Looking back now, the mistakes we made seem so obvious and if we had the opportunity to start all over again, we'd do it all differently. But, at the time, technology was just starting to open up global communication and our project was the first of its kind, so others have since been able to learn from our mistakes. The first problem we had was that our 28 board members all spoke different languages, so everything had to be translated at least five ways. If we'd let the groups in the different countries work autonomously and report back individually, we'd have been able to work much faster. We wouldn't have insisted on holding big multi-national meetings if we'd known how much trouble they'd cause because of the challenges of cross-cultural communication. For example, when we asked some of the team leaders if their teams were going to finish something on time, they usually answered 'Yes'. But we didn't understand that this 'Yes' actually meant, 'Yes, we're trying as hard as we can to finish this', so we got completely the wrong idea about how much progress they were making. The worst mistake we made was the progress chart. The chart had stars on it – blue stars to show the teams on schedule, white stars for the teams that were a little bit late and red stars for the teams who were seriously behind. After we introduced it, some of the leaders whose teams had received a red star simply refused to talk to us anymore. Of course, if we'd understood more about the cultural context, we'd have realised that this way of communicating a problem was too direct. It caused people to lose face and was highly insulting to the teams with the red star. Such mistakes ended up costing us nearly everything. Although we eventually completed the work, we were four months behind schedule and because some of our partners had opted out of the project, it was a commercial failure. Akrun nearly went out of business and were forced to sell the satellite system to another company at a very low price. If I could pass on just one piece of advice to anyone working on cross-cultural projects, it would be this: do your homework – you really can't afford not to.

4 Elicit or pre-teach *lose face* (to be put in a position that is embarrassing, or that could make people lose respect for you). Allow the students time to read the questions, then play the audio again for them to note down the answers. Allow them to compare their answers before taking feedback from the class.

ANSWERS

1 the global communication satellite
2 translating everything five ways so that the 28 board members, who all spoke different languages, could communicate with each other in big multi-national meetings
3 big multi-national meetings
4 they meant, 'Yes, we are trying as hard as we can to finish this by the date you need' not 'Yes, we will definitely finish by the date you need'
5 the progress chart, which gave them red stars when they were behind schedule
6 to do your research when working on a cross-cultural project

Grammar

5 Ask the students to match the two parts of the sentences, then check the answers.

ANSWERS

1 b 2 e 3 d 4 a 5 c

6 Allow the students time to answer the questions and complete the rules, using the Grammar reference to help them if necessary. Check the answers.

ANSWERS

1 1 and 5   2 2, 3 and 4   3 simple, perfect

Students can find more activities at www.richmondatwork.net

Speaking

7 Ask the students if they know of any other situations where cultural differences have caused problems and discuss any they mention as a class. Then ask the students to read the texts and note down their answers to the questions. Give them time to discuss their answers in pairs. Take feedback from the class, then read the explanations on page 99 together. Encourage discussion and write any useful vocabulary on the whiteboard.

Extra activity

On the whiteboard, write: *A different life*. Underneath, write five dates that refer to key events in your life, e.g. 7/6/09 September 2012   4 January 2005   23/12/99   July 1998
Say what each refers to, and how your life could have been different if things had gone differently (e.g. *On June the 7th 2009 I graduated from university. If I hadn't passed my degree, I would have had to retake the exams, and I wouldn't have trained to be a teacher.*). Encourage questions. When you have finished, ask a strong student to give an example, then ask the students to continue in pairs.

Lesson 3: When things go wrong, page 68

LESSON OBJECTIVES:

Students will learn and practise ...
avoiding making mistakes
apologising

Warm up

Write on the whiteboard: *an embarrassing mistake*. Tell the students about an embarrassing mistake you made as a child or teenager. Encourage questions. Then ask the students to think of an embarrassing mistake they made when they were young, and tell their partner.

Start up

1 Allow the students time to read the quotes and discuss the questions, then take feedback from the class, and write any useful vocabulary on the whiteboard.

POSSIBLE ANSWERS

2 don't say anything at all, speak to a colleague, speak to your boss, send an email to explain the situation

Reading

2 Look at the title and ask a volunteer to paraphrase it (what to do when you make a very big mistake). The students should remember *screw up* from lesson 1, including the fact that it is not considered a polite expression by many people. Allow the students time to read the text and discuss the questions before taking feedback from the class.

3 Elicit or pre-teach *own up to something* (to admit that it was you who made a mistake), *face up to something* (to accept the result of a mistake, even if it is unpleasant), *heartfelt* (really and sincerely felt), *put something right* (to correct the bad situation that your mistake caused). Ask the students to read the text again and note down key words in answer to the questions. Then allow them time to discuss their answers in pairs before taking feedback from the class.

Culture 7

ANSWERS

1 Sending a confidential email to the wrong person; making a mistake with key figures that your boss is about to use in an important presentation.
2 Because you will look worse if someone else breaks the news.
3 Take responsibility and offer an explanation for why it happened, without making excuses.
4 and 5 Students' own answers.

Listening

4 ◉ **7.2** Play the audio for the students to note down answers. Allow them to compare their answers in pairs before taking feedback from the class.

ANSWERS

1 train station announcement – train has been delayed by 50 minutes
2 overseas visitor – wrong type of room booked
3 a spokesperson for the government – 'mistakes' that were made with regard to another nation with whom they were in conflict (we don't know what)
4 supplier – delay in delivery of items ordered
5 staff member (to manager) – forgot to bring copies of the report to a meeting

◉ **7.2**

1
We regret to inform passengers that the ten twenty-five departure to Glasgow Central from platform seven will be delayed by approximately 50 minutes due to engineering problems on the line at Berwick. We apologise for any inconvenience caused.

2
Please accept our sincere apologies for the misunderstanding, Mr Kim. Our administrator had not understood that Mr Park was a senior member of staff and so she reserved a standard room for him instead of a suite. We sincerely hope that Mr Park was not too uncomfortable yesterday evening and we have reserved a penthouse suite for him at the Oakland for the rest of his stay.

3
Clearly, we in this government recognise that mistakes were made in the past. But mistakes are made in every conflict between nations and this one was no exception. At the present time, however, I really believe that relations between our two countries are improving, there is progress being made and that we can be optimistic about the future.

4
I'm so sorry to hear about the delay receiving your delivery, sir. We had an unusually large number of orders last week, which disrupted our normal delivery schedule. I do apologise. I've checked on the computer and it should be with you tomorrow morning.

5
I'm sorry, Karen. I did print out several copies of the report before I left, but I think I must have left them in the printer in the office. I'm afraid we'll have to manage without them for the meeting this morning, but I'll ring the office now and ask Cindy to get us a copy sent over as soon as possible.

5 Read the questions with the class, then play the audio again for the students to note down answers. Allow them time to discuss their answers in pairs before checking as a class.

ANSWERS

1 No, the railway company hasn't taken any action other than informing passengers about the delay. As far as we know the train will eventually arrive, but behind schedule.
2 Yes, he's booked into a better room for the coming night.
3 No, this is a non-apology so the speaker doesn't take responsibility for anything. The use of the passive 'mistakes were made' doesn't specify what the issues might be and doesn't attribute them to anyone.
4 Yes, the order will be with the client by the next day.
5 Yes, she will get the office to email through a copy of the report.

Functional language

6 Play the audio again, pausing after the sentences to allow the students time to write the missing words. Ask them to check their answers with the audioscript on page 128.

ANSWERS

a regret to inform passengers b apologise for any inconvenience c accept our sincere apologies d are made in every e so sorry to hear f afraid we'll have to

Fluency

7 ◉ **7.3** Read the rubric with the class. Demonstrate the activity by saying the sentence *I'm so sorry to hear about the delay in receiving your delivery* in a soft, sincere-sounding way, then in a cold and insincere way. Ask the students which sounded more since, and which style they would prefer to hear if they were the customer. Then play the audio for the students to tick the apology that sounds more sincere. Check the answers.

ANSWERS

1 b 2 a 3 b

◉ **7.3**
See **7** in the Student's Book.

8 Play the audio for the students to repeat the apologies in **7**. Encourage them to exaggerate the tone of voice.

Speaking

9 Ask students to read the situation, and invite volunteers to paraphrase the problems. Then read questions 1–3 with the class, and set a time-limit of 20 minutes for the students to follow the instructions in pairs. Monitor as they talk, and note down any language problems to deal with later. Ask several pairs to 'perform' one of the apologies to the class.

79

Extra activity

Write on the whiteboard:

scr_ _ up / me_ _ up (screw up / mess up)
o_ _ up to something (own up)
fa_ _ up to something (face up)
apo_ _ _ _ _ _ _ _ _ _ something (apologise for)
bla_ _ something _ _ someone (blame … on)
bla_ _ someone _ _ _ something (blame … for)
It's my fau_ _. / Whose fau_ _ is it? (fault)

Ask the students to look back through the lesson and complete the verbs and expressions. Then ask the students to work in pairs to write a dialogue including all the verbs and expressions. Ask pairs to perform their dialogue for the class.

Scenario: Losing Luis Lima, page 70

SCENARIO OBJECTIVE:

Students will decide how to persuade a top player to return to the club.

Warm up

With books closed, write on the whiteboard:

Who is the most brilliant young sportsperson from your country at the moment?

What do you know about him/her?

Ask the students to discuss the questions with a partner, then take feedback from the class, and write any useful vocabulary on the whiteboard. In a monolingual class, each student in a pair should choose a different person.

1 Elicit or pre-teach *rising star* (a person who is becoming famous), *spot* (to discover someone with talent), *talent scout* (a person who tries to find young people who are good enough to play professional sport), *scholarship* (an amount of money awarded to someone to allow them to study at a college without paying, because they are exceptionally talented) and *fan base* (total number of fans). Give the students time to read the article and note down key words for their answers. Allow them time to compare their answers in pairs before taking feedback from the class.

ANSWERS

1 (Manaus in north-east) Brazil, six years
2 He's exceptionally talented, has a huge fan base and will draw in large crowds to watch the matches.
3 Possible answers: Luis might have secretly been offered a better deal with another club; he might have found he has a terrible illness or be suffering from stress; he might be homesick and have gone back to Brazil; he might have had a change of heart about making a career out of hockey.

2 🔊 **7.5** Elicit or pre-teach *miserable* (very unhappy), *clubbing* (going out to nightclubs), *nervous breakdown* (a mental crisis which makes you unable to deal with normal life) and *take someone under your wing* (to take responsibility for taking care of someone). Read the questions with the class, then play the audio for the students to note down answers. Allow them time to compare their answers in pairs before taking feedback.

ANSWERS

1 none 2 the recently retired coach 3 He's been generally a bit depressed and miserable recently. He's been out late a lot and coming it late for training and exhausted. He's angry.
4 He's rebelling – he's angry with the club for their treatment of him when he first arrived. He also misses the old coach (Uncle Enzo), who was a father figure to Luis. He's also angry with his family for pushing him too hard, even when he was very young.

🔊 **7.5**

T = Tyler, B = Beto

T: So, Beto, what's up with Luis? I haven't heard a thing from him since he left. He's seemed generally a bit depressed and miserable recently. Do you think this is to do with Enzo Ribeiro retiring? He was almost like an uncle to him.

B: I don't know. Cooper's definitely no Enzo Ribeiro, but he's only trying to get the best out of us.

T: Well, Luis's behaviour has been getting worse and worse lately. He's always late for training and he's obviously completely exhausted because he's been out all night clubbing, or whatever. Not that it makes any difference to his game; he's so talented! Anyone else would have been fired for such behaviour or at least given a warning. And as it is, I'm sure they'd still take him back – he only has to ask. Do you think he's having some kind of a nervous breakdown?

B: No, I'm sure he isn't. I think he's just rebelling. He seems to be really angry with the club. Yesterday evening he was talking about how lonely he felt when he first came here because he couldn't speak any English and everybody seemed so cold and distant. Enzo really took him under his wing so it must be tough now that he's gone. It's true that he hasn't really learnt much English as he used to spend so much time with 'Uncle' Enzo. Do you think the club could have done more to help him with his English or to integrate him better with the other players?

T: Yeah, maybe, but the club's given him a lot of opportunities. He's always said how great it feels to send money home to his family.

B: I don't know, Tyler. He sounds pretty angry with his family at the moment as well, especially his mother. He's been talking about how she made him practise for at least two hours a day ever since he was four years old and how he wishes he had time to do other things. He's had this huge pressure on him to work hard and succeed all his life and it seems like he just can't take it anymore.

3 Emphasise that the students' sentences need to be based on the situation, but will have to be rephrased in their own words. Ask the students to make notes as you play the audio, then allow them time to finish the sentences and compare answers in pairs before taking feedback from the class.

Culture 7

ANSWERS

1 Even if Cooper isn't like Ribeiro, he's only trying to get the best out of the players.
2 If Luis weren't so talented, the club would have given him a warning or fired him before now.
3 The club would probably take Luis back if he asked.
4 He might not have been so angry with the club if they had done more to integrate him when he first arrived.
5 If he hadn't had such pressure on him to succeed, perhaps he wouldn't be so angry with his family at the moment / be rebelling.

4 Arrange the students into AB pairs. Ask Student A to read the article on page 100, and Student B the article on page 104. Ask them to note key words to help them remember the most important information, and then talk about the article with their partner. Then allow pairs time to work together to complete the text. Check the answers.

ANSWERS

1 Brazil 2 Hawks Hockey High School / Hawks Junior League Team 3 sixteen 4 Connecticut 5 training 6 tired 7 visa 8 retire 9 ice hockey 10 style

5 ◢))) **7.6** Play the audio for the students to answer the question. Allow them time to discuss their answer before taking feedback.

ANSWER

No, they don't.

◢))) **7.6**

A = Alex, C = Colby

A: Thanks for agreeing to meet me so quickly. We really have a problem here. I have my star player who has decided to leave the team and a new coach who shows great promise for the club, but hasn't started off well with Lima. I need to know if I should be worried about Coach Cooper.
C: Cooper's fine. He's only just arrived so hasn't had a chance to make a mark yet. He's much more direct than Coach Ribeiro ever was, but a lot of the players really like his style. He's a real motivator. Lima had a special relationship with Ribeiro so his departure has been tough for him.
A: But Lima has really helped us turn the club around and I really don't want to lose him. Losing him will be incredibly bad for the club. His fan base has increased our mid-season ticket sales by almost 50% recently.
C: So, what do you suggest? Should we try to get him back? What about Coach Cooper?
A: For the sake of the club, I think we need to offer Lima something to come back.
C: He won't want to work with Cooper though, so are you suggesting we get rid of the coach?
A: If we want money to keep coming, then Lima is the guy to help us with this. That said, finding a different coach is going to be almost impossible at this stage in the season.
C: I don't know. I don't think Lima knows what he wants at the moment. He was very emotional when I last spoke to him. He kept saying he'd been pushed into hockey as a child and had no real passion for it, which is ridiculous when you think of how passionate he is as a player: it's what defines him. Can we offer him a salary increase?
A: Well, we probably could offer him more. It's no secret that he's not that well-paid in comparison with many other hockey players of his talent. Considering his recent bad behaviour, missing training, etc. though this might cause even more bad feeling amongst the other players. But he is our star player.
C: If he agrees to come back, we'll need to do something about his relationship with the new coach.

6 Read the questions with the class, then play the audio again for the students to mark the statements true or false. Then ask the students to work in pairs to correct the false statements. Check the answers.

ANSWERS

1 T
2 F (Cooper's fine. He's only just arrived so hasn't had a chance to make a mark yet.)
3 F (finding a different coach now is going to be almost impossible at this stage in the season.)
4 T
5 F (It's no secret that he's not that well-paid in comparison with many other hockey players of his talent.)

7 Read the instructions with the class. Set a time-limit of ten minutes for pairs to compose their email.

8 Ask each pair to exchange their email with another pair. Set a time-limit of ten minutes for pairs to write a response to their email. Take feedback on the result of the exchange.

9 Allow pairs time to agree on the action the club should take. Take feedback from the class, and encourage discussion.

Extra activity

Write the verbs *start up* and *calm down*. Elicit or tell the students the name given to this type of verb (phrasal verbs). Ask the students to look back through the unit and choose two phrasal verbs from each lesson that they would like to add to their repertoire, and to write two sentences that include them. Then give the students a chance to compare their lists. Ask several students for their favourite in their list.

Writing emails

Go to **Writing emails 7** on page 50 and do the exercises. Teacher's Book reference on page 65.

8 Marketing and selling

UNIT OBJECTIVES:

Students will practise …	and they will learn how to …
comparative and superlative structures	give persuasive presentations
extreme adjectives	use rhetorical techniques
marketing and advertising vocabulary	
discussing brands and branding	

Lesson 1: Legalised lying?, page 72

LESSON OBJECTIVES:

Students will learn and practise …
marketing and advertising vocabulary
comparative amd superlative structures

Warm up

Write the following marketing slogans on the whiteboard. Elicit what each of the companies makes if you think there is any doubt.
1 I'm _____ it! (lovin' – McDonald's – burgers)
2 Eat _____ (fresh – Subway – sandwiches)
3 It gives you _____ (wings – Red Bull – 'energy' drink)
4 Just _____ it (do – Nike – sportswear)
5 Ideas for _____ (life – Panasonic – electrical equipment)

Ask the students to discuss in pairs what the missing word is in each, then ask pairs to discuss which of the slogans is most effective, and why.

Start up

Write on the whiteboard:
Think of a well-known TV ad in your country at the moment.
Describe it to your partner.
Who is it aimed at?
What is it trying to make them think?

Ask the students to describe their ad and discuss the questions with a partner. Take feedback from the class and write any useful vocabulary on the whiteboard.

1 Allow the students time to read the quotes and discuss their answers with a partner before taking feedback from the class.

Reading

2 Focus on the pictures. Ask the students if they know anything about the marketing techniques used for the products/performers pictured. Elicit or pre-teach *feud* (a disagreement between two people or groups that lasts for a long time). Then ask the students to read the texts quickly and put in the three words. Check the answers.

ANSWERS
1 green 2 small 3 feud

3 Allow the students time to reread the texts and answer the questions. Ask them to compare answers and discuss question 6 before taking feedback from the class.

ANSWERS
1 Kayne West and 50 Cent 2 Lucky Strike 3 Volkswagen Beetle 4 Volkswagen Beetle 5 Kayne West and 50 Cent
6 Students' own answer.

Vocabulary

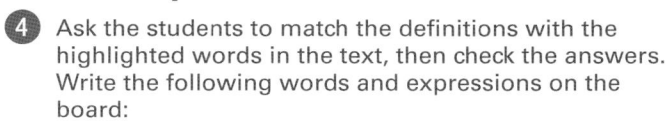

4 Ask the students to match the definitions with the highlighted words in the text, then check the answers. Write the following words and expressions on the board:

slogan, sponsor, status symbol, rivals, trend setters, baby boomers

Ask the students to write down one of the most famous current examples of each one in their country at the moment (e.g. for *sponsor*, they could name a company that spends lots of money sponsoring a team or competition, and for *baby boomer*, they should name the most famous person born between 1945 and 1965).

ANSWERS
1 slogan 2 sponsoring 3 ploy 4 status symbol 5 rivalry
6 trend setters 7 baby boomer

Students can find more activities at www.richmondatwork.net

Grammar

5 Read the **Grammar** box with the class, and then allow the students time to complete the rules and find examples of uses 1–5 in the text. Check the answers.

ANSWERS
er / est – smaller, the smallest
more / the most – more expensive, the most expensive
1 the older, tougher, more streetwise of the two
2 the bigger the better
3 ads were getting bigger and bigger and more and more colourful
4 West's album was far more successful
5 by far the most recognisable

/ Marketing and selling 8

6 Ask the students to work in pairs to complete the sentences with the comparative and superlative forms. Check the answers.

ANSWERS
1 most annoying, clever 2 the more expensive, the higher
3 by far the most influential 4 more, more popular
5 most memorable 6 more appropriate, of the two

Students can find more activities at www.richmondatwork.net

Speaking

7 Ask the students to take turns choosing one of the questions in **6** for their partner to answer. Monitor as they talk, and note down any problems with the comparative and superlative forms to deal with later.

Extra activity
Ask the students to look back through the lesson and choose five adjectives that they would like to add to their repertoire, then compare their list with a partner. Tell pairs to exchange their two lists of words with another pair, so that each of the pair has one list. Pairs take turns drawing pictures to describe the adjectives without speaking or using gesture, so that their partner can guess it.

Lesson 2: Why the brand matters, page 74

LESSON OBJECTIVES:
Students will learn and practise ...
talking about brands and branding
extreme adjectives

Warm up

With books closed write the names of these well-known international companies on the whiteboard (or substitute others if any are not well known in your students' country):

Microsoft

Domino's

Volkswagen

Toyota

Ask the students to draw the companies' logos from memory, then compare their results with other students. If possible, take in the actual logos for students to compare, or look them up on the Internet.

Start up

1 Allow the students time to look at the ads and the slogans and discuss their ideas for the products. Then take feedback from the class.

ANSWERS
a Coca-Cola b diamonds c soap d petrol e trainers

Reading

2 Elicit or pre-teach *outlive* (to live longer than another thing or person). Set a five-minute time-limit for the students to discuss the question in the rubric and note down five bullet points to represent their ideas. Then ask them to read the text to see if any of the ideas are the same. Take feedback from the class. Ask the students if there is anything in the text that they don't completely agree with.

POSSIBLE ANSWER
A brand is a unique design/packaging, logo or symbol (or a combination of these) that identifies a product and differentiates it from its competitors. Companies try to make their brand match the lifestyle ambitions and self-image of the people they want to buy their products. Ideally, they would like consumers to see their product or company as a 'friend'.

3 Allow the students time to reread the text and underline the correct options, then check the answers.

ANSWERS
1 exposure, T (this is only true according to the author of the text, whereas studies would show that they still have an effect, even if subliminal) 2 irrelevant, F 3 associations, T
4 conscious, F 5 rationalise, attraction, T

Listening

4 8.1 Play the audio for the students to listen and guess the brands. Allow students to confer after the first playing, then play it a second time and take feedback.

ANSWERS
1 Coca-Cola 2 McDonald's 3 Nike 4 Intel Pentium processors 5 Disney

8.1
1
One of the keys to the success of this brand, originally created in Atlanta in 1886, and now the most recognised in the world, is its universal appeal. Its target market is literally everybody and the brand has come to be a symbol of happiness and democratic freedom. As well as the product's unique taste – the recipe remains a closely-guarded secret – it has highly recognisable packaging. The classic bottle, created in 1915, has a shape resembling the silhouette of a woman and the red and white cans are also recognised all over the world.
2
This brand, originally created in 1940, owes its success to the fact that it successfully targeted a highly profitable market segment – children. By making itself so attractive to children, the company also managed to sell many of its products to their accompanying parents. The brand's mascot, a clown character invented in the 1960s, was the master stroke. He represented a world where food was quick, delicious and also came with brightly-coloured plastic toys. Children couldn't get enough of it.
3
In the late 1970s and early 80s, this company decided it needed 'to do something' about its very small market share. From

83

this declaration, a famous slogan was born and a brand which represented a positive, energetic, 'can do' approach not just to sport, but to life itself. The company produced a series of funny ads showing popular sports stars doing incredible things effortlessly thanks to the kit they were wearing. They were extremely popular and the brand's market share more than doubled.

4
This company was extraordinarily successful in building a high-profile brand for an 'invisible' product – a tiny, but vital component used in electronic devices that most consumers didn't even know existed. In the 1990s, they ran a series of high-profile TV ads featuring the memorable 'inside' slogan and four-note jingle to educate consumers about the importance of their product in technology. They persuaded the manufacturers of electronic devices, that were made using their component, to add a sticker with their 'inside' slogan so that BOTH brands would be visible to consumers.

5
This brand was born in the 1920s in a production studio in California. It was originally based on one man's vision and a series of funny, memorable characters that he created, including a pair of mice and a bad-tempered duck. They became so successful that the brand grew and grew throughout the 20th century and expanded into other areas of the entertainment industry. Its appeal is based on fantasy, story-telling and dreams coming true and although the products are developed for children, they are also attractive to many adults.

5 🔊 **8.1** Play the audio again for the students to complete the sentences, then check the answers. Then ask them to reread the sentences, and discuss the question in pairs. Take feedback from the class.

ANSWERS
1 unique taste, recognisable packaging 2 plastic toys
3 funny ads, sports stars 4 'invisible' product
5 fantasy, story-telling

GRAMMAR

6 Write on the whiteboard: *cool, warm, hot, cold, boiling, freezing*.

Ask the students to order the adjectives from hottest to coldest (Answer: *boiling, hot, warm, cool, cold, freezing*). Then ask which ones you can't use with *very* (*boiling* and *freezing*). Explain that these two adjectives are 'extreme' or 'non-gradable'. Read the **Grammar** box with the class. Then ask the students to replace the adjectives in sentences 1–8 with extreme adjectives and modifiers. Elicit the meaning and pronunciation of *minute* /maɪˈnjuːt/ in the box. Check the answers.

ANSWERS
1 absolutely astounding 2 utterly exhausted, absolutely filthy
3 completely packed, absolutely delighted 4 absolutely minute 5 utterly terrified 6 absolutely hilarious 7 utterly furious 8 absolutely gorgeous

🅡 Students can find more activities at www.richmondatwork.net

Speaking

7 Demonstrate the activity yourself. Show all the brands you are carrying and wearing, and list the brands you own. Ask the students if they think you are 'heavily-branded'. Then ask the students to do the same in pairs, and discuss the questions. Take feedback from the class.

Extra activity

Write on the whiteboard:
A: You look tired.
B: Yes, I'm c_____ e_____! I had to work late at the office.
A: You must be angry.
B: Angry? That's not all. I'm a_____ f_____! Someone stole my wallet so I had to walk home!

Elicit what adverb and extreme adjective could go in the gaps (*completely exhausted, absolutely furious*).

Ask the students to work in pairs to write a similar dialogue including four extreme adjectives with intensifying adverbs. Then ask pairs to perform their dialogue for the class.

Lesson 3: The art of persuasion, page 76

LESSON OBJECTIVES:

Students will learn and practise ...
persuasive presentations
rhetorical techniques

Warm up

Ask the students to study the picture in **2** for one minute for a memory test. Then ask them to close their books and try to write the answers to the following questions in pairs:

1 How many people are in the picture? (five)
2 What are the main colours of the carpet the men are holding? (red and blue)
3 What is on the small table? (nothing)
4 What is on the floor in front of the woman on the right? (a rucksack/bag)
5 Does the male tourist have long or short hair? (short)
6 Which of the women is holding a camera? (the one on the left)
7 What colour are her trousers? (red)
8 What is on the seat next to the woman nearest the carpet men? (a hat)

Ask how many questions pairs got right, and congratulate the winners.

Marketing and selling 8

Start up

1 Write the following sentences on the whiteboard:
1 *Persuasion is the art of getting people to do things that are in their own best interest that also _____ you.*
2 *The first art of persuasion is learning how to consistently talk to people about _____ .*

Ask the students to discuss what they think the missing words are (Answers: *benefit*, *them*). Check the answers then ask them to tell their partner how far they agree with the quotes, and, if possible, to tell a true story that illustrates one of the quotes. Read the questions with the class, and give the students time to discuss them in pairs. Take feedback from the class, and write any useful vocabulary on the whiteboard.

Reading

2 Pre-teach *draught-proofed* (treated so that is doesn't allow cold air to get in). Allow the students time to match the techniques with the presentation beginnings. Ask the students to compare answers in pairs before checking as a class.

ANSWERS
1 e   2 a   3 b   4 c   5 d

3 Ask the students to match the presentations with the products. Allow the students to discuss the clues that led them to their answers before taking feedback from the class. Don't confirm the answers at this stage.

ANSWERS
1 pension plan   2 management training for women
3 language-learning software   4 roof insulation
5 a gym-based fitness programme

Listening

4 🔊 **8.2** Play the audio for the students to check their answers to **3**. Ask the students to read the first sentence of each presentation in audioscript 8.2 on page 130, and discuss which they think is most effective, and why.

🔊 8.2

1
So, an old man goes to see his doctor with a whole list of complaints – 'This hurts, that's stiff, I get tired very quickly, etc. 'But Mr Williams', the doctor replies, 'You really can't expect to feel the same as you did when you were younger. As we get older, our body inevitably starts to wear out. After all, who wants to live to 100?' The old man looks him straight in the eye and replies, 'Anyone who's 99, young man, anyone who's 99.' You probably haven't given much thought yet as to what you might be doing when you get to 99, but one thing's for sure: it's never too early to start putting money aside for your old age. If you don't start looking after your future, your future won't look after you.

2
It was once said about Ginger Rogers' famous dancing partner, Fred Astaire: 'Sure, he was great, but don't forget that Ginger Rogers did everything he did, backwards ... and in high heels.' Unfortunately, it's still true today that women's efforts often go unrecognised. Despite our so-called equal society, in many industries, men are still paid up to 20% more than female colleagues in the same job. Shouldn't more women be fighting back? Of course they should. That's why our executive training programmes are specifically tailored for women to help them overcome the challenges that still exist in …

3
I was only 20 years old when I suffered one of the bitterest and most painful disappointments of my life. I don't come from a rich family and when, after many difficult years of study and preparation, I won a scholarship to the top engineering school in France, we were all delighted. But then, something terrible happened. Although the school wanted to have me, I also had to pass their entrance exam and … I failed. Most of my grades were excellent, but I had failed and failed badly in one subject, so I lost my place. That subject was English and the night I got my results, I promised myself that I was going to find a way to help people like me …

4
Did you know that if every house in the UK was fully draught-proofed, the nation would save enough energy to easily heat all the homes in Belfast and Cardiff combined? Do you have any idea of just how much you could actually save by insulating your roof? Were you aware that there are new government grants available for energy-saving home improvements? Well, I'm here today to tell you about our fast and efficient insulation plans that can actually help you save money whilst making your home cosier, more comfortable and considerably more cost effective to run.

5
It's a sad fact that an incredible 80% of members either never actually come to the gym, or come very rarely. Fifteen per cent of any membership is usually composed of people who joined in January, probably after eating too much at Christmas, but stopped coming entirely by the end of February. Does any of this sound familiar? If the answer is yes and you are one of the many millions for whom, when it comes to exercise, the spirit is willing, but the body is weak, then you've come to the right place.

Functional language

5 Read the **Help** box with the class. Look at question 1, and ask a volunteer to explain what a rhetorical question is (a question that someone asks for effect, which does not require an answer). Ask the students to look at the audioscript on page 130 and find a rhetorical question. Once everyone has had the chance to find it, confirm the answer (*Shouldn't more women be fighting back?*) and ask the students together to answer the rest of the questions. Check the answers.

> **ANSWERS**
> 1 Shouldn't more women be fighting back?
> 2 I was only 20 years old when I suffered one of the bitterest and most painful disappointments of my life.
> 3 When it comes to exercise, the spirit is willing but the body is weak.
> 4 cosier, more comfortable and considerably more cost effective
> 5 If you don't start looking after your future, your future won't look after you.
> 6 I had failed and failed badly.

Fluency

6 •))) **8.3** Play the audio for the students to listen and underline the stressed words in the sentences in **5**, before discussing what the importance of these words is in the sentences. Then play the audio again for the students to repeat the sentences.

> **ANSWERS**
> 1 Can we <u>really</u> expect this situation to continue? (This emphasises the speaker's incredulity – he/she just can't believe the situation is as it is.)
> 2 Imagine being thrown out into the street, <u>cold</u>, <u>lonely</u> and <u>frightened</u>. (These are the three things the speaker wants the audience to imagine.)
> 3 To do <u>nothing</u> is impossible; to <u>act</u> is to take a terrible risk. (They represent the two opposing courses of action.)
> 4 What <u>they</u> want is sun, sand and sea. (To stress that it is this particular group who want sun, sea, and possibly to go on to contrast with another a group who want something else.)
> 5 Sometimes we have to be <u>cruel</u> to be <u>kind</u>. (They represent the two opposing ways of behaving which speaker wants to contrast.
> 6 Good <u>fences</u> make good <u>neighbours</u>. (The two important elements in the sentence that balance each other out – one is the result of the other.)

•))) **8.3**
See Answers above.

Vocabulary

7 Ask the students to close their books, then read the first sentence of the text to them. Ask the students to work in pairs to write down three words that they think may be among these powerful words. Then ask them to read the text and check. Look at the example and ask the students to work in pairs to choose two topics from the list and write three 'powerful' sentences for each. Take feedback from the class.

8 Ask pairs to take turns reading their sentences to the class. Encourage positive comments.

> **POSSIBLE ANSWERS**
> 1 You'll love having a dog. Not only will you have a new friend, but research has proven that walking the dog is one of the best and safest ways of taking exercise and improving your health. It's so easy!
> 2 Today cosmetic surgery is both incredibly safe and amazingly good value for money. We can guarantee The results can be life changing and you'll feel like a new person. You'll love all the compliments you will suddenly start receiving and ask yourself why you didn't do it sooner.

Students can find more activities at www.richmondatwork.net

Speaking

9 Ask the students to work in pairs to choose a topic and prepare the introduction to a presentation. Encourage them to prepare the introduction orally and just write down key words. Tell them to try to use:
- at least three rhetorical devices from **5**.
- powerful words including extreme adjectives and modifiers.

Set a time-limit of 15 minutes, then ask pairs to take turns to perform their introductions. Ask the students to vote for the best one.

> **Extra activity**
>
> Ask the students to look up each of the positive italic words in the text in **7** (*money, save, new*, etc.) in an Advanced Learner's dictionary and note down at least two things about the meanings or use of each word that surprises them (e.g. additional meanings, collocations, idioms), then write a sentence for each relating to a product or service that their company sells (or for a typical product or service in their industry).

Scenario: Rebranding Ibiza Joy, page 78

> **SCENARIO OBJECTIVE:**
> Students will decide on an alternative sector of tourism for a holiday company.

Warm up

Write on the whiteboard:

What are the most popular holiday destinations for the following groups of people in your country?
- *single 20–30 year olds*
- *families with young children*
- *older couples whose children have left home*

Why do they choose these places?

Ask the students to discuss the questions in pairs, then share their ideas with the class.

1 Ask what the students know about Ibiza. What type of holiday do they think Ibiza is famous for? (It's an island off the east coast of Spain. It's most famous for holidays where young people go to dance to electronic music and 'party' – although families go there on holiday too).

Marketing and selling 8

Read the questions with the class, then allow the students time to read the text and discuss their answers in pairs. Take feedback from the class. Ask for a volunteer to explain *change hands* (to be bought by a new owner).

ANSWERS
1 clubbing holidays for techno fans
2 suggested answers: early twenties, predominantly male, from London or large UK cities …
3 bookings are down and their two main hotels have decided not to renew their contracts with Ibiza Joy

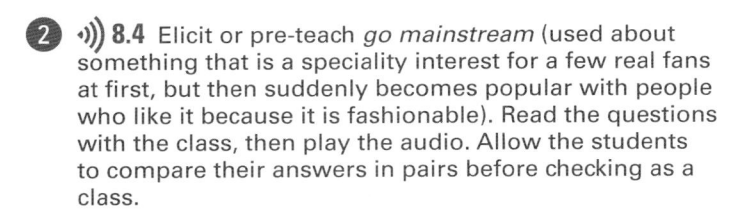

2))) **8.4** Elicit or pre-teach *go mainstream* (used about something that is a speciality interest for a few real fans at first, but then suddenly becomes popular with people who like it because it is fashionable). Read the questions with the class, then play the audio. Allow the students to compare their answers in pairs before checking as a class.

ANSWERS
1 Med-Clubbers and Twenty-Up
2 Their reps know who the best DJs are and how to get into the best club nights.

))) **8.4**

C = Carmen, J = Joe
C: It's a bit of a shock to lose both the Rafael and the Libertad deals at the same time. It won't be a problem to get more rooms, but we'll never be able to negotiate such good rates again. We're just going to have to put our prices up: I just don't see any other solution.
J: I don't either, but raising our prices is going to put us in an even worse position in relation to the big package suppliers like Med-Clubbers and Twenty-Up Holidays. They already offer more or less what we do, but at a lower price. And if we put our room rates up, we'll be much more expensive instead of just slightly more expensive.
C: Yes, I know. There are too many companies trying to get in on the market for low-budget, clubbing and beach holidays for twenty-somethings. I mean, apart from the fact that we were here first, how are we different from Med-Clubbers or Twenty-Up? All our brands are about being young and partying and having fun, aren't they?
J: Yes, but we started out as something a bit different. Originally, Ibiza Joy was meant for people who were seriously into dance music and techno. But then electronic music went mainstream and got very popular and suddenly everyone wanted to come clubbing in Ibiza. So these days we're competing with Twenty-Up and Med-Clubbers for the same customers … and it's getting more and more difficult to differentiate ourselves and what we offer. The Med-Clubbers tend to be a bit younger and wilder than our customers and seriously interested in partying – the louder the music, the more crowded the club, the better; whereas the Twenty-Up crowd is a bit more sophisticated, they're a slightly older crowd, with a bit more cash and they stay in more expensive hotels, but where does that leave us? I can't think of a single thing we offer that they don't.
C: Well, thanks to Richie, our reps really do know who the best DJs are and how to get into the best club nights … but then our customers, who aren't serious techno music fans – and that's most of them these days – don't appreciate this because they wouldn't know the difference anyway.

3 Allow the students time to read the questions, then play the audio again for them to choose the correct options. Check the answers.

ANSWERS
1 go up   2 much more   3 beach and clubbing holidays
4 going to the beach and appreciating techno music
5 differentiate themselves from the competition
6 more sophisticated   7 Very few

4 Allow the students time to discuss the questions in pairs and note down their ideas. Then take feedback from the class, and encourage discussion.

ANSWERS
The holidays are no longer catering for serious music fans since the music went mainstream. More people want a beach holiday with clubbing, and don't mind with which company, as long as it's cheap. They can't tell the difference between good and bad music.
Possible answer: Perhaps it could aim its brand at the older, 'real' fans of techno music that came in the early days. They may like to be treated differently from the young people who don't really like the music. They would probably have more money to spend now they are older, too.

5))) **8.5** Play the audio for the students to listen and answer the question. Allow them to compare their answers in pairs before checking as a class.

ANSWER
They propose to leave the techno scene and start catering for a completely different holiday maker.

))) **8.5**

R = Richie, L = Loli, C = Carmen, J = Joe
R: Loli and I completely agree with everything you and Joe have been saying, Carmen. You're absolutely right that we don't have a strong identity anymore, but actually, and this is something we've been thinking about for a while, this is an opportunity for us to make some changes. You're quite right, Joe; the original techno scene that we started the company for doesn't really exist anymore. Most of the clubs in San Antonio have become totally commercial and mass market, and anyway our customers these days aren't especially into techno music, they're just young people who want a cheap holiday in the sun with lots of partying … and yes, there are now too many other suppliers offering more or less what we offer. We could hang on and fight for our market here, but we think we could do better than that, don't we, Loli?
L: We do! As we all know, there's more to Ibiza than bars and beaches. There's the watersports for example. There seems to be a constant stream of spa facilities opening and yoga is getting very popular. There's eco-tourism and cultural tourism. We could still use our clubbing contacts,

for example, to offer our guests exclusive back-stage passes to the big techno events. We don't have to concentrate on the low-cost end of the market any more … and nobody is forcing us to restrict ourselves to the youth market. We could totally rebrand ourselves!

C: Eco-tourism is an idea worth exploring – I wrote my thesis for my Masters in Tourism on it, so I'd be really enthusiastic. And you know what, José-Luis from the Libertad hotel is going to be managing an eco-hotel in Las Salinas … maybe we could just transfer our contracts there?

J: Um … I'm slightly in shock. Do you really think we can change so completely? What would our new customer profile be?

R: Well, that's what we've got to talk about …

6 Before listening again, ask the students what alternative sectors they remember. Then play the audio as the students make notes. Allow them to discuss their answers in pairs before taking feedback.

ANSWERS

Some ideas suggested are: water sports, spa facilities, yoga, the eco tourist, cultural tourism, older holiday makers, and not restricting themselves to the budget market. Carmen wrote her thesis on eco-tourism and also a contact from one of the hotels they used to use is going to be managing an eco-hotel on the island.

Extra activity

Write these synonyms on the whiteboard:

1	affluent	a	activity
2	disposable income	b	fashionable
3	leisure	c	free time
4	lucrative	d	health
5	niche	f	profitable
6	on trend	g	quite rich
7	pursuit	h	specialised area
8	sustainable	i	money available for non-essential things
9	wellness	j	that could continue for a long time

Ask the students to work in pairs to match the synonyms, sharing their knowledge and using their dictionaries (Answers: 1 g, 2 i, 3 c, 4 f, 5 h, 6 b, 7 a, 8 j, 9 d).

7 Arrange the students in groups of three, A, B and C. Focus on the bullet-point headings they need to make notes under, then ask them to look at their texts on page 79, 104 or 107. Set a time-limit of 15 minutes.

ANSWERS

Student A
- Market profile and characteristics: over 55 years old
- What Ibiza has to offer this market: good weather lots of sun and relaxing surroundings, quiet cultural destinations
- Potential advantages: large and fast-growing sector of population, significant amounts of disposable income, lots of leisure time, happy to spend money, if they feel getting value for money
- Potential disadvantages: Stereotype of Ibiza as a destination for young people, this age group might need special facilities – low beds, lifts in hotels, etc.

Student B
- Market profile and characteristics: adventure and sports tourism – covering a broad cross section – thrill seekers, young professionals with a lot of disposable income, dabblers and enthusiasts
- What Ibiza has to offer this market: beautiful beaches and sea for all manner of watersports, mountainous regions for climbing, etc
- Potential advantages: customer profile overlaps current profile so can use a lot of existing contacts
- Potential disadvantages: company's limited range of contacts and expertise in sports provision. Would need to build up a portfolio of reputable contacts, employ a different sort of (more expensive because more knowledgeable) seasonal rep. Insurance and safety issues need to be investigated.

Student C
- Market profile and characteristics: eco-tourism / wellness tourism – two overlapping sectors, both attracting affluent, well-educated tourists
- What Ibiza has to offer this market: many places of outstanding natural beauty on island, new hotels with spas and wellness facilities – island has provision for types of tourist
- Potential advantages: hotel contact moving into this sector, currently growing sector – very much on trend
- Potential disadvantages: The fact that this is two sectors rather than one might make for mixed messages in the marketing. The customer profile is very different from the one that Ibiza Joy currently targets and although Richie and Loli have a lot of contacts within the sector which is still relatively new, they are likely to face strong competition in area that is considered desirable and 'on trend' by new developers.

8 Ask the students to reform their groups and share their information, discussing and making notes to address the bullet points. Allow 15 minutes.

9 Ask the students to continue working in their groups of three. Allow them 15 minutes to prepare the basic content of their introduction, then make it more effective by adding rhetorical devices and powerful adjectives. Ask them to work from key words rather than writing out the introduction.

Ask groups to take turns performing their introduction. Ask the listening students to note down two positive points about each of the groups' presentation.

Extra activity

Ask the students to look back through the unit and find ten combinations of adjective + noun that they would like to add to their repertoire. Arrange the students in groups of three. Ask them to take turns to draw one of their collocations, without speaking, for the others in the group to guess. Ask several students for their favourite in their list.

Writing emails

Go to **Writing emails 8** on page 51 and do the exercises. Teacher's Book reference on pages 65–66.

9 Problems and solutions

UNIT OBJECTIVES:	Students will practise ...	and they will learn how to ...
	verb patterns	talk about developing a product
	phrases using prepositions	talk about adapting products
	phrases for suggesting and agreeing solutions	discuss decision-making

Lesson 1: Creating, page 80

LESSON OBJECTIVES:
Students will learn and practise ...
verb patterns
talking about developing a product

Warm up
Write the following words on small pieces of paper and give them out to the students, telling them to keep their word secret (if you have more than eight students, write some words more than once:

bicycle, ballpoint pen, glasses, tin-opener, water wheel, telephone, refrigerator, wheel

Ask the students to stand up and find a partner, and take turns to give a purely physical description (e.g. for ballpoint pen: *a 15 cm thin plastic tube with another tube inside which is filled with ink. The inner tube is attached to a metal point with a tiny metal ball inside*). When they have each guessed their partner's word, they swap papers and find a new partner. Stop after five minutes and write the words on the board. Ask the students to work in pairs to write the words in the order they think they were invented, and to guess the year. When most pairs have finished, give the answers (1 wheel – 8,000 B.C 2 water wheel – 31 B.C. 3 glasses – 1286 4 tin-opener – 1810 5 refrigerator – 1850 6 bicycle – 1860 7 telephone – 1876 8 ballpoint pen – 1938).

Start up

1 Focus on pictures a–d but not the texts, and ask the students to discuss question 1 in pairs. Listen to students' ideas of what the items are before giving the answers.

Write *a eureka moment* on the board, and elicit or teach the meaning (a sudden moment of inspiration experienced by inventors, scientists, etc. It comes from the Ancient Greek word meaning 'I have it!', and is said to have been shouted by the Ancient Greek scientist Archimedes in the bath). Then ask pairs to continue discussing questions 2–4. Take feedback from the class and write any useful vocabulary on the whiteboard.

ANSWERS
1 a computer mice **b** plastic objects – two cups and a telephone **c** Velcro **d** a wind-up radio
2 a as part of most computers, it helps us with work and leisure **b** it allows the production of strong, light articles; it is very versatile and is used in many vital everyday objects **c** it allows us to fasten and unfasten items quickly **d** it can be used where there are no batteries or electricity
3 and **4** Students' own answers.

2 Ask the students to read the texts quickly and match them with the pictures. Quickly take feedback and check their answers.

ANSWERS
1 d **2** c **3** b **4** a

Listening

3 Ask the students to discuss the question very briefly in pairs, then take feedback.

ANSWERS
In an airport. Students' own answers.

4 Focus on picture 2. Ask the students if they have seen a Trunki, or if they know anyone who has one. Then ask the students to discuss the question in pairs, and note down their ideas for each bullet point. Take feedback from the class.

5 🔊 9.1 Play the audio for the students to listen to Rob Law, and tick the points they noted that he mentions. Take feedback from the class.

ANSWERS
material: strong, cheap and able to be made in any colour
shape: comfortable to sit on, safe for children, stable so won't fall over
size: maximum luggage space whilst complying with airline regulations about carry-on luggage size

🔊 **9.1**
This all started when I was a student, actually. I was studying project design at university, and there was a design competition sponsored by a plastic manufacturer, with a good prize. So, to enter the competition I needed to come up with a product made of plastic. Now, I'd always thought that luggage was mostly very uninteresting in design, so I went into a department store to look at what was there – it was all black and boring, but I was struggling to come up with a novel idea. Anyway, I wandered into the children's section without expecting to find inspiration, but in fact that was when I had my eureka moment. I was looking at the colourful tractors that children ride on, and it suddenly hit me I could combine the manufacturing techniques that gave the toys their strength, with the different techniques, that enabled suitcases to have maximum luggage space. So, I spent a lot of time making

89

models to find the right shape. I researched data on children's body sizes, and took my models into schools for children to try, and that all helped me to arrive at the final shape. All children's products have to meet extremely strict safety standards to prevent anyone getting hurt, so I had to do lots of tests to make sure the shape was stable and wouldn't fall over, and children couldn't hurt themselves in any way. I was also limited by size – it had to be small enough for airlines to allow it on a plane as hand-luggage. The obvious material was the most common plastic, polypropylene, because it's very strong, cheap, and it allows you to use colour freely. I managed to find a manufacturer in China that would produce it cheaply, and a warehouse – my bedroom was already full of models. Eventually, I had to employ someone so I had to find premises. I decided to take really beautiful photos of kids using the product, to make it stand out from the crowd. Because of that, the press were really interested in it from the start. They thought it was an interesting and different product, and they knew they'd get a great photo. So, we've featured in over a thousand newspapers and magazines, and that has saved us having to pay for any publicity. I made a few mistakes. I regret not going to China to do the quality control on the first production run, because there was a problem that was expensive to correct. We started winning design awards, which started to attract the attention of the big stores. That encouraged me to carry on growing the company, and it helped me persuade investors to put money into Trunki. Suddenly Trunki was very successful. Next time you're at an airport, notice how many there are. Now, I'm looking forward to taking Trunki into more markets around the world.

6 Allow the students time to read the summary sentences. Tell them to fill the gaps with a maximum of three words and play the audio again. Allow the students to compare answers in pairs before checking as a class.

ANSWERS
1 win a competition   2 department store   3 into schools
4 employed someone   5 beautiful photos
6 won (design) awards

Grammar

7 Ask the students to work together to choose the correct verb forms. Then play the audio again for them to check.

ANSWERS
1 to come   2 to have   3 getting   4 to use   5 to take, stand out   6 having   7 going   8 winning, to attract
9 to carry on, persuade, to put   10 to taking

Students can find more activities at www.richmondatwork.net

8 Focus on the **Grammar** box. Ask the students what the first verb they will write in the box is (*enable*). Then allow them time to write down verbs from **7** and the audioscript in the correct category. Check the answers. Ask which verb in **7** can be followed by either of the first two patterns (*start*).

ANSWERS
- verbs followed by infinitive with *to*: try, enable, allow, decide, expect, encourage, start, persuade, help, need, manage, struggle
- verbs followed by *-ing*: prevent, save, regret, start, carry on, spend (time)
- verbs followed by other forms: make, look forward, help

Speaking

9 Focus on the pictures. Ask the students if they know what the people invented; if not, ask them to guess. Arrange the students into AB pairs, and ask Student A to look at page 100, and Student B at page 105. Set a time-limit of ten minutes for them to read and absorb the content of their texts and to write down the bold verbs that will help them remember. Then ask them to turn back to page 81 and tell their partner about their entrepreneur. Monitor as they talk, and note down any problems with verb forms to deal with later.

10 Set a time-limit of 15 minutes for the discussion. Take feedback from the class, and write any useful vocabulary on the whiteboard.

Extra activity

Write each of the following verbs on a small piece of paper: *admit, avoid, carry on, consider, delay, deny, enjoy, look forward to, mention, miss, practise, prevent someone, regret, save someone, thank someone for, agree, allow, decide, enable someone, expect, learn, manage, offer, prepare, persuade someone, pretend, refuse, seem, struggle, try, want attempt, continue, hate, like, love, prefer, start*

Arrange the students in pairs or groups of three. Explain that you will give each group some words, face down, and they have to make up a story using the words, starting with *You'll never believe what happened to me yesterday!*

Demonstrate the activity by randomly taking one of the words and starting a story, for example (if you took *refuse*): *You'll never believe what happened to me yesterday! I was driving along when suddenly a man stepped into the road in front of me and refused to move …*

Then indicate for a student to take another word and say 'Continue the story'. Explain that the students in the group should take turns to add one or two sentences to continue their group's story, including the word they pick up. Tell each student to note down the verbs so that they will be able to retell the story. Set a ten-minute time-limit for the stories.

After ten minutes, form new groups, and ask the students to retell their story. Monitor as they speak, and note down any problems with verb patterns to deal with later.

Problems and solutions 9

Lesson 2: Adapting, page 82

LESSON OBJECTIVES:

Students will learn and practise ...

phrases using prepositions

talking about adapting products

Warm up

With books closed, ask the students in pairs to brainstorm what they know about India. Take feedback, and write up students' ideas on the whiteboard. Ask volunteers to draw an outline of India on the whiteboard, with key cities marked. If possible, take an atlas to the lesson so the class can compare the students' map to the actual shape.

Start up

1 Focus on the pictures, and elicit what they show (an Indian couple riding a Vespa/scooter, a razor, an Indian McDonald's menu). Then read the fact file with the class. Ask if any of the information was mentioned in the **Warm-up** activity.

Ask the students to discuss the questions in pairs, making a list for question 2. Take feedback from the class and write any useful vocabulary on the whiteboard. Finally, focus on the **Help** box, and read the definition of *glocalisation*. Ask the students if they know any other examples of successful glocalisation.

ANSWERS

1 Possible answers: the population of India is 1.2 billion, which is about a sixth of the world population
2 Students' own answers. From the information in the fact file, product price would be a factor, also the high percentage of the population who don't eat beef or who are vegetarian.

Listening

2 9.2 Focus on the incomplete sentences. Emphasise to the students that these are summary sentences so they will not hear these actual words in the audio. Play the audio once or twice for the students to complete the summaries. Allow the students to compare their answers in pairs before checking as a class.

ANSWERS

1 beef   2 sit, bigger   3 wheels, higher   4 handle, cheaper

9.2

I = Interviewer, R = Rahul

I: This week we've been looking at glocalisation, and today in the studio we're pleased to welcome today's guest, expert on the Indian economy, Rahul Gupta.
R: Good morning.
I: So Rahul, with its rapidly growing economy and large population, India is a popular market with global companies. What kind of changes do companies need to make for the Indian market?
R: It depends on the product, of course. Successful companies always start with a thorough investigation of what Indian consumers want, and then decide whether to make changes to the product. McDonald's is a company that depends on glocalisation, and it's growing fast in India despite big challenges.
I: What particular challenges does it face in India?
R: The first one is the diet. McDonald's main product is a beefburger, but most Indians don't eat beef! So, they had to adapt the menu to the Indian diet, and in fact they came up with a menu that uses vegetables and chicken for the burgers. There are items on it that are specially designed for Indian tastes, like the Maharaja Mac and the Veg McCurry – in fact, some McDonald's in India are 100% vegetarian.
I: And was changing the menu enough?
R: No. In India, people are used to sitting down for meals, not buying them to take away. McDonald's understood this, and so their restaurants are bigger in India, with a lot more tables – which is more expensive to set up, of course.
I: So, cultural differences can shape the product.
R: Yes, and sometimes subtle things. Vespa, for example, made some changes to their scooters to make them suitable for India, where they're very popular. Indian roads can be quite rough, so they made the wheels easier to change. But they also noticed that women often sit sideways to ride on the back of the scooter because they wear long saris. To make this easier, they made the seat slightly higher, but with lower footrests.
I: And is pricing an important factor?
R: It's crucial, yes. A great example of this is Gillette razors. They adapted one of their most popular models and designed a new razor aimed specifically at the Indian market. They based the new design on a detailed study of Indian men's shaving needs. They studied how Indian men hold the razor, and changed the design of the handle slightly. By simplifying the design, they produced a razor which sells at just 30 cents – that's 30 times less than the original razor costs in the USA!
I: And was the strategy a success?
R: An incredible success – they succeeded in grabbing 50% of market share – in just three months!
I: So, what are the lessons here?
R: Have a clear strategy, and research, research, research!
I: Rahul Gupta, thank you.

3 Ask the students to work in pairs to try to complete the sentences. Then play the audio again for them to check. If possible, show the students how they can find information on which preposition to use in a good monolingual dictionary (for example, look up *adapt* in an Advanced Learner's dictionary), being careful to search for the correct sense.

ANSWERS

1 with   2 to   3 for   4 to, for   5 at   6 on   7 in

Reading

4 Focus on the picture that accompanies the text in **5**, and elicit what it shows (A woman cleaning her teeth). Ask them what message the company wants to put in our minds with this picture (e.g. *This will give you strong, healthy teeth / white teeth / nice breath / make you beautiful*).

Read the questions with the class, then set a time-limit of ten minutes for the discussion. Take feedback from the class and write any useful vocabulary on the whiteboard.

5 Allow the students time to mark the sentences true or false, then ask them to work together to make changes to the False sentences so that they are true. Check the answers.

ANSWERS

1 T 2 F (They rate spending time with family and security more highly.) 3 T 4 T 5 F (It sells well all over the world.)

Speaking

6 Set a time-limit of ten minutes for the discussion. Take feedback from the class and write up any useful vocabulary on the whiteboard.

7 Allow the students time to note the two main core values for each country and compare answers before checking as a class.

ANSWERS

Country A: security and physical attractiveness
Country B: showing that you have money and innovation
Country C: reliability and spending time with family

8 Elicit an example of how you might need to adapt one of the products in the box for one of the countries (for example, a car for country A may need additional security features). Set a time-limit of ten minutes for the discussion, and tell the students to make a note of their main ideas, as they will need to remember them for the next exercise.

9 Take feedback from the class. Encourage questions and discussion. Alternatively, so that students get the chance to speak more, form two groups for feedback, with one student from each pair joining each group. Then reform the class, and ask the students what the most interesting idea they heard was.

Extra activity

Ask the students to close their books. Explain that you are going to dictate the text they have just read, but you are going to leave out groups of three words. When you say 'Gap', they should draw three lines to write the missing words on. When they are ready, read the text, saying 'gap' where the bracketed words are (these are the answers). So begin with: *As you read this, millions of people ... GAP! ... are cleaning their teeth ...*

As you read this, millions of people GAP! (around the world) *are cleaning their teeth with Colgate toothpaste. They GAP!* (are experiencing the) *same taste, and are equally happy with how clean it GAP!* (makes their teeth). *And yet when* (they saw the) *toothpaste advertised, they felt different emotions. So, how is it that GAP!* (companies such as) *Colgate manage to sell their product GAP!* (across a wide) *range of different countries and cultures, while other companies are less successful? One market research company in Toronto, Canada, has GAP!* (been studying this) *phenomenon. The first step in their study was to GAP!* (find out what) *people in different countries saw as the most GAP!* (important things in) *life – that is, their 'core values'.*

After dictating the gapped text, ask the students to work in pairs to work out the three missing words in each case. When the first two pairs have finished, ask them to look at page 83 to check their answers.

Lesson 3: Group problem-solving, page 84

LESSON OBJECTIVES:

Students will learn and practise ...
discussing decision-making
phrases for suggesting and agreeing solutions

Warm up

Tell the students you are going to give them a puzzle to solve. Read this scenario:

Three men had lunch in a café and paid £30. As they were leaving, the waiter realised he'd made a mistake, and the meal should only have cost £25. He ran after them and told them, and gave them £5 back. As they couldn't divide the £5 by three, they took £1 each and gave the waiter a £2 tip for being so honest.

Ask the students how much each man has now paid (£9).
Ask how much the men have now paid in total (£27).
Ask how much the waiter has (£2).
Ask what it adds up to (£29).
So where is the missing £1? Ask the students to try to work out why there is one pound missing. Take feedback from the class.

(Solution: The question is false – there is no reason to add the £2 to the £27, as it is already contained in the £27 that the men paid. No money is missing – the men paid £25 to the café, gave £2 to the waiter, and got a £3 refund: 25 + 2 + 3 = 30.)

Start up

1 Arrange the students in groups of three or four and allow them time to solve the problem. When most groups have a solution, ask one or more groups for their solution. Finally, ask them to turn to page 100 to read the solution.

ANSWER

Students refer to page 100 in the Student's Book for the solution.

2 Allow the students time to discuss the questions in pairs, then take feedback from the class.

Reading

3 Ask the students to read the text quickly before discussing the meaning of *groupthink* with a partner and agreeing on a definition. Take feedback and write the suggested definitions on the whiteboard.

Problems and solutions 9

ANSWERS

Students' own answers. Key elements are: decisions made without proper consultation; one person (especially someone senior) dominating; some people not speaking out. 'Group mentality' becomes strong and takes on momentum, but may be headed in the wrong direction.

4 Ask the students to read the text again and tick the ideas that are in the text. Allow the students to compare their answers in pairs before checking as a class.

ANSWERS

Tick: 1, 3, 4, 6 and 7

Listening

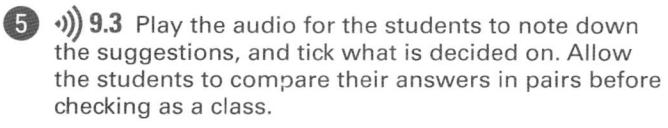

5 9.3 Play the audio for the students to note down the suggestions, and tick what is decided on. Allow the students to compare their answers in pairs before checking as a class.

ANSWERS

hot dog and disco night
music and curry night

9.3

V = Victor, I = Ivy, P = Pavel, J = Jo

V: Ivy, hi. Not late, am I?
I: Hi Victor. No, right on time. Seen the others?
V: No, I … oh wait, here they come.
P: Hi, hi.
I: Hi Pavel.
V: How's it going?
P: Good, thanks. Do you know … er, Jo, isn't it?
J: Jo, that's right.
I: Nice to meet you, Jo.
V: Welcome to the party committee.
J: Hello.
I: Well, thanks for coming. So our end-of-year party is only ten days away, so we need to get it all settled at this meeting. I've been thinking a bit more about the idea for a burger and disco night that I mentioned last time, and I really think that's the way to go.
P: Erm, sorry – I wasn't here last time – burger and disco night, you're saying.
I: That's it – nice and simple, and everyone's guaranteed a good time. Victor's with me on that, so maybe we could start thinking about the details …
P: … er, hang on a minute. If you remember last year, I looked into the cost of hiring a disco, and it was way too much for our budget.
V: You were asking the wrong people, Pavel. And you don't just listen to their first price, you know.
P: No, I got several quotes. But the letters to the student magazine said that people were sick of discos.
I: Oh, the people who write letters to the magazine are just boring. We don't need to take any notice of them.
P: Anyway, I think we should think up some alternatives. Jo, what do you think?
J: Well, obviously I haven't been involved before, but I do think that we could do something a bit more, erm, unique. There are some really good student bands and musicians at the college who would play for free. And I have two friends who cook fantastic Indian food. So, how about a music and curry night?
I: Like you said, Jo, it's your first time here – great idea, but not really the kind of thing that's been successful in the past. And not everyone eats curry …
V: No, if I had to choose between burgers or curry, I'd go for burgers every time.
P: But not everyone eats meat! We could have a vegetarian curry, and …
I: Look, Pavel, you've come here with a very negative attitude – we need positive voices on the committee.
P: I'm just saying we should come up with a few more ideas …
I: Seriously, I need to go in about, erm, twenty minutes, so we just need to settle on something and make some kind of action plan. So, Victor, you're happy with burgers and disco, aren't you?
V: Sure. I'll start looking for a cheap quote.
I: Jo, do you have any objections to the idea, given the time pressure?
J: Well, I suppose not, I don't really …
I: So, that's settled, then. We're all agreed on a burgers and disco night … erm, I'll order the food. Pavel, can you print some tickets for this, and Jo, you said you'd make posters, so if you could show me some ideas tomorrow …

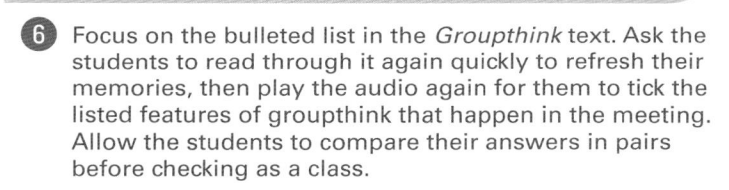

6 Focus on the bulleted list in the *Groupthink* text. Ask the students to read through it again quickly to refresh their memories, then play the audio again for them to tick the listed features of groupthink that happen in the meeting. Allow the students to compare their answers in pairs before checking as a class.

ANSWERS

- A senior group member makes it clear from the start what decision they want – Ivy says, 'I've been thinking … about the idea … that I mentioned last time, and I really think that's the way to go.'
- One person or several people dominate the meeting – Ivy and Victor don't accept any one else's ideas and interrupt people.
- Someone can put pressure on others … – Ivy says, 'Jo, do you have any objection, given the time pressure…?'
- One person assumes what opinion another will have, without asking) – Ivy says, 'Victor's with me on that … without asking him.'
- People outside the group are stereotyped – Ivy says, '… the people who write letters to the magazine are just boring.'
- Objective information is rejected – Pavel says, 'I looked into the cost of hiring a disco, and it was way too much for our budget… I got several quotes.'

Functional language

7 Allow the students time to try to complete the sentences, then play the audio again for them to check.

ANSWERS

1 way, go   2 think up, alternatives   3 choose between, go for   4 come up with   5 settle on   6 objections to   7 settled, agreed on

Speaking

8 Allow the students time to discuss the question and note their ideas, then take feedback from the class.

POSSIBLE ANSWERS

Allow group members to write suggestions anonymously. Set rules – every suggestion must be treated with respect. Choose a chairperson to keep the discussion fair and effective. Don't include the manager in the meeting, but present him/her with the ideas generated afterwards. Bring in a specialist to evaluate ideas or run the meeting. Tell group members that conflict is a natural part of decision-making – they don't have to agree with a person. Make sure there are different types of people in the meeting, e.g. creative, practical, financially aware. Give people roles in the meeting, e.g. one focuses on sensible solutions, one on crazy, one on deliberately bad. Collect all ideas before evaluating any.

9 Arrange the students in groups of four (or three if the total is not divisible by four): A, B, C and D. Ask them to turn to page 100, 105, 106 or 107, depending on their letter, and read about their particular technique. Ask them to note down a key word for each idea in the text, as they will have to talk about it afterwards. Set a time-limit of ten minutes for the students to read and note down words, then take turns to explain their technique to the group. Encourage questions and discussion.

10 Ask each group to agree on a 1–4 ranking for the techniques, then take feedback from the class.

11 Arrange the students in groups of four or five, and ask them to agree on one of the techniques they described in **9** to use in their meeting. Once they have decided, tell them they have 15 minutes to decide how best to raise money.

12 Ask groups to take turns to explain their idea to the class. Alternatively, ask each student to form a new group with a student from each other group. In this way, each student in the class will have the chance to explain their idea. Take feedback on the most interesting ideas.

13 Allow the students to discuss the questions in pairs, then take feedback from the class.

Extra activity

Ask the students to look at the on pages 100, 105, 106 and 107 and make a list of verbs and verb + noun collocations relating to thinking. Elicit the first two (*look at a problem, come up with a plan*).

Scenario: Breaking into America, page 86

SCENARIO OBJECTIVE:

Students will finalise plans for a UK pilot supermarket in the USA.

Warm up

Write the following on the whiteboard, with the right-hand column in random order:

sweets	candy
handbag	purse
lift	elevator
ground floor	the first floor
trousers	pants
rubbish	garbage
petrol	gas
car park	parking lot
toilet	rest room
shop	store
underground	subway
queue	line

Explain that some are used in the UK, and some are used in the US. Ask the students to match the pairs.

1 Focus on the picture and ask the students if the supermarket is similar to the supermarkets in their country. Pre-teach *ready meal* (a meal that requires no preparation, often frozen), *own-brand* (a product made by the supermarket to compete with well-known brands), *upmarket* (designed for people who think they have a higher social status), *aisles* (the spaces between supermarket shelves where you can walk) and *coupons* (pieces of paper that give you discounts on certain products). Allow the students time to discuss the questions. Take feedback on question 1, then go through each bullet point in question 2, asking students whose supermarket has that feature to raise their hands. Ask one or more students each time for their opinion of the feature. Encourage discussion.

2 Point out the boxes under the text. Ask the students to read the text and then paraphrase the information with a partner. Check that students know the meaning of *pilot store* (a single shop which, if successful, will be used as a model for many more). Take feedback to check everyone understands the scenario. Then ask pairs to agree on two more aspects of its new store that Brookes must get right, and then rank all from 1–7. Allow pairs to compare their rankings before taking feedback from the class. Write any useful vocabulary on the whiteboard.

ANSWERS

Possible other aspects: layout, location, special offers, slogan, advertising

Problems and solutions 9

3 🔊 **9.4** Tell the students they just need to tick the +/– columns on the first listening. Play the audio for them to tick the appropriate column. Allow students to compare answers in pairs before checking as a class.

ANSWERS

See **4**.

🔊 **9.4**

G = George, W = woman, M = man

G: So, first I'd like to show you some of our products ... so, here is a roast turkey dinner ...
W: So, that's a ready meal, to cook in the microwave ...
M: It's so small! Is it for a child?
G: No, it's for an adult. This meal is very popular in the UK.
W: Well, turkey is popular here, of course, but it's a family meal, and we'd always cook it fresh. We do eat ready meals, but usually Mexican food. Do you sell them?
G: No, we don't, actually, so ...
M: They wouldn't sell in my neighbourhood – there are lots of Hispanic families, and they always cook Mexican food fresh. You could sell the ingredients.
G: OK, so ... like this? Fresh chicken? It's our own brand ...
M: Own brand? Oh, I see – it's a 'Supernova' chicken! Sounds funny, but if it's cheap, it's fine with me.
G: That's right! Three dollars, so cheaper than a brand.
M: Yes, that's pretty cheap. I'd try that, I suppose.
W: So, I'm not clear – is Supernova a cheap store or not? I'm sorry, but that has to be clear if you want me to use your store.
G: We have a large range of our own-brand produce, which is low-priced. But we also sell brands, of course. So, for example, you can buy Supernova Cola, or Coca-Cola.
W: I always buy brands, because I know I can trust them.
M: Is the Coca-Cola cheaper than other stores?
G: Mm, medium price, but we do lots of in-store special offers you know, two-for-one.
M: So sometimes I might go in your store, and find I can buy two bottles of Coke for the price of one.
G: Sometimes, yes. OK ... so, I wanted to ask you ... Where do you buy your groceries? Are you loyal to one store?
W: No, I'm not loyal.
M: No, I'm not loyal.
W: It depends. I need to know how much I'll pay before I go shopping. I collect money-off coupons from the newspapers.
M: Yeah, so do I. So, like, if we need meat that week and I have meat coupons from the local newspaper, I'll go to the store I have meat coupons for.
G: So you don't have a loyalty card, obviously.
W: I've never had one – I follow the offers!
M: I'd try it, if it gave me good discounts.
G: Right, that's interesting. OK, so can I show you some more of our produce? OK ... erm these 'Supernova' apples ... oh, by the way, what do you think of the name, 'Supernova'?
W: Mm, that doesn't sound like a store to me! I'm not sure why, but it doesn't seem right.
M: The name appeals to me – sounds like a really big store. What kind of store is it, again?
G: It's a neighbourhood store – 'Simple and fresh, every day' – that's our slogan.
M: That makes it sound like a deodorant!
W: 'Simple and fresh, every day' – yes, nothing wrong with that. So, these Supernova apples – why are they all prepackaged?

That's not simple, and it makes them look, well, not fresh. I'm used to loose fruit, not pre-packaged.
G: The plastic packaging actually keeps them fresh.
M: So, this pack of apples would be how much?
G: That would be ... erm ... I think, $1.98.
M: That's expensive!
G: But as I say, we have lots of special offers, two-for-ones instore, and ...
M: I'm confused. Is this supposed to be a cheap store or not?
G: It's high-quality in, erm, a convenient location.
M: Mm. Well, it's interesting, but you need to sort out your pricing!

4 🔊 **9.4** Play the audio again for students to note down details. Allow the students to compare their answers in pairs before checking as a class.

ANSWERS

	Woman		Man	
roast turkey ready meal	✓	cooks turkey and chicken fresh, not microwave	✓	portion size is too small, thinks it's for a child
own brand chicken	✓	if it's cheap, it's alright with her	✓	cheap so happy to try
money-off coupons	✓	will use Brookes' Supernova store for these items	✓	will use Brookes' Supernova store for these items
loyalty cards	✓	don't use them	✓	would try if offered good discounts
name	✓	sounds funny, doesn't sound like a store to her	✓	name appeals – sounds like a really big store
slogan	✓	nothing wrong with that	✓	sounds like a deodorant
apples	✓	not keen on all the packaging, don't look fresh	✓	too expensive
pricing strategy			✓	confused about whether it's a cheap store or not

5 Allow the students time to examine the map and key, and discuss the locations before agreeing on the best one. Take feedback from the class, and encourage discussion, without giving any indication of which location could be best.

POSSIBLE ANSWER

A would not be suitable because you have to drive to it, so it wouldn't be a 'neighbourhood' store, and you might as well drive a little further and go to Walmart. C is in a neighbourhood, but there is already a lot of competition. B would be best.

6 Focus on items 1–7 with the class, then ask the students to read the texts and write E or R next to each item. Allow the students to compare their answers in pairs before checking as a class.

ANSWERS

1 E 2 R 3 E 4 R 5 E 6 R 7 E

7 Arrange the students in new pairs. Then set a time-limit of 15 minutes for each pair to agree on a plan for the supermarket, filling in the details in the table.

POSSIBLE ANSWERS
- best location: B (see question 5)
- name and slogan: probably change name, as woman said the name 'doesn't sound like a store to me! I'm not sure why but it doesn't seem right', and the man said it sounds like a big store, which it isn't; also, some students may notice that the name could be interpreted in Spanish as meaning 'supermarket doesn't work'
- price level: medium rather than everyday low is more realistic as it would be impossible to compete with large chains on price; money-off coupons seem a good idea as both the woman and the man in the research said they used these; there is no evidence either way for 2-for-1 offers, so students can justify using them or not
- store design features: Rachel clearly has the best first-hand knowledge of what US shoppers like, so the layout should be conservative, and busy rather than with lots of space, and definitely not with self checkouts
- product types to include and avoid: ready meals could be OK, but the research session suggested that portions should be larger and meals should be locally researched, e.g. Mexican and roast turkey dinner both rejected here; own brand produce seems OK from the research, and brands must certainly be sold; research needs to be done how fresh food is sold, e.g. the woman thought pre-packaged apples didn't seem fresh.

8 Arrange the class in two groups, with one student from each pair in **7** in each group. Tell the group secretaries they need to copy the table in **7**, and use it to record the group's joint decision.

9 Re-form the class, and ask a spokesperson from each group to explain their plan. Encourage discussion of the differences.

Note that this is based on a real scenario involving a UK supermarket in the USA. The venture failed despite huge investment. Based on what analysts said about the reasons for failure, the best chance for Brookes to succeed would be to:

- have a traditional, busy layout with lots of products in display stands; US shoppers tend to see a modern, open design as cold and unfriendly.
- sell mainly brands, and if selling any own-brands, they must be well-researched, and not appear strange to US shoppers, who are generally conservative and not experimental.
- decide on a clear price strategy – shoppers who are confused will avoid the shop. In this case, it would be difficult to compete with Walmart on price, so the best strategy would probably be to have consistently medium prices, but with plenty of special offers; coupons are very popular in the US, and loyalty cards work well when introduced from the start.
- be located in an area where people walk rather than drive to the shops, otherwise they may as well drive to Walmart. It should therefore be in the centre of town, but away from the competition of other neighbourhood stores. In this case, B is the best location.

- change the name: it must sound 'right' to shoppers, but in this case they didn't particularly identify with it (also, 'Supernova' can mean 'supermarket doesn't work' in Spanish!).
- change the slogan: again, it needs to give the right message to US shoppers, which the market research in this case shows it not to. What works well in one country may not work in another, so very careful market research is needed.
- the product range should be very carefully researched and matched to the exact area – US shoppers like the food they are used to. In this case, if the store is located at B, then the product range should have more of a Hispanic feel.

Extra activity

Ask the students to choose two items of vocabulary from each lesson of the unit that they would like to add to their repertoire, and write a definition for each. Then arrange the students in small groups, and ask them to take turns reading a definition for the rest of the group to guess the word or expression.

Writing emails

Go to **Writing emails 9** on page 52 and do the exercises. Teacher's Book reference on page 65–66.

10 The rules of work

UNIT OBJECTIVES:	Students will practise ...	and they will learn how to ...
	modal verbs	express rules and expectations
	the past form of modals	describe sanctions
	vocabulary related to honesty and responsibility	describe unethical practices

Lesson 1: Office relations, page 88

LESSON OBJECTIVES:

Students will learn and practise ...
modal verbs
vocabulary related to honesty and responsibility

Warm up

Ask the students to imagine they had to share an office with another person. Ask them to write five words or expressions that describe the type of person they would happily share with, and five words or expressions to describe the type of person that would annoy them. Then ask them to compare their lists in pairs before taking feedback from the class. What are the three most popular qualities? What are the top three most annoying?

Start up

1. Arrange the students in groups of three or four. Allow them time to look at the cartoon story and discuss the question. Take feedback from the class, and write any useful vocabulary on the whiteboard.

Vocabulary

2. Focus on the **Help** box. Ask the students if they ever have to fill out travel expense claims, and if so, what evidence they have to provide. Ask if it would be possible, in their experience, for someone to overclaim expenses. Ask the students to read the email and then, with a partner, write one sentence to summarise the situation (e.g. Emma discovered her colleague had overclaimed on his travel expenses). Take feedback, and write good summaries on the whiteboard.

Ask the students to read the email again, and find words to complete the questions. Check the answers.

ANSWERS

1 fault 2 dishonest 3 guilty 4 blame 5 trust
6 truth, lie

3. Allow the students time to read the complete questions and the email again, and think about their answers. Then ask them to discuss the questions with a partner. Take feedback from the class, and encourage discussion. Write any useful vocabulary on the whiteboard.

POSSIBLE ANSWERS

1 Emma feels it is partly her fault.
2 He overclaimed travel expenses.
3 Because she looked at her colleague's claim form.
4 She is not to blame for her colleague overclaiming but she is to blame for looking at the claim form.
5 Emma feels she can trust him.
6 She certainly shouldn't lie, as she would be in trouble – but maybe she doesn't need to tell the whole truth.

🌐 Students can find more activities at www.richmondatwork.net

Listening

4. 🔊 **10.1** Focus on the **Help** box. Ask the students to read sentences 1–5, and decide together in each case which of the options is the best advice. Then play the audio once or twice for them to choose the advice the presenter actually gives. Check the answers.

ANSWERS

1 chat informally 2 she's sorry 3 avoid sounding too serious
4 correct his expenses form 5 will probably survive

🔊 **10.1**
Well, Emma, I can see why the situation must be a worry for you – on the one hand you have to be honest, but on the other you don't want to fall out with your friend. And I think, here, you need to talk to your colleague about it. You don't need to make a big thing of it – just make it seem like a casual chat as you pass. You can start by apologising for looking at his expenses form. I'm sure you didn't mean to do it, and you're certainly not to blame, and then explain about the awkward situation you're in now. If you do it in a friendly and direct way, he'll be fine about it. But you mustn't accuse him of not being honest if you want to maintain your relationship. Just focus on your position, and smile and try to keep the conversation light. Ask him if he'd mind contacting Finance and changing his claim, saying he thinks he's made some mistakes. You don't have to discuss the matter in more detail, but he may want to – I'd leave that up to him. If he refused to cooperate, it might be difficult to stay friends. But he sounds like basically a good guy, so I feel sure you can. If not, well ... you won't really have lost anything in any case. I hope that helps. I'm sure you needn't worry. Please let us know what happens!

97

5 Allow the students time to discuss their opinion in pairs, and suggest other ideas if possible. Then take feedback from the class.

> **ANSWERS**
>
> Students' own answers. An alternative might be to avoid mentioning that she's seen his expense form and just let him know in passing that finance want to see her about her expense form.

Grammar

6 Play the audio again, pausing after sentences 1–8 for the students to complete the sentences. Check the answers.

> **ANSWERS**
>
> 1 must 2 have to 3 need to 4 don't need to 5 can
> 6 mustn't 7 don't have to, but he may 8 needn't

7 Write on the whiteboard:
   1 I _____ go (have to / must)
   2 She _____ go (has to / must)
   3 I'll _____ go (have to)
   4 I apologise for _____ go (having to)

Ask the students to work in pairs to complete the sentences using *have to* and *must*. Highlight the fact that *have to* and *must* have very similar meanings, but are formed in different ways (e.g. the third person singular of *must* doesn't end in *s*, there is no infinitive or gerund form of *must*). Explain that *must* is a modal verb and ask the students if they can think of any others which follow the same rules (*must, may, might, can, could, will, would, shall, should*). Focus on the **Grammar** box and ask the students to match the modal verbs with their uses. Check the answers.

> **ANSWERS**
>
> 1 c 2 d 3 a 4 e 5 b

Students can find more activities at www.richmondatwork.net

Fluency

8 •)) 10.2 Write on the whiteboard:
   1 A: What are you listening <u>to</u>? B: I'm listening <u>to</u> jazz.
   2 A: I've asked <u>them</u> to take part in the meeting.
      B: You've asked <u>them</u>?! Why?
   3 A: <u>Can</u> you see the problem? B: I certainly <u>can</u>!

Ask the students to discuss in pairs how the underlined words are pronounced in each case. Read the sentences and establish the pronunciation (1 /tuː/, /tə/ 2 /ðəm/, /dem/ 3 /kən/, /kæn/), and get the students to say both the underlined words and the whole sentences. Elicit or explain why the different forms are used. (The stronger-sounding form is used when the word is emphasised, either because it comes at the end of the sentence or when the speaker emphasises it for meaning.)

Play the audio twice for the students to read and listen. Allow the students time to discuss the questions in pairs, then take feedback. Explain that certain words in English have two pronunciations, 'weak' and 'strong'. Words that act in this way are 'grammatical' words such as prepositions (e.g. *to, of*), pronouns (e.g. *her, them*), and modal and auxiliary verbs (e.g. *can, would*). The italic words in the sentences are examples of weak forms, and use the sound /ə/. The bold words are examples of strong forms of the same words, as explained above.

Ask the students to work together to underline where they would put the main stresses in each sentence, i.e. on the stressed part of the words that carry the meaning. Then ask them to practice pronouncing the sentences, focusing especially on the stressed syllables and the weak forms. Monitor and help as they do this. Finally, play the audio again for the students to listen and repeat.

> **ANSWERS**
>
> The italics words are weak forms and therefore unstressed. The bold words are strong forms and are stressed.

> •)) **10.2**
>
> See **8** in the Student's Book.

Speaking

9 Demonstrate the activity by telling the students where you place your cross. Think of two examples which illustrate your attitude to conflict. Allow the students time to place their cross, and to think of two real-life situations that show their attitude. Set a time-limit of ten minutes for them to explain to their partner. Take feedback from the class, and write up any useful vocabulary on the whiteboard. Note any problems using modal verbs to deal with later.

10 Arrange the students in new AB pairs. Ask A to look at page 101, and B to look at page 105. Ask them to read the situations and write down three or four key words to help them remember each situation. Allow them time to do this, then ask them to close their books and take turns to explain one of the situations and ask their partner to say and justify what he/she would do in that position. Take feedback from the class.

Extra activity

Ask the students to write six pieces of advice for a person starting at their place of work or study. They should use all the verbs studied in this lesson, and three of their sentences should be positive and three negative. The advice can be serious or humorous – whichever you feel is more appropriate for your class. Ask the students to compare their sentences in pairs, then ask some students to read their advice to the class.

The rules of work 10

Lesson 2: Whistleblowing, page 90

LESSON OBJECTIVES:

Students will learn and practise ...
words to describe unethical practices
past form of modals

Warm up

With books closed, arrange the students into AB pairs. Ask Student As to open their books at page 90 and study the pictures at the top of the page for one minute, ready to be tested. After a minute, ask them to close their books, and ask Student Bs to open their books at page 90. Student B has to ask Student A five questions to test his/her memory of the picture. Make sure that the students who were tested in unit 8 now have the chance to ask questions. Alternatively, ask the class to work in pairs to answer the following questions after studying the pictures and closing their books:

1 *How many wind turbines are there?* (eleven)
2 *What colour are the capsules that are out of their packaging?* (red and white)
3 *How many cranes can you see on the construction site?* (one)
4 *Which direction are the motorbikes going in – towards the right or towards the left?* (right)
5 *How many people are in the office?* (four)
6 *What's the woman in the grey jacket holding?* (a pen)
7 *What colour skirts are the store models wearing?* (black and orange)

Start up

1 Ask the students to work in pairs to match the pictures with the industries, then check the answers. Read the names of the industries for the students to repeat and underline the main stress in each word (*pharma<u>ceu</u>ticals, cons<u>truc</u>tion, <u>cloth</u>ing, fi<u>nan</u>cial <u>ser</u>vices, <u>en</u>ergy, <u>sports</u>*). Then ask students to listen to their partner saying the words.

POSSIBLE ANSWERS
1 e   2 b   3 d   4 c   5 f   6 a

2 Allow the students time to discuss the questions. When most pairs have finished, take feedback from the class, and write any useful vocabulary on the whiteboard.

ANSWERS

Students' own answers. (Of these industries, energy companies are consistently among the most profitable worldwide, as are banks and other financial services. Pharmaceutical companies can potentially make enormous profits, but it depends on the success of particular drugs, so is probably less consistent. At a particular time and place, however, any of these industries could be the most profitable.)

Vocabulary

3 Tell the students a true or made-up story about an occasion when you were expected to pay someone a bribe (give them an illegal and secret payment) in order to get good service. For example, you could say you wanted to eat in a restaurant, but the waiter said you would have to wait a very long time get a table. He made it clear that if you paid him £10 (or equivalent), he could find you a table immediately. Ask the students what they would have done in that situation, and whether they think it's acceptable. Ask them if there is an expression for this kind of payment in their language. Encourage any stories volunteered by students, but be aware this could be a sensitive area.

Allow the students time to match the unethical practices with their definitions, using their dictionary to help them. Allow the students to compare answers in pairs before checking as a class. Then, as in **1**, read the vocabulary items for the students to underline the main stresses (*un<u>eth</u>ical <u>prac</u>tices, <u>bri</u>bery, fraud, cre<u>a</u>tive ac<u>coun</u>ting, exploi<u>ta</u>tion of <u>wor</u>kers, in<u>sid</u>er <u>deal</u>ing, price <u>fix</u>ing, tax e<u>va</u>sion*).

ANSWERS
1 g   2 c   3 f   4 b   5 d   6 a   7 e

4 Set a time-limit of 15 minutes for discussion. Monitor as the students talk, and note down any language problems to deal with later. Take feedback from the class. Encourage discussion, and write any useful vocabulary on the whiteboard.

ANSWERS

Students' own answers. (Students may have heard, for example, of price fixing in the pharmaceutical industry; bribery in construction; exploitation of workers in the clothing industry; fraud, creative accounting and insider dealing in financial services; price fixing in energy; bribery in sport. However, any answer is possible.)

Students can find more activities at www.richmondatwork.net

Listening

5 🔊 **10.3** Read the definition of *whistleblower* in the **Help** box with the class, and ask students how they would express this in their own language. Then play the audio for the students to listen and identify the unethical practice. Allow the students to compare their answers in pairs before checking as a class.

ANSWER

creative accounting

🔊 10.3

I worked as an accountant at Company X, and was promoted to a senior position after several years. So, then it became part of my job to check the monthly accounts. The first time I did this, I noticed that a lot of figures had been entered incorrectly – they were much too high. I thought there might have been a mistake, so I contacted my boss. He said it would be investigated, and I heard nothing more. But it was worrying me, and the following month when I looked at the figures, they were again way too high – I mean millions of pounds too high.

This time I contacted the CEO, and – I must have been so naïve because I thought he would thank me! – he asked me to come and see him. When I did, he asked me to write down the incorrect figures, on paper and from memory. I couldn't understand why he asked me to do that – it was impossible, I told him. He said he wasn't at all happy with my performance in my new job, and I didn't have to come into work the next day because I was suspended while my findings were investigated. I should have realised at that point what was happening.

I was allowed back after two weeks, but I noticed that people were avoiding me, and because I wasn't allowed access to the IT network, I was unable to do my job. Two weeks later was my performance review, and my boss said I was incompetent, and should consider resigning. I did resign, and it was difficult to get a new job because they gave me terrible references. At first I thought I should have just kept quiet – I needn't have put my career at risk because nothing changed. But then, a couple of months later, I got a call from an ex-colleague, who said a similar thing had happened to her, and I realised I had to do something, so I reported the company – on the government website there was an email address for reporting fraud. I couldn't prove anything, and, of course, I ought to have collected evidence while at the company. But the company was investigated, and the people responsible for the dishonest accounting were fired. I eventually got some compensation, but that's not why I did it. I feel proud of myself now – I can't have been the first to discover what was going on, but I was the first to report it.

6 Allow the students time to read the questions and discuss which options they think are correct based on what they remember. Then play the audio again for them to choose the correct option. Check the answers.

ANSWERS

1 c 2 a 3 a 4 b

Grammar

7 Write on the whiteboard:

He _____ have gone to the conference.

Elicit which modal verbs could go in the gap, and write them underneath, then elicit how each one changes the meaning. Suggestions should include *must* (= I'm sure he went), *may/might* (= It's possible he went), *could* (It's possible he went OR He was able to go, but he didn't), *should* (= He didn't go, and that was a mistake), *shouldn't* (= He went, and that was a mistake), *needn't* (= He went, but it wasn't necessary), *wouldn't* (= part of a third conditional sentence).

Ask the students to work in pairs to underline the correct option, then listen again to check.

Ask the students to discuss the questions, then take feedback (We use this type of past modal when we are analysing the past, and thinking how things could have been different; This type of past modal is formed with modal *verb + have + past participle*). Write the formation on the whiteboard.

ANSWERS

1 might 2 must have been 3 couldn't understand 4 didn't have to 5 should have realised 6 should have just kept 7 needn't have 8 had to do 9 ought to 10 can't have been

🌐 Students can find more activities at www.richmondatwork.net

8 Ask the students to work in pairs to do number 1. Take feedback from the class, listening to different suggestions, if there are any, before revealing the correct answer. Ask pairs to continue with numbers 2–11, then check answers. Check the students understand the difference in meaning between the two possible options in number 6. Write them both on the whiteboard, and ask the students which form means that it wasn't necessary to contact the supplier (both), and which means that we did contact the supplier (*needn't have*). Similarly, elicit the difference between the two options in number 7 (*We were able to* = we had that possibility and we may have taken it; *we could have tried* = we had the possibility but we didn't take it).

ANSWERS

1 I should have updated my CV.
2 He ought to have saved the data.
3 I had to finish the report.
4 You couldn't / weren't allowed to be late.
5 You didn't have to go to the meeting.
6 We didn't need to contact / needn't have contacted the supplier.
7 We were able to try / could have tried emailing the customer.
8 He could speak German.
9 He can't have been in the meeting.
10 She could/might/may have been travelling by train.
11 They must have been happy with the result.

Speaking

9 Arrange the students in new AB pairs. Ask Student A to look at page 101 and follow the instructions, and Student B at page 105. Set a time-limit of ten minutes. Then ask Student As to stand up and go and find another Student A and practise telling their story, and the same for Students Bs. After five minutes, ask them to rejoin their original partner and take turns to tell their story, asking questions to clarify the story they listen to. Then ask the students to list the characters in their partner's story, and put a tick or a cross next to each one according to whether they did the 'right' or the 'wrong' thing, in the student's opinion. Finally, ask the students to explain their opinions on how each character behaved. Before they do this, remind them to use the grammar of the lesson.

Take feedback from the class. Encourage discussion, and note down any problems with the past form of modals to deal with later.

Extra activity

Prepare a number of pieces of paper with the following (or similar) sentences on them:
You should have brought a map!
You must have made a mistake.
You shouldn't have opened the box!
You must have felt embarrassed.
You should have called the police.
You can't have done it very well.
You must have been very happy.
You shouldn't have told anyone.
You can't have been warm enough.
You must have had to hurry.
Tell the students that you will give them a sentence, and they have to invent and explain a situation so that others can guess the sentence.
As an example, write on the board:
You _____ have _____ .
Demonstrate the activity for the sentence *You should have gone by car.* (e.g. say to students, *I arranged to meet my friend in town. It was a nice evening so I decided to walk, but I got there really late, and he'd already gone*). Point to the words on the board, and elicit the exact sentence. Then give the students the pieces of paper and arrange the students in small groups to take turns explaining their situations.

Lesson 3: The right rules, page 92

LESSON OBJECTIVES:

Students will learn and practise ...
expressing rules and expectations
describing sanctions

Warm up

Write on the whiteboard:
se_ / m_ _ _ (set, make)
sti_ _   _ _ / ob _ _ (stick to, obey)   the rules
bre_ _ _ / ig_ _ _ _ (break, ignore)
ben_ (bend)

Ask the students to complete the verbs in pairs, using their dictionary and sharing their knowledge. Check the answers, then write on the whiteboard:
Are there times when it's OK to bend or break rules?
Did you stick to your school's / your parents' rules when you were a teenager?
Ask pairs to discuss the questions, then take feedback from the class.

The rules of work 10

Start up

1 Write the following adjectives on the whiteboard:
wacky, dull, conventional, stimulating, nspiring, lifeless
Ask the students to work in pairs to decide which picture each adjectives goes best with (*dull, conventional* and *lifeless* with the picture on the left; *wacky, stimulating* and *inspiring* with the one on the right). Then ask each pair to use their bilingual dictionaries or share their knowledge to find one more adjective for each picture. Then allow the students a short time to discuss the questions, then take feedback.

POSSIBLE ANSWERS

1 The company on the left probably has the stricter rules.
2 The company on the left would be most suitable for administrative companies such as accountancy. The company on the right would be suitable for creative companies such as website design.

2 Ask the students to read the quotes and then discuss the questions in pairs. When some pairs have finished, take feedback from the class.

POSSIBLE ANSWERS

The first quote could be explained as 'If you have too many rules, you prevent creative thinking', and the second one as 'Rules limit progress'; however, many different interpretations are possible.

3 Talk about your own personal experience of a place where you found the rules too strict or not strict enough, and encourage questions and comments. Then allow the students time to discuss the questions. Take feedback, and write any useful vocabulary on the whiteboard.

Reading

4 Elicit or pre-teach *stock-checking* (the process of checking what things in a shop have been bought, and therefore need replacing) and *weird* (strange). Ask the students for examples of the rules the two employees might have to obey, based on the pictures and their job titles. Ask the students to read the texts quickly to check their ideas. Check the answers.

ANSWERS

1 yes **2** For Barney, there aren't any obvious rules and all that seems to matter is the end result. He feels trusted to get on with his job without having to adhere to rules about dress code or office hours. For Petra there are rules for almost everything and the company trusts them to follow these rules.

5 Allow the students time to reread the texts and write B or P (or both) next to each sentence. Allow the students to compare answers in pairs before checking as a class.

ANSWERS

1 P   **2** B/P   **3** B/P   **4** P   **5** P

101

6 Ask the students to discuss in pairs what word is missing from the first sentence. Check the answer, and ask which employee used the word (Petra). Then allow the students time to complete each remaining gap with one word from the text. Allow the students to compare their answers in pairs before checking as a class.

POSSIBLE ANSWERS

1 tightly controlled / strict, break   2 has the right, allowed
3 guidelines, free and easy / relaxed

Listening

7 🔊 **10.4** Emphasise that Barney and Petra are talking about their previous, not current, jobs. Allow the students time to read the options before playing the audio for them to choose the correct options. Check the answers.

ANSWERS

1 enforce   2 compulsory   3 fined   4 fired after being warned   5 have lunch at your desk   6 could wear your own clothes

🔊 **10.4**

Barney
I had a job in a construction company, in the office. Of course in construction there are millions of health and safety rules, but this company was really slack about enforcing them. Like, for example, you were meant to wear a hard hat and safety boots at all times on site, but a lot of people didn't. And all the workers were supposed to have safety training when they started work, but the company didn't bother with that. The strange thing was, my boss knew they'd get into trouble if there was an inspection, but he didn't seem to care. Anyway, that actually happened just after I left. A safety inspector arrived without warning, and apparently they got a massive fine – fifty thousand pounds or something like that.

Petra
I worked in a call centre where you weren't allowed to use the internet or phone for non-work related purposes. They monitored use, and if they caught you, you got a warning. One person actually got fired after they'd got two warnings for making personal calls – I don't know why they didn't use their mobile, but it wasn't fair. It's a grey area, but I'm not sure if companies are allowed to read all your emails and listen to your calls. They also had some really petty rules, like you weren't supposed to eat at your desk. I mean, what's the point of that? And you had to dress smartly, even though it was a call centre! I couldn't stand it, so I handed in my notice after six months.

8 Allow the students time to complete the sentences, using their dictionary to help them, then play the audio again. Check the answers.

ANSWERS

1 slack, enforcing   2 meant   3 supposed   4 get, trouble
5 caught, warning   6 grey area   7 petty

Speaking

9 Allow the students time to read the questions, and set a time-limit of 15–20 minutes for the discussion. Monitor as they talk, and note down any problems with the language of the lesson.

Take feedback from the class, and write any useful vocabulary on the whiteboard.

POSSIBLE ANSWERS

2 To encourage standard behaviour, quality, etc. where necessary, but also to allow room for individuality and creativity where appropriate; staff should be able to see the purpose of workplace rules.
3 A company without any employees, i.e. completely run by the founder(s), would not need formal rules, although there would still be standards (e.g. production standards, safety standards, etc.) and norms (e.g. expected dress and behaviour when meeting clients) to follow; as soon as employees are hired, it becomes more necessary to have rules.

Extra activity

Write these strange laws on the whiteboard:
It's illegal to ...
1 eat or drink near _____ in Rome. (monuments)
2 _____ while walking through the town of Daytona Beach, Florida. (spit)
3 step on _____ in Thailand. (banknotes)
4 feed _____ in Venice. (pigeons)
5 fight _____ in Alabama. (bears)
6 _____ while driving on the Autobahn in Germany. (run out of petrol)
7 _____ in the village of Sarpourenx, France. (die)
8 wear _____ to the Houses of Parliament in the UK. (metal armour)

Ask the students to discuss the laws in pairs, and guess the missing word. Encourage discussion and comments.

Scenario: Environmental dilemma, page 94

SCENARIO OBJECTIVE:

Students will discuss the ethics of four people involved in the pollution levels of a chemical company.

Warm up

Write the following (real) headlines and words on the whiteboard:
1 CLIMATE CHANGE DRIVES CROP PEST SPREAD
2 BP SEEKS TO HAVE OIL SPILL SETTLEMENT PAYMENTS SUSPENDED
3 EMERGING ECONOMIES URGED TO GO GREEN
4 SEA ICE REACHES SEASONAL LOW
5 HUGE TIDAL ENERGY PROJECT APPROVED
a Arctic   b waves   c farmers   d fuel   e drilling

The rules of work 10

Ask the students to work in pairs to match words a–e with the story they are likely to appear in, and to discuss briefly what they think each story is about. Check the answers. (Answers: 1c – Insects that eat farmers' crops are affecting more areas because of the increase in temperatures. 2e – The oil company BP is currently refusing to pay any more money to people affected by the accident in the Gulf of Mexico which caused oil to pollute the sea. 3d – Countries whose economies are growing fast are being encouraged by a US expert to invest in alternative fuels and other technology that helps the environment. 4a – There is much less ice in the Arctic Ocean than is normal at this time of year. 5b – The Scottish government has given permission for a company to make electricity from the movement of waves in the sea around Scotland.)

1 Focus on the pictures. Elicit what the students can see in each one. Ask the students to discuss the link between them, then take feedback from the class.

ANSWERS
From left to right: Industries located on the banks of a river, crops being sprayed with fertiliser/pesticide, a scientist carrying out an experiment, a dead fish, presumably from polluted waters. Possible link: waste chemicals from industry and farming pollute rivers and kill wildlife.

2 Elicit or pre-teach *protest* (noun = a public meeting to show that you strongly disagree with something, verb = to take part in a protest), *pour* (to put liquid into something) and *waste* (materials that are thrown away because they are no longer needed). Ask the students to read the text and discuss the questions in pairs, then take feedback.

ANSWERS
1 Following a report published last week, environmental groups claim that Waring Chemicals are pouring too much waste into the river. Other companies aren't producing as much waste.
2 farming

3 🔊 **10.5** Read the information about Freya MacNeil, and ask the students what they think she wants to talk with Lou about. Focus on the **Help** box and read the questions with the class. Then play the audio for the students to answer the questions. Allow them time to discuss their answers before taking feedback.

ANSWERS
1 He says they are well within the legal limits for this type of waste.
2 She says the limits are too high in that case.
3 He says they need to concentrate on expanding before they can spend money on a waste treatment facility.
4 Because he has spent years building a reputation as an environmentally friendly company.
5 Freya probably feels angry and disappointed in her boss. Lou probably feels angry at being criticised by a member of staff. He possibly also feels guilty given his environmental credentials in the past but feels (justifiably or not) that his hands are tied while he builds up his business.

🔊 **10.5**
F = Freya, L = Lou
F: Have you read this report, Lou?
L: From the Science Institute? Yes, yes, I have.
F: Well ... it's shocking ... isn't it? I mean, I had no idea of the effects our waste was having – assuming the research is correct.
L: It looks correct, actually – I mean ...
F: But we need to reduce our waste. We can do it – we just need to build a waste treatment facility, and ...
L: Now wait a minute. Even the report admits that we are well inside legal limits for this type of waste.
F: Well, in that case, the limits are too high! And they've actually made Waring's limit higher – it's unbelievable! Look at the effect it's having on fish in the river.
L: I know, and in the future we'll have to build a treatment facility, but we can't at the moment. We are just starting to do really well. This is our chance to grow. We can't grow if we spend all our money building a waste treatment facility. And we would have to stop production for weeks. We'd lose our advantage, and ... well, maybe that would be the end of the company.
F: I can't believe you're saying this. Look, you've spent years establishing a reputation for this company as being environmentally friendly. Now we've got protesters outside. That's what's going to cost jobs.
L: The government environment agency decides the limits, and we are well within them.
F: I don't believe it ... I've got journalists leaving messages on my phone. What should I tell them?
L: Tell them we're working closely with the government environment agency to make sure we obey all waste regulations, because we care about the environment.
F: Well ... OK, but I must say I'm disappointed. I thought you cared.

4 Read the information about Malik Khan. Ask the students what Malik and Kelly's jobs are (Malik gives government permits to local companies, which allow them to put a certain amount of waste into rivers; Kelly, his boss, decides what 'certain amount' each company is allowed to put in the river). Then ask the students to read the email exchange and answer the questions. Allow them time to discuss their answers in pairs before taking feedback.

ANSWERS
1 Because the limits have been increased despite reports that the number of fish in the river is falling. (Also later that Kelly is reluctant to discuss the matter.)
2 There may have been a mistake.
3 He wants to spend a few days doing some research and talking to people at the institute.
4 He probably feels frustrated because he can see that there's a problem and his boss is reluctant to discuss it.

5 Arrange the students into AB pairs. Check that the students know who they are, Freya or Malik. Allow them time to read the instructions, then tell them they have five minutes to think about what they want to say. After this time, set a ten-minute time-limit for 'Freya' and 'Malik' to talk about their worries and ask for advice.

103

6 Ask pairs to get together with another pair and compare their conversations in **5**.

7))) **10.6** Play the audio for the students to answer the questions. Allow them time to discuss their answers in pairs before taking feedback.

ANSWERS
1 As a favour, to repay Lou for his help furthering her career in the past.
2 To resolve the pollution levels by the following year.
3 Students' own answers.

))) **10.6**
K = Kelly, L = Lou
K: Kelly Deans.
L: Kelly, hi – it's Lou.
K: Oh Lou, hi! How are you?
L: Great, thanks. How about you and the family?
K: Yes, all good. So, what can I do for you, Lou?
L: Well, I just wanted to thank you for your help. Those permits with the higher levels will really help, because, well … it's an important time for us.
K: I know it is, and that's OK, Lou. It was the least I could do, because you helped me so much when we worked together early in my career.
L: I did, but anyway, I really appreciate your help here.
K: You do realise, though, that I won't be able to do the same next year. There's a lot of pressure on me over this. I feel bad that I can't be open about it with my staff – they wouldn't understand that in the long term, it's the best thing for the town.
L: I'm sure – I'm under pressure too. There's the press, and I can't talk to my employees about it, either, even though it's their jobs I'm protecting. But anyway, I wanted to say thanks. Without your help, we would have lost the advantage we have with our product. We're just starting to do well, and I'd hate it if we had to lose any jobs.
K: Yes, Waring's is good for the town. To be honest, though, I am worried about these pollution levels. I trust the Institute's report, but it's only for a year, so the river will recover.
L: Me too. I'm not happy about it, but we'll start to build the waste treatment facility in six months, and it'll be open in a year's time. Then we'll voluntarily set our own levels, and they'll be the lowest in the industry.
K: Promise?
L: I have the plans on my desk. The bank has said yes, so it's definite.
K: Well, you know I trust you, Lou.
L: So, we should get together again soon – come for dinner with Joe next weekend, maybe.
K: That would be great. I'll speak to Joe and get back to you. OK then, love to Maria, and speak to you later.
L: Yes, will do. Bye then, Kelly.

8 Arrange the students into AB pairs. Read the rubric and the unfinished sentences, then ask Student A to look at page 101, and Student B at page 105. Ask them to note down key words, then report the information they read to their partner. Then ask them to reach agreement on a way to finish each sentence. Take feedback from the class.

POSSIBLE ANSWERS
- Lou Waring did the right thing because he did what was necessary to protect local jobs / … because he eventually reduced pollution from his factory by 80%.
- Lou Waring did the wrong thing because he allowed pollution from his factory to run out of control / … because he secretly (and possibly unlawfully) used a personal relationship to gain an advantage.
- Kelly Deans did the right thing because she helped to protect local jobs without doing long-term environmental damage.
- Kelly Deans did the wrong thing because she caused environmental damage in order to do a friend a favour / … because she was secretive/dishonest in a government job / … because she caused Malik to lose his job.
- Freya MacNeil did the right thing because she challenged her boss about environmental damage / … because she played a part in reducing her factory's waste by 80%.
- Freya MacNeil did the wrong thing because she allowed Malik to lose his job, while she kept hers.
- Malik Khan did the right thing because he acted when he suspected corruption / … because he risked his job in order to protect the environment.
- Malik Khan did the wrong thing because he accused his boss of acting illegally without being able to prove it.

Extra activity

Give out ten very small pieces of paper to each student, and ask them to look back through the unit and write ten useful nouns, adjectives or verbs on the pieces. Then pass around a bag or other container and ask the students to fold up each piece of paper and put them all in.

Divide the class into two teams and toss a coin to see which team goes first. Ask who is going first on that team, and tell them they have one minute to take one word at a time from the bag and explain it for their team to guess (without using gestures!). When it's guessed, they put it aside and quickly go on to the next one. If they think the team can't guess, they can fold up the word and put it back in the bag. Tell them to start, then after one minute say 'stop' and add up their points for correctly guessed words. Then the other team does the same with the remaining words for one minute. Carry on like this until everyone has had a turn (or two in a small class). If all the words have been guessed before everyone has had a turn (or two in a small class), put all the words back in and continue as before – this will speed the game up as the students have heard all the words, so just a reminder is necessary. The team with the most points after everyone has played is the winner.

Writing emails
Go to **Writing emails 10** on page 53 and do the exercises. Teacher's Book reference on page 66.